The Which? Guide to Renting and Letting

About the authors

PETER WILDE is a practising and consultant solicitor who has specialised in landlord and tenant law. He is also a senior lecturer at the College of Law, Chester.

PAUL BUTT, LLB, is a solicitor and an associate professor at the College of Law, Chester. He is the author of several books, on landlord and tenant issues, conveyancing and other property matters, and a lecturer to the profession.

JOHN STOCKDALE, MA (Cantab), who wrote the text relating to tax, combines practice as a solicitor with lecturing to the profession. He was formerly head of tax and a principal lecturer at the College of Law, Chester.

DEREK O'CARROLL, author of the chapters on Scotland, is an advocate at the Scottish bar. He speaks and writes frequently on housing issues and is the author of many publications, including the Model Scottish Secure Tenancy Agreement.

The Which? Guide to Renting and Letting

Peter Wilde and Paul Butt

 CONSUMERS' ASSOCIATION

Which? Books are commissioned and researched by
Consumers' Association and published by
Which? Ltd, 2 Marylebone Road, London NW1 4DF
Email address: books@which.net

Distributed by The Penguin Group:
Penguin Books Ltd, 80 Strand, London WC2R 0RL

First edition June 1994
Second edition May 1995
Reprinted 1996
Revised October 1996
Revised September 1997
Reprinted February 1998
Revised October 1999
Revised March 2002

British Library Cataloguing in Publication Data
A catalogue record for this book is available from the British Library

ISBN 0 85202 894 6

For a full list of *Which?* books, please write to Which? Books, Castlemead, Gascoyne Way,
Hertford X, SG14 1LH or access our website at www.which.net

Editorial and production: Joanna Bregosz, Nithya Rae
Cover photograph: Pictor

Typeset by Saxon Graphics Ltd, Derby
Printed and bound in England by Clays Ltd, St Ives plc

Contents

	Introduction	7
1	Letting in the private sector	13
2	Assured shorthold tenancies	16
3	Assured tenancies	40
4	Finding a tenant	62
5	Granting a shorthold tenancy	70
6	Granting non-shorthold tenancies	89
7	Lettings prior to 28 February 1997	90
8	Houses in multiple occupation	110
9	Housing benefit and council tax	114
10	Public-sector tenancies	120
11	Housing associations and registered social landlords	135
12	Repair and maintenance of rented property	140
13	Harassment and unlawful eviction	157
14	Possession proceedings	170
15	Defending possession proceedings	197
16	Finance and tax	200
17	Long leases of houses: the right to buy or extend the lease	213
18	Long leases of flats: acquiring the freehold or an extension of the lease	221
19	Service charge disputes	242
20	Commonhold	265

21 Practical tips for landlords and tenants   269

22 In Scotland: private-sector tenancies   274

23 In Scotland: public-sector tenancies   289

Appendix I   Assured tenancies: grounds for possession   302

Appendix II   Sample agreement for letting a whole house on a shorthold tenancy   311

Appendix III   Sample agreement for letting a whole house on an ordinary assured tenancy with a ground 1 notice   320

Appendix IV   Sample agreement for letting part of a house, not on an assured or a shorthold tenancy   331

Appendix V   Sample guarantee agreement for residential tenancies   341

Addresses and websites★   344

Index   346

Throughout this book for 'he' read 'he or she'

★An asterisk in the text indicates that the address of the organisation can be found in this section

Introduction

If you are thinking of letting a house, flat or bedsitter, or of renting one, you will find yourself involved with a complex area of law: the law of landlord and tenant.

Many changes in the law of residential landlord and tenant have taken place recently. The rights of tenants – especially long-term tenants – have been modified significantly. Also, the passage of the Commonhold & Leasehold Reform Bill through Parliament could mean that new blocks of flats are sold commonhold rather than leasehold (see Chapter 20).

This guide is intended to help residential landlords and tenants, whether potential or actual, understand the legal framework within which they will be operating. Although the book also touches on the economic and practical aspects, it is the legal side that can create the biggest headaches and this, therefore, is its main focus. However, it is not a substitute for seeking professional help, nor does it set out to provide a comprehensive explanation of the law.

The rules on renting and letting have evolved over many years. Some of the basic principles go back centuries and reflect decisions made by judges: this is called 'common law' (judge-made law), but nowadays most of the rules are found in Acts of Parliament, such as the Rent Acts and the Housing Acts, both of which are considered in this guide. Chapter 1 briefly describes the different types of tenancy in existence in the private sector (public-sector tenancies are considered separately, in Chapter 10).

Legal definition of a tenancy

A tenancy is an arrangement under which exclusive possession of a property is granted for a fixed or ascertainable period of time. It is,

Chart 1: Public-sector tenancies

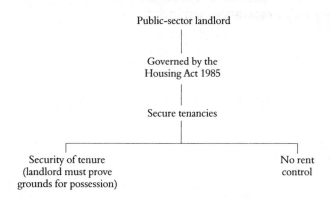

Public-sector landlord

Governed by the
Housing Act 1985

Secure tenancies

Security of tenure
(landlord must prove
grounds for possession)

No rent
control

Chart 2: Private-sector tenancies

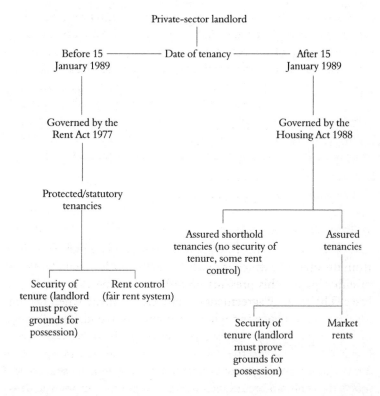

Private-sector landlord

Before 15 ———— Date of tenancy ———— After 15
January 1989   January 1989

Governed by the   Governed by the
Rent Act 1977   Housing Act 1988

Protected/statutory
tenancies

Assured shorthold
tenancies (no security of
tenure, some rent
control)

Assured
tenancies

Security of
tenure (landlord
must prove
grounds for
possession)

Rent control
(fair rent system)

Security of
tenure (landlord
must prove
grounds for
possession)

Market
rents

Chart 3: Registered social landlord (housing association) tenancies

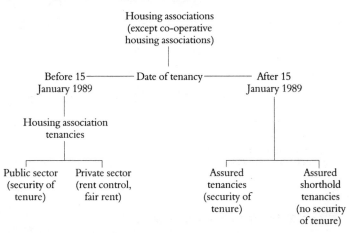

Housing associations
(except co-operative
housing associations)

Before 15 ——— Date of tenancy ——— After 15
January 1989   January 1989

Housing association
tenancies

Public sector
(security of
tenure)

Private sector
(rent control,
fair rent)

Assured
tenancies
(security of
tenure)

Assured
shorthold
tenancies
(no security
of tenure)

of course, usually granted in return for rent but rent is not, legally, an essential part of a tenancy (although landlords who do not charge rent are few and far between). A lease is exactly the same as a tenancy, although in practice the expression 'lease' usually indicates that the property is let for a *fixed* term, such as six months or a specified number of years, whereas a tenancy usually indicates a *periodic* letting, for example, where property is let from week to week or from month to month until terminated by notice. However, the key requirements of any lease or tenancy are:

- a letting for a 'fixed or ascertainable period of time'
- the granting of 'exclusive possession'.

Fixed or ascertainable period

A tenancy or lease must be granted for a period which is defined from the outset or which is capable of being made certain by the act of either party. This presents no difficulty in the vast majority of cases. The tenancy agreement or lease will stipulate when the tenancy is to commence and when (or how) it is to end. The duration of the term is thus known or ascertainable from the outset. Sometimes, however, the situation is less clear. A case involving land adjoining a highway concerned a lease which was granted 'until the land was required for road-widening purposes'. It was

9

held that the land could not be leased for this indefinite period of time as no one could say in advance when the land would be required for this purpose: a 'fixed' or 'ascertainable' period could not therefore be set.

In the case of periodic lettings, although the letting is for an indefinite period, the requirement of certainty is still satisfied. The distinction is that although the tenancy may be allowed to carry on indefinitely, either party may terminate by giving a notice to quit which expires at the end of a relevant week or month of that tenancy. The only uncertainty is *when* the landlord or tenant will choose to give notice; the termination of the letting is not an uncertain duration, dependent upon some future or uncertain event, but can be made certain by either landlord or tenant.

Exclusive possession

Exclusive possession of the property or a defined part of it needs to be specifically granted to the tenant. If the occupier is merely given the right to *share* occupation, for example, with the owner, but not given the *exclusive* use of a specific part of the property, the arrangement would amount to a licence, not a lease or a tenancy. This point is very important since tenants have substantial statutory protection (under the Rent Acts and Housing Acts) which does not, generally, apply to licensees. This point is considered in more detail on pages 18–21. A lodger who merely shares a house with the owner, where the owner has unrestricted access to the lodger's bedroom for cleaning, providing bed linen or services, is usually regarded as a licensee with very little protection under the law. If the owner dies, or sells the house to someone else, the lodger's rights (which are merely personal rights of occupation) would not be binding against the owner's successor. A tenant, on the other hand, is regarded as having an 'interest' in the property, which can be binding on the landlord's successor. Although this book is primarily concerned with the rights of landlords and tenants rather than licensors and licensees, residential licences are covered where appropriate.

The landlord/tenant relationship

The private letting market is expanding. Many would-be landlords are buying property for occupancy by tenants, particularly now that mortgage lenders offer 'buy-to-let' schemes and property for this purpose is widely regarded as a good investment. However, anyone intending to become a landlord should be aware of what can go wrong – and tenants, too, can fall foul of landlords with a cavalier attitude to their responsibilities.

Common problems that arise in renting and letting

Apart from the question of which regime applies to a tenancy (Chapter 1 provides a brief guide to the private-sector ones), disputes frequently occur over:

- rent arrears – what happens if the tenant fails to pay the rent?
- the deposit – how much should it be, what is it for, who holds it, what amounts can be deducted from it, and how does the tenant get it back?
- repairs and maintenance – whose responsibility are they and how can the tenant ensure that the work gets done?
- gas, electricity and telephone bills – how does the landlord ensure that the tenant pays these, especially at the end of a tenancy?
- council tax and water rates – who is liable?
- nuisance or annoyance on the part of the tenant – what powers does the landlord have to control this?
- fluctuating occupiers – how can the landlord keep track of tenants and occupiers that come and go?
- houses in multiple occupation – what powers does the local authority have?
- recovering possession – does the landlord need a court order and, if so, how is this obtained?
- defending possession proceedings – can the tenant stop the landlord recovering possession?

The first of these is one of the most serious. Tenants can fall behind with their rent, or, worse still, build up huge arrears and then move out, with very little chance of being traced or the money recovered. Even tenants who provided good references can fall on hard times after entering into a tenancy agreement, making the recovery of rent difficult for the landlord. For the landlord to seek possession through the courts (which most landlords are legally obliged to do) can be expensive and take several months, especially if the tenant disputes the claim or makes a counter-claim against the landlord –

for example, by claiming that the property has fallen into disrepair and that compensation is therefore due to him because the landlord is in breach of his obligation to repair.

While such problems can never be totally eliminated, some elementary precautions can be taken to reduce them, such as taking care to obtain and check out references, including one to confirm financial status, and making sure that the tenancy agreement covers all potential areas for dispute in clear, explicit terms.

Tenants, on the other hand, could find themselves in a difficult situation if a landlord with a mortgage on his property has failed to obtain his mortgage lender's consent to granting a tenancy. This could lead to the tenants being evicted – not by the landlord, but by his mortgage lender.

This guide aims to alert both sides to potential difficulties, explaining the legal position and, where appropriate, how to obtain redress.

Chapter 1

Letting in the private sector

What follows is a brief overview of the rules that apply in the private sector where the landlord is either a private individual or a company. (Public-sector tenancies are dealt with in Chapter 10.)

For private landlords and tenants there are broadly two regimes. Prior to 15 January 1989 most private residential tenancies were governed by the Rent Acts, which gave most tenants substantial security of tenure: the landlord was unable to gain possession without proving a 'ground' or 'grounds' for doing so; the tenancy could pass on the death of the tenant to the tenant's relatives; and the amount of rent charged was controlled, which meant that landlords could not increase the rent without the approval of a rent officer.

The Rent Acts were good news for tenants but not for landlords, with the result that the private-sector rentals market dwindled over the years. However, some of these Rent Act tenancies, known as 'protected' or 'statutory' tenancies, still exist and will continue to exist for many years (they are covered in Chapter 7).

The second regime was introduced by the Housing Act 1988, itself substantially amended by the Housing Act 1996. This legislation covers assured and assured shorthold tenancies, which came into operation on 15 January 1989. The rationale behind them was to give private landlords choice in how much security of tenure they granted to tenants.

Under an assured tenancy, tenants had some security of tenure in that a ground for possession had to be cited before the landlord could re-possess the property, but there was no restriction on the amount of rent that could be charged.

Alternatively, the landlord could grant an assured shorthold tenancy, which had to be for a minimum of six months but gave no security of tenure after that time and the landlord, after getting a court order, was entitled to possession. A shorthold tenant had some protection against excessive rents, but no security of tenure after six months.

These rules were changed for tenancies granted on or after 28 February 1997 to make most private tenancies assured shortholds unless the landlord opts for an ordinary assured tenancy (sometimes called 'fully assured tenancies' because of the full security of tenure they confer on the tenant). Needless to say, most private landlords prefer assured shorthold tenancies.

Originally, certain formalities applied to assured shorthold tenancies: those granted before 28 February 1997 had to be for a fixed term of at least six months and the landlord was required, before the grant of the tenancy, to serve the tenant with a prescribed form of notice properly informing the tenant of the consequences of the tenancy being shorthold. Failure to comply with this meant that the tenancy was not an assured shorthold but was an ordinary (or fully) assured tenancy with full security of tenure. Many landlords who failed to comply found, to their cost, that they could not evict the tenant even when the six month term expired.

Tenancies granted on or after 28 February 1997 are normally assured shortholds. Even so, the landlord cannot generally obtain possession in the first six months, even if the tenancy was granted for less than six months or was granted on an indefinite or periodic basis. In any event, in order to obtain possession the landlord must still serve proper termination notices and the rules here can still cause problems.

To summarise, the private sector comprises:

- Rent Act tenancies granted prior to 15 January 1989, under which tenants continue to have full security of tenure and control over the amount of rent they pay.
- Housing Act 1988 tenancies granted on or after 15 January 1989 but before 28 February 1997, which will be ordinary (or fully) assured tenancies giving the tenant full security of tenure *unless* the landlord created a proper assured shorthold tenancy for a minimum of six months and complied with the formalities for the creation of an assured shorthold tenancy (in which case the tenant has no security after the minimum fixed term of six months has expired)

- Housing Act 1996 tenancies granted on or after 28 February 1997, which will automatically be deemed assured shorthold tenancies unless the landlord has specifically opted to grant an ordinary (or fully) assured tenancy (a rare occurrence).

Sometimes neither the Rent Acts nor the Housing Acts apply to the tenancy. Certain tenancies are excluded altogether. For example, if the landlord is a resident landlord living in another part of the same building containing the rented accommodation, subject to certain conditions neither regime will apply – hence, the tenant will have none of the rights granted to Rent Act or Housing Act tenants.

Chapter 2

Assured shorthold tenancies

The Housing Act 1988 'invented' two different types of tenancy of residential property: assured tenancies and assured shorthold tenancies.

An assured tenancy gives the tenant extensive security of tenure, which means that at the end of the agreed term of the letting the tenant does not have to leave but has a legal right to stay on for as long as he or she wants, unless and until the landlord can establish one of the grounds for possession laid down by the Act. These include, for example, rent arrears or the fact that the landlord wants to live in the property himself.

Assured tenancies are sometimes referred to as 'ordinary assured tenancies' to distinguish them more clearly from assured shorthold tenancies (which are usually referred to simply as 'shortholds' for the same reason).

An assured shorthold tenancy gives the tenant no security of tenure after the ending of the contractual term of the letting. So the landlord is certain to obtain possession on or after the end of the term agreed between the parties. However, to do so he will still need to go to court and follow the correct procedure, giving the tenant at least two months' notice in writing. But there is no need for the landlord to give reasons as to why he wants possession. This is why shortholds have proved so popular with landlords. As far as rent is concerned, however, shortholds do have one slight advantage for tenants in that if the tenant considers the rent excessive, he can refer it to the Rent Assessment Committee, which will decide the appropriate rent for the property. As we shall see, there are various time limits within which this right can be exercised and no question of the rent being reduced below the open market rent for the property. The provision only prevents the landlord from over-charging. It has to be said that, although this right exists, it is comparatively rare for tenants to avail themselves of it, partly, no doubt, because tenants are unaware that they have the right; certainly the landlord is not obliged to inform them of it.

Virtually all lettings of residential property starting on or after 28 February 1997 will be shortholds.

Advantages of shortholds for landlords

In most parts of Britain it is very difficult to find property to let on anything other than a shorthold basis. Not only does this give the landlord the absolute right to possession, but if a shorthold landlord wishes to obtain it he can use the accelerated possession procedure (see Chapter 14), a special process that is both quicker and cheaper than normal court procedures for obtaining possession.

As well as having an absolute right to possession at the end of the agreed term of the letting, the landlord can also obtain possession from a tenant during the tenancy in certain circumstances, including non-payment of rent. This right is, however, dependent upon a special term being incorporated in the letting agreement (see Chapter 5).

Old shortholds and new shortholds

The Housing Act 1988 gives landlords the choice of the type of tenancy to use. But the rules as to when a letting could be a shorthold changed as from 28 February 1997. So we have 'new' shortholds (i.e., those granted on or after that date), and 'old' shortholds (i.e., those granted before it).

Until 28 February 1997, to be a shorthold a letting had to comply with various conditions: one of these was that the landlord had to serve a notice on the tenant prior to the letting stating that it was going to be a shorthold. If the conditions were not complied with, the letting would be an ordinary assured tenancy giving the tenant full security of tenure. As many current lettings were initiated prior to 28 February 1997, this guide outlines both sets of rules. 'Old' shortholds are further discussed in Chapter 7.

All lettings granted on or after 28 February 1997 are shortholds unless a notice was served to say the letting was to be an ordinary assured tenancy, so the 'default' position has been completely reversed. Note, however, that if the letting is a renewal of a tenancy originally made before that date, the pre-28 February 1997 position must be considered as well.

New shortholds (lettings made on or after 28 February 1997)

Although it is most likely that any letting of residential property made on or after this date is a shorthold, various conditions have to be fulfilled before this can be confirmed. To be a shorthold, a tenancy must satisfy the definition of an assured tenancy in the 1988 Act, so these conditions apply to all lettings made on or after 15 January 1989, whether assured or shorthold tenancies (and whether new or old shortholds). Unless these conditions are complied with, the 1988 Act will not apply at all and the tenant will have no security of tenure or recourse to rent control.

A tenancy under which a house is let as a 'separate dwelling' will be an assured tenancy if and so long as *all* the following requirements are met:

(1) the tenant or each of the joint tenants is an individual
(2) the tenant or at least one of the joint tenants occupies the dwellinghouse as his only or principal home, and
(3) the tenancy is not specifically excluded by other provisions of the Act.

Some of the terms used in these requirements have particular meanings, as described below.

'Tenancy'

The letting must be a 'tenancy', not simply a licence to occupy the property. (If an occupier does not have the right to the sole possession of some part of the house, he will be a licensee and not a tenant: see also the section on the legal definition of a tenancy in the Introduction.)

'House'

There is no precise definition of 'house', but in this context it is wider than the everyday use of the word. Any building designed or adapted for living in is capable of being a house – hence, the definition could include not just lettings of whole houses but lettings of flats and also lettings of, for example, converted barns, windmills and so on.

'Let as a separate dwelling'

The property which is let, as well as being a 'house', must be let *as* a 'dwelling'. So the purpose of the letting is relevant; hence, if a building that would otherwise qualify as a house is let for business purposes (for example, as an office), the tenant cannot claim that it is let on an assured or shorthold tenancy merely because he decides to move in and live there. (A tenant of business premises is, however, likely to have other statutory protection, but this is beyond the scope of this book.)

The property must be let as 'a' dwelling – that is, one single dwelling only. So if the property let comprises two or more residential units, each intended for separate occupation (for example, a house which has been converted into several flats), that tenancy cannot be an assured tenancy. The subletting of each of the individual flats, however, could be within the definition.

The property must be 'separate': hence, accommodation which lacks some essential feature of a dwelling, such as a kitchen, is excluded. So the letting of a single room without kitchen and bathroom facilities would not be capable of being an assured or shorthold tenancy even though the tenant 'lived' in the room. If the tenant of such a room were given the right to share such essential facilities with others in another part of the building, the letting could then be an assured tenancy. However, the tenant must have the right to the exclusive possession of at least one room (otherwise the arrangement cannot be a tenancy at all).

Note that if the facilities are shared with the landlord, the tenancy will be excluded from the definition of an assured or shorthold tenancy for different reasons: see 'Resident landlords', on page 32.

These rules are important in, for example, the common situation where a house has been converted into flatlets and each tenant is given exclusive occupation of his own bed-sitting room but shares a bathroom and kitchen with other tenants. The lettings of each flatlet could well fall within the 1988 Act.

But if each of a group of people were given a right to share the occupation of the whole of the house with the others, and no one had the right to exclusive possession of any part of the house, the arrangement could give rise only to a licence, not a tenancy of any kind. In such 'sharing' cases, care must be taken to ascertain precisely what rights are being given to the occupiers. If, say, five people were each given a separate right to share the whole house and were left to decide between them who has which bedroom, this would be a licence. On the other hand, if the owner of the house were to give each of the same five people the right to the use of a specified room and then to share the rest of the house with the others, each of them could have a shorthold.

'If and so long as'

The status of the tenancy is not to be determined once and for all at the commencement of the letting. Whether a tenancy is a shorthold can fluctuate during its subsistence according to changed circumstances. For example, one requirement of the definition is that the tenant must be occupying the house as his only or principal home. This may have been the case at the start of the tenancy, which puts the tenancy within the 1988 Act, but if subsequently the tenant were to cease to reside there, the tenancy would no longer be within the Act. The landlord would then be able to obtain possession without having to follow the procedure laid down by the Act; he would still need a court order, however (see Chapter 14).

The tenant must be an 'individual'

'Individual' in this context means a human being. So the letting must be to a human being, or to several human beings. Lettings to companies are therefore excluded from the definition, even though a human employee or director of the company may well be in occupation of the house. Lettings to limited companies were in the past sometimes used by landlords as a way of avoiding the grant of an assured tenancy with its security-of-tenure implications. However, as all lettings to individuals will now be shortholds without any security, there is no longer any need for this device.

The tenant must occupy the property as his 'only or principal home'

A person's 'home' is the place in which he intends to live permanently, as opposed to occupying it temporarily. The law recognises, however, that it is possible for a person to have more than one 'home' (some, for example, live near their place of work during the week and elsewhere at weekends). If that is the case, the circumstances will decide which is the tenant's principal home. Only a tenancy of the principal home can be an assured or shorthold tenancy. A 'holiday home' would not, therefore, be entitled to the protection of the Act.

Although the provision requires 'occupation', this does not mean continuous occupation. A temporary absence, due to holidays or hospitalisation, for example, would not deprive a tenancy of its status within the 1988 Act.

Tenancies specifically excluded from the definition within the 1988 Act

Various lettings which satisfy the basic definition of an assured tenancy will not, in fact, be protected if they constitute one of the following exceptions.

Tenancies entered into before the commencement of the 1988 Act

The Housing Act 1988 came into force on 15 January 1989. Only lettings entered into on or after that date can be assured or shorthold tenancies. Any tenancy already in existence on that day will, if it has any protection at all, still remain subject to the provisions of the Rent Act 1977 (see Chapter 7).

High-value properties

Owing to the abolition of domestic rates, a distinction is drawn between those tenancies granted before 1 April 1990 and those granted on or after that date. For tenancies granted before 1 April 1990, a tenancy of a house with a rateable value in excess of £750 (£1,500 in Greater London) cannot be an assured or shorthold tenancy.

If the tenancy was granted on or after 1 April 1990, it cannot be assured or a shorthold if the rent payable is £25,000 or more per annum.

Tenancies at a low rent

This exclusion has also been affected by the abolition of domestic rates. Lettings made before 1 April 1990 cannot be assured or a shorthold if the annual rent is less than two-thirds of the rateable value of the property. For tenancies granted on or after 1 April 1990, the exclusion applies to tenancies in which the rent does not exceed £250 per annum (£1,000 per annum in Greater London).

Business tenancies

A tenancy in which the premises are occupied for the purposes of a business, or for business and other purposes, is excluded from being an assured tenancy. Lettings of property used partly for business and partly for residential purposes cannot be assured tenancies, even if they are occupied by the tenant as his only or principal home, and so on. Hence, a letting of a traditional corner shop with living accommodation over it would be excluded, although such a tenancy may well have some protection under the statutory protections given to business tenancies.

Tenancies of agricultural land

Tenancies of agricultural land will be excluded even though the tenant lives on the property. Such tenants will probably have other statutory rights under the legislation relating to agricultural holdings (beyond the scope of this book).

Lettings to students

Lettings to students by specified educational bodies, such as universities and colleges, are outside the definition of an assured tenancy. Note that this exception does not apply to lettings to students by landlords other than the institutions themselves; lettings to students by private landlords are capable of being assured tenancies, subject to the normal requirements being fulfilled.

Holiday lettings

A letting for the purpose of a holiday cannot be an assured tenancy. In the past, some landlords tried to exploit this exception by purportedly granting holiday lettings in non-holiday areas and for excessively long periods of time in order to avoid granting an assured tenancy with security of tenure. However, as all lettings are now shortholds without any security, there is no longer any need for them to use this ploy – which, in any event, did not succeed in deceiving the courts.

Lettings by resident landlords
If the landlord lives in another part of the building occupied by the tenant, it is likely that there will not be an assured tenancy (see below).

Crown, local authority and housing association lettings
Although these are excluded from the definition of an assured tenancy, lettings by local authorities and housing associations may have other protections: see Chapters 10 and 11 respectively. Lettings by the Crown Estate, which administers property owned by the Queen in her private capacity, will be within the 1988 Act.

Existing Rent Act tenants

The 1988 Housing Act gives assured tenants less protection in some areas (and particularly with regard to rent) than those given to tenants protected by the 1977 Rent Act. Although new tenancies were to be covered by the 1988 Housing Act, existing Rent Act tenants were not to lose their existing protections. In case unscrupulous landlords contrived to grant new tenancies to their existing tenants after the 1988 Housing Act had come into force, thus depriving the tenants of their existing Rent Act protections, anti-avoidance provisions were written into the 1988 Act.

Therefore, a tenancy granted to a person with a subsisting Rent Act tenancy by that person's landlord (or one of joint landlords) will still be Rent Act-protected, even if it was granted on or after 15 January 1989. This will be the case even if the house let under the new tenancy is different from that let to the tenant under the original tenancy: hence, a landlord cannot deprive his existing Rent Act tenants of their protection by granting them a new letting of a different house. Note that this rule applies only where there is no gap between the end of the Rent Act tenancy and the new letting. If, for example, the tenant were to move out for a short period and then be granted a new tenancy, it is likely that the new tenancy would be within the 1988 Act and the Rent Act protection would be lost.

The only exception to this provision occurs where the tenant was a protected shorthold tenant under the Rent Act 1977. Protected shortholds were the forerunners of today's assured shortholds and like them gave no security of tenure. Any new letting to a protected shorthold tenant will always be an *assured* shorthold. For further information on protected shortholds, see Chapter 7.

Rent under a new shorthold tenancy

There is no restriction on the amount of rent which can initially be charged on the grant of a shorthold tenancy. (This is so even if there is an existing registration of a fair rent for the purposes of the Rent Act 1977: see Chapter 7.) The amount of the rent paid under an assured tenancy is whatever landlord and tenant agree. Market forces will therefore prevail.

However, if the landlord subsequently wishes to *increase* the rent, he may not be able to do so unless he follows the correct procedure.

Also, a tenant may have a right to challenge the amount of the rent originally agreed by referring it to the Rent Assessment Committee.

Contractual increases in rent

Under contract law, a landlord cannot unilaterally vary the terms of a tenancy after it has been granted. He cannot, therefore, change the amount of the rent payable without the consent of the tenant, *unless* the terms of the tenancy allow the landlord to do so. Some landlords seem unable to grasp this point.

From a landlord's point of view, therefore, it is wise to include a term in any tenancy agreement allowing the landlord to increase the rent. The kind of provision to be included is discussed in Chapter 5 and a landlord wishing to increase the rent must follow the procedure set out in the tenancy agreement.

Many informally granted tenancies, however, contain no such provision. This could disadvantage the landlord, who, in the case of a long-term tenancy, might find the value of the rent being eroded by the effects of inflation.

To relieve this potential unfairness, the 1988 Housing Act contains provisions enabling a landlord to increase the rent even though this is not permitted by the terms of the agreement. These provisions, however, apply only to periodic (i.e. weekly or monthly) tenancies and the procedure is somewhat complex. It is therefore still advisable to include a provision for rent increase even in a periodic tenancy, to avoid the need to resort to the procedure. See Chapter 5 for the form the provision should take.

Statutory increases for periodic tenancies

If there is no provision in the tenancy agreement for an assured or shorthold tenancy allowing the landlord to increase the rent, he can do so by following the procedure laid down by the 1988 Act. This is a complex procedure requiring the landlord to serve a notice, in the prescribed form, on the tenant suggesting a figure for the new rent. The tenant can then refer this notice to the Rent Assessment Committee (an independent, public body which operates on a regional basis) for arbitration if agreement on the new rent cannot be reached.

The Rent Assessment Committee is directed to determine the rent at which the premises might reasonably be let in the open market. This is not, however, like the old 'fair rent' system under the 1977 Rent Act, which permitted a rent below the open market rent to be imposed (see Chapter 7). None the less, if a term in the tenancy agreement expressly permits rent increases, there will be no need to rely on the statutory procedure. Any other increase of rent imposed without following this procedure would be unlawful and could not be recovered from the tenant.

Rent increases for fixed-term tenancies

There are no statutory provisions providing for a rent increase in a fixed-term tenancy (for example, one for 18 months); the provisions apply only to periodic tenancies. In the absence of any express provision in the tenancy agreement the landlord will be unable to increase the rent during the fixed term without the agreement of the tenant. It is, therefore, advisable to include in the agreement for any fixed-term tenancy of over (say) 12 months an express provision allowing the rent to be increased. However, the attempt to do so may be frustrated by the tenant referring the original rent to the Rent Assessment Committee (see below).

Once the fixed term has ended the tenant will continue in possession as a statutory periodic tenant (see below). The above provisions concerning the statutory right to increase rent in a periodic tenancy would then apply to enable the landlord to increase the rent. Alternatively, at the end of a shorthold the landlord has an absolute right to possession and could therefore obtain possession and grant a new tenancy at a higher rent. This could be granted to the same tenant, if the tenant wanted to stay on, without the need to obtain possession. The tenant would then be faced with Hobson's choice – either agreeing to a new tenancy at a higher rent or potentially losing his home – as the landlord has an absolute right to possession under a shorthold.

Referring the rent to the Rent Assessment Committee

A shorthold tenant can refer the rent originally agreed on the grant of the tenancy to the Rent Assessment Committee, which will then determine the amount of rent payable. The referral can be made only during the first six months of the tenancy. Furthermore, the committee can make such a determination only if there is a sufficient number of similar dwellinghouses in the locality let on assured tenancies *and* the rent payable under the shorthold is significantly higher than the rent which the landlord might reasonably be expected to obtain in the light of the level of rent paid under these other tenancies. The committee compares the rents being charged for similar properties in the locality and then decides what the rent for the premises in question should be – which will never be lower than the market rent.

A landlord is at risk of a lower rent being fixed only if he is charging 'significantly' more than the market rent for the house. Applications by tenants to the Rent Assessment Committee are comparatively few in number.

Rent Assessment Committee decisions

The effect of a rent being fixed by the Rent Assessment Committee differs depending upon whether it is a fixed-term tenancy or a periodic tenancy.

In the case of a fixed-term tenancy, the rent will become the maximum rent chargeable for the property throughout the remainder of the fixed term. This is despite anything to the contrary in the tenancy agreement, and there is no provision for this figure to be increased during the fixed term, no matter how long that might be. It is for this reason that landlords are advised to avoid the grant of long shortholds. In the case, for example, of a 21-year shorthold, a rent fixed in the first six months would continue to apply for the remainder of the term, despite any provisions in the tenancy agreement allowing the landlord to increase the amount of the rent.

On the ending of the fixed term, and assuming that no new tenancy has been granted, a statutory periodic tenancy will arise. The landlord can increase the rent payable under this tenancy above that assessed by the committee by following the statutory procedure for periodic tenancies mentioned above. Twelve months must have passed, however, since the assessment before this procedure can be followed. As the statutory procedure is somewhat complex and long-winded, it would be more sensible for the landlord to grant a new tenancy at an increased rent. As mentioned above, this could be to the same tenant if that tenant were to agree; if he did not, possession could be obtained against him.

In the case of a periodic tenancy, the rent will remain as fixed by the committee unless and until the landlord is able to increase it using the statutory procedure for increasing rents in periodic tenancies. Note that the landlord may not use this procedure until 12 months have expired since the rent was assessed by the committee. Note also that the statutory procedure is available only where there are no provisions in the tenancy agreement allowing the landlord to increase the rent, in which case the landlord would have no need of it.

But, of course, the landlord has an absolute right to possession and can terminate the tenancy by giving two months' notice (see Chapter 14) and then granting a new tenancy. As before, this could be to the same tenant, if he was agreeable; if not, possession could be obtained and a new tenant found.

The right to apply for the rent to be assessed is a once-and-for-all right given to the tenant. Once the rent has been determined by the committee no further application for the fixing of a different figure can be made by either landlord or tenant, even if market rents change in the meantime.

The rent determined by the committee applies only during the particular tenancy in question, however. It will not limit the amount of rent chargeable under any subsequent letting of the same property, even if this is between the same landlord and tenant.

When an application to the Rent Assessment Committee is not possible

A tenant can apply to the committee only within the first six months of the tenancy. If a tenant has a succession of lettings (for example, two successive lettings for three months), he can apply within six months of the grant of the first tenancy to him. Apart from this situation, a tenant who does not apply for the rent to be assessed during the first shorthold granted to him will not be able to apply during any subsequent letting; this is irrespective of whether an application was made during the original shorthold. Note also that only one application to the committee can be made. Once the rent has been determined by the committee, it cannot be resubmitted for a further determination, even if the original determination was many years before.

Transferring the tenancy and subletting

A tenancy 'belongs' to the tenant in just the same way as his car would. He can therefore freely 'assign' it, i.e. sell it or give it away, to whomsoever he likes. Alternatively, he can sublet – that is, grant a lease shorter than his own, or take in lodgers.

This is all well and good from the point of view of the tenant but will not be acceptable to the landlord; there is little point in the landlord carefully checking the references of a tenant only to find that the tenant has later assigned the tenancy to a person who would have been unacceptable to him. It is usual, therefore, to find in the tenancy agreement a clause expressly prohibiting assignment and subletting. If the landlord has included such a provision this will be binding on the tenant. Sometimes the landlord will not completely prohibit assignment and subletting but will state that such arrangements require his consent. This would give him the opportunity to vet any prospective new occupant of the premises in the same way as he would check up on any other would-be tenant.

A risk remains that such a 'consent' clause could be used unfairly by a landlord, any request for consent being arbitrarily refused or simply ignored altogether. The Landlord and Tenant Act 1927 and the Landlord and Tenant Act 1988 provide, however, that a landlord cannot unreasonably withhold his consent and must respond to a tenant's request within a reasonable period.

However, if there is no such express provision, the 1988 Housing Act may be of some assistance to the landlord as it implies a term prohibiting assignments, subletting and so on. The Act applies only to periodic shortholds (including statutory periodic tenancies); like the provisions allowing increases of rent, it does not apply to fixed-term shortholds. Thus, in the absence of an express contractual prohibition, a fixed-term tenant will be able to assign or sublet as he chooses.

Statutory prohibition

The term implied into a periodic tenancy by the 1988 Act is that the tenant shall not without the consent of the landlord assign the tenancy *or* sublet or part with possession of all or part of the property.

These prohibitions do *not* apply if a premium was paid on the grant or renewal of the tenancy. 'Premium' includes any money payments in addition to rent (such as a lump-sum payment on the grant of the lease) and also returnable deposits exceeding one-sixth of the annual rent.

Note also that this statutorily implied prohibition does *not* prevent the taking in of lodgers or the sharing of accommodation with someone else, for example, a cohabitee.

The statutory rules noted above whereby a landlord may not withhold his consent unreasonably do not apply to consents required under this statutory rule. So a landlord can be as unreasonable as he likes in refusing consent.

As these statutory restrictions do not apply to fixed-term tenancies, this is a potential problem for landlords granting assured shortholds. Although an assured shorthold tenant has no security of tenure, any subtenancy granted by an assured shorthold tenant is capable of being an assured tenancy with full security of tenure which can be binding upon the head landlord. The head landlord will therefore be entitled to possession in respect of the assured shorthold head tenant but not the subtenant, which is hardly satisfactory from the head landlord's point of view.

In *all* cases, a landlord granting a shorthold must avoid this potential problem, by ensuring that the tenancy agreement contains an express provision prohibiting subletting. With such a provision, no subletting would be binding upon the head landlord. See Chapter 5 for the wording of such a provision.

Death of a tenant

Fixed-term tenancies

As explained above, a tenancy 'belongs' to the tenant, therefore his tenancy does not die with him; it will pass on in the same way as the deceased's other property. So, on the death of one of two or more joint tenants, the tenancy will become the sole property of the survivor(s). On the death of a sole tenant the tenancy will pass to the person nominated in his will. If the tenancy is not expressly given to a particular person, it will pass with the 'residue' of the estate – hence, it will pass to the person who is given all the remainder of the deceased's property which has not been otherwise disposed of.

If the tenant dies without leaving a valid will (intestate) the laws of inheritance will decide to whom his property will pass; often this will be his spouse.

Periodic tenancies

The 1988 Housing Act contains specific provisions concerning the succession to a periodic tenancy on the death of a sole tenant which override other inheritance laws.

On the death of a sole periodic tenant the tenancy will pass to the tenant's spouse, provided that the spouse has been occupying the dwellinghouse as his/her only or principal home immediately prior to the death, notwithstanding the terms of the deceased's will.

The word 'spouse' can include a person who was living with the tenant as his or her wife or husband even though they were not actually married. Because of the requirement that a partner must be living with the tenant 'as husband or wife' the courts have held that a same-sex partner cannot succeed under this provision. This finding may be subject to challenge under the Human Rights Act.

These succession rights will not apply if the deceased tenant was himself a 'successor', under the terms of the definition: that is, the tenancy became vested in him:

(1) by virtue of this provision
(2) under the will or intestacy of a former tenant
(3) he is the sole survivor of joint tenants, or
(4) he succeeded to the tenancy under the provisions of Rent Act 1977 (see Chapter 7).

Therefore only one statutory succession is possible. If X, the tenant, dies and Y succeeds to the tenancy under this provision, there can be no further passing-on of the tenancy under the Act, even if Y was living in the house with his/her spouse.

If there is no statutory succession, for example, because there is no qualifying 'spouse', or there has already been a succession, or the tenancy is for a fixed term, the tenancy will then pass under the will or intestacy of the deceased as set out above.

Subtenants

A subtenancy occurs when the person granting the lease is himself merely a tenant of the property. The law recognises that a tenant can himself grant a lease giving the right of exclusive possession of the property to someone else, who then becomes a subtenant. The only restriction is that this sublease must be for a shorter duration than the length of time as yet unexpired of the landlord's own lease. So a tenant with two years of his lease unexpired could grant a sublease for any period not exceeding one year and 364 days. The tenant would continue paying his rent to his landlord in the normal way, but would himself receive rent from the subtenant. This might be a sensible arrangement if the rent being paid by the subtenant were more than the rent due from the tenant to his landlord.

As between any particular landlord and tenant, it is irrelevant whether the landlord owns the freehold interest in the property or is himself merely a tenant. If the conditions are complied with for the creation of a shorthold tenancy, then the subtenant will have a shorthold. This will be the case even if the lease under which his landlord owns the property ('the head lease') prohibits subletting (see above).

The problem, however, is that this subtenant may not have any rights in relation to the head landlord. Hence, although the subtenant's own landlord will not be able to evict him until the end of any fixed term, and then only by following the correct shorthold procedure, it may be possible for the head landlord to obtain possession against him immediately.

If the head lease prohibits the granting of subleases, either expressly or otherwise (see above), the subtenant will have no protection against the head landlord once the head lease has come to an end. Once the head lease has come to an end the head landlord will have an immediate right to possession without the need to prove any reason or grounds for possession, or to serve the normal two months' notice, or to wait until the end of any fixed term. Although the head landlord still may not evict the subtenant without obtaining a court order, this will be available as a matter of right.

If, on the other hand, the subtenancy was *not* prohibited by the terms of the head lease, the subtenant will have a tenancy binding against both his own landlord and any head landlord, irrespective of whether the head lease comes to an end or not.

This is a potential problem for landlords granting assured shortholds. Although an assured shorthold tenant has no security of tenure, any subtenancy granted by an assured shorthold tenant is capable of being an assured tenancy with full security of tenure, which can thus become binding upon the head landlord. (Chapter 3 covers the grant of assured tenancies which are not shortholds.) So the head landlord will be entitled to possession in respect of the assured shorthold head tenant but not the subtenant, which is hardly satisfactory from the head landlord's point of view. Remember, the statutory restriction on subletting is not implicit in a fixed-term shorthold tenancy.

A landlord granting a fixed-term shorthold can avoid this potential problem, by ensuring that the tenancy agreement contains an express provision prohibiting subletting. With such a provision, no subletting would be binding upon the head landlord. (See Chapter 5 for the wording of the provision.)

Resident landlords

Most lettings by resident landlords occupying another part of the same building are excluded from the definition of an assured or a shorthold tenancy; their tenants will therefore have no security of tenure, and may also have only limited protection under the protection-from-eviction legislation (see Chapter 13). This situation is often referred to as the 'resident landlord exception'.

For the resident landlord exception to apply, various conditions must be fulfilled (see below); however, as all lettings starting on and from 28 February 1997 will be shortholds and as shortholds have no security of tenure anyway, the main significance of the resident landlord exception will be for tenants whose tenancies were entered into prior to 28 February 1997. In the case of lettings starting on and after that date, the effect of the resident landlord rule will be that:

- the tenant has no right to refer the rent to the Rent Assessment Committee
- the tenant is not entitled to the minimum two months' notice required to terminate a shorthold

- the tenant may not have the protection of the protection-from-eviction legislation (see Chapter 13)
- the statutory succession provisions do not apply
- the statutory rules on increasing the rent and not assigning will not apply.

For the letting to be excluded from the definition of an assured or a shorthold tenancy all of the following conditions must be complied with:

- the dwellinghouse which is let must form only part of a building
- the building must not be a purpose-built block of flats
- the tenancy must have been granted by an individual (i.e. not a limited company) who at the time of the grant occupied another part of the same building as his only or principal home, and
- at all times since the tenancy was granted the interest of the landlord has continued to belong to an individual who continued so to reside.

Hence, the resident landlord exception covers the situation where the tenant lives in part of a building and the landlord lives in another part of the same building, provided that the building is not a purpose-built block of flats. So if a landlord lives in a large house and lets part of it, or converts a house into several flats, lives in one and lets the others, the lettings will be outside the definition of an assured or a shorthold tenancy.

However, if the building was constructed in flats (as opposed to being converted into flats) the lettings will be capable of being assured tenancies or shortholds even if the landlord lives in one of the flats himself.

The reason for the exception is that it is thought unwise to give security of tenure to tenants when they are living in close proximity with the landlord – forcing people to live together, as it were. In a purpose-built block of flats there is less chance for the sort of incident that can sour relationships, hence the exception to the normal rule.

It is not sufficient for the landlord just to have been in residence at the commencement of the tenancy: he must be in occupation throughout the tenancy. If he ceases to reside at the premises the exception will cease to apply and the letting will once again be capable of being an assured tenancy with full security of tenure.

However, if the landlord is two or more individuals, only one of those persons need be in residence at any one time.

Note that periods of absence by the landlord whilst on holiday, in hospital and so on will not end his residence. Also, although on a change of landlord the new landlord must also take up residence for the exception to apply, certain periods of absence, on a change of ownership or on the death of the landlord, for example, will not invalidate the exemption from security of tenure.

The landlord must be resident at the start of the tenancy. If he is not, the exception will not apply, even if he moves in at a later date and is still in residence when possession is being sought. Furthermore, if a tenant has an assured tenancy (i.e. there is no resident landlord), and the landlord then moves in and grants him a further tenancy this second tenancy will *not* be subject to the resident landlord exception even though the landlord was in residence at the start of the second tenancy and remains so throughout the letting. This is an anti-avoidance provision designed to ensure that a landlord does not deprive existing tenants of their protection as assured tenants by moving in and then granting a new tenancy to them.

Expiry of a shorthold

On the ending of a fixed term, the tenant is allowed to remain in possession as a statutory periodic tenant. However, the tenant still has no security of tenure. The court must still make an order for possession if the landlord follows the correct procedure (he must serve the tenant with not less than two months' notice stating that he requires possession: see Chapter 14).

In the case of a shorthold which is a periodic tenancy, this can only be brought to an end by the landlord if he obtains a court order for possession and will again require the service of not less than two months' notice.

Note, however, that in the case of both fixed-term and periodic shortholds, the court cannot order the tenant to give up possession before six months have passed since the grant of the tenancy. This is so even if the fixed-term letting was for a shorter period – for example, three months. A landlord wishing to let for a period shorter than six months – and be sure of obtaining possession – will be able to do so only if he can grant an ordinary assured tenancy and rely on one of the ordinary assured mandatory grounds for possession (see Chapter 3).

Termination of tenancy by the tenant

It is not always appreciated by tenants that a tenancy is a contract, placing obligations on them as well as on the landlord. So if a tenant enters into a 12-month fixed term, he cannot terminate the letting before the end of those 12 months without the landlord's consent. If he does attempt to terminate it within the period without consent – by just leaving, or sending the keys back to the landlord, the landlord is entitled to claim the full amount of rent from him until the end of the fixed period.

In the case of a periodic tenancy, the tenant can terminate it only, unless the landlord agrees otherwise, by serving notice on the landlord in writing: one month's notice in the case of a monthly tenancy and four weeks' notice in the case of a weekly tenancy. As well as being served at the correct time, the notice must also expire at the end of a completed period of the tenancy. This is sometimes referred to as the 'corresponding day rule', as the notice always has to expire on the same day of the week or month. This means, for example, that for a weekly tenancy beginning on a Monday, the notice must expire on a Sunday (technically, the tenancy ends at midnight on the Sunday, so a notice terminating on a Monday would also be acceptable). For a monthly tenancy commencing on the 23rd of a month, the notice must expire on the 22nd of a subsequent month, although the 23rd would also be acceptable: no other day would be acceptable, however.

Obtaining possession

The court must order possession on or after the ending of a shorthold, provided that the landlord follows the correct procedure, serving a 'Section 21 notice' on the tenant and giving the tenant at least two months' notice that he requires possession (see Chapter 14). As previously stated, however, in the case of both fixed-term and periodic shortholds, the court order cannot order the tenant to give up possession before six months have passed since the grant of the tenancy. This is the case even if the fixed-term letting was for a shorter period, such as three months.

Other grounds for possession

As a shorthold is a type of assured tenancy the mandatory and discretionary grounds which apply to ordinary assured tenancies can also apply (see Chapter 3 for these). Of course, as a landlord has an absolute right to possession under a shorthold, he would normally have no need to use these grounds.

However, the normal shorthold procedure to obtain possession can be used only after any fixed term granted has expired. So, for example, in the case of a 12-month fixed-term tenancy, the landlord can obtain possession under the shorthold procedure only at the end of that 12 months. This could be a problem for a landlord faced with a tenant who refuses to pay the rent.

However, some of the ordinary assured tenancy grounds can be used during a fixed term, including mandatory ground 8 and discretionary grounds 10 and 11 (all of which relate to rent arrears). As with other assured tenancies, these grounds can be used during the fixed term only if the tenancy agreement contains provisions allowing them to be used. These grounds are considered in detail in Chapter 3 and Chapter 5 contains advice on drafting the tenancy agreement so that the grounds can be used. Without provision within the agreement to use the grounds for possession, the landlord cannot obtain possession from a defaulting tenant until the end of the fixed term. He would, of course, be able to sue the tenant for the arrears, but the tenant might not be able to pay.

If faced with a periodic shorthold tenant who defaults on the rent, the landlord can make use of the normal shorthold procedure for obtaining possession and immediately serve the usual two months' notice.

As previously explained, however, possession can still not be ordered until after the expiry of six months from the commencement of the tenancy.

Statement of the terms of the tenancy

It is always advisable to have a written tenancy agreement that sets out all of the terms relating to the letting. However, many tenancies are still granted orally, which often leads to a dispute between landlord and tenant concerning what was agreed. The 1996 Housing Act therefore places an obligation on the landlord of a new shorthold tenancy to provide the tenant with a statement of at least the more important terms of the tenancy.

The landlord must provide details of the following terms:

* the tenancy's commencement date
* the rent payable and the dates on which it is due
* any terms providing for rent review
* the length of a fixed-term tenancy.

The tenant may make a request in writing for these details. It is a criminal offence for the landlord to fail to provide the information within 28 days, unless he has a reasonable excuse (for example, being away on holiday when the request was served).

This provision relates to oral tenancies, or those which are in writing but contain no reference to one or more of the points listed above.

The provision might seem a strange one, as it might appear to allow the landlord to dictate the terms of the tenancy, which should have been the subject of agreement between the parties. However, the Act makes it clear that a statement by the landlord is not to be regarded as conclusive evidence as to those terms, as this can be only his version of what was agreed and his version could be challenged by the tenant.

The procedure whereby the tenant requests details of the terms of the tenancy is little used in practice.

Q *I have a 12-month shorthold tenancy with six months left to run but I need to move to a different town because of my job. Can I leave if I give the landlord a month's notice?*

A Legally speaking, you can leave at any time, but you will still be obliged to continue paying the rent until the end of the 12 months. You agreed to pay the rent for the full 12 months and unless there is something written into the tenancy agreement allowing you to leave early, the rent is still due from you. Your only hope is to approach the landlord on an informal basis and explain your problem. He may be sympathetic and agree to let you off future payments of rent, particularly if you find someone to take over the flat when you leave.

Q *I have a 12-month shorthold with six months left to run. Last week the landlord told me that he was putting up the rent next week. Can he do so?*

A Only if there is something in the tenancy agreement which gives him the right to do so. If there is not, the rent must remain fixed until the end of the fixed term. He can then increase the rent, but if you do not accept that the proposed increase is reasonable, you can insist that he follows the procedure laid down for assured tenancies (see page 25) and the matter can then be referred to a Rent Assessment Committee for an independent assessment of the correct amount of rent payable. Remember, however, that at the end of the 12 months, the landlord has an absolute right to obtain possession from you. An amicable settlement is obviously preferable.

Q *Before I took my tenancy, my landlord told me that it was going to be a shorthold, but no written notice was ever given to me. The tenancy has now come to an end and the landlord says I must move out next week. Do I have to go?*

A This depends on the date your tenancy was granted, but in any event the landlord needs to obtain a court order for possession.

If your tenancy was granted after the Housing Act 1996 came into operation and the landlord has given you the appropriate two-month termination notice (see Chapter 14), the court must order possession. If, however, your tenancy began before the Housing Act 1996 came into force your tenancy cannot be an assured shorthold as the landlord did not give you the correct form of notice before the commencement. This means you have an ordinary assured tenancy (see Chapter 3) and so you have security of tenure. The landlord must show that a ground for possession exists and (if he is relying upon a discretionary ground) that it is reasonable for the court to order possession.

Q *I granted a six-month shorthold tenancy which expired three months ago. Since then I have continued to accept rent from the tenant on a monthly basis, but there has been no further agreement between us. I now want the tenant to leave, but she says she does not have to do so as she now has an ordinary assured tenancy with full security of tenure. Is she right?*

A No. On the ending of a shorthold and in the absence of the grant of a new tenancy, the tenant remains in occupation as a statutory periodic tenant. But this implied tenancy is still a shorthold, unless the landlord informs the tenant that it is not to be a shorthold. Even if a new tenancy had been expressly granted, that too would be a shorthold unless the landlord tells the tenant otherwise. So you have an absolute entitlement to possession, provided you follow the correct procedure (see Chapter 14).

Q *I have a 12-month shorthold, which has four months left to run. I have been working away for the past few weeks and have let my boyfriend stay in the flat to make sure that everything is okay while I am away. My landlord now says that he wants possession immediately as I have ceased to reside in the flat. Can he claim possession in this way?*

A No. You have a fixed-term letting for 12 months. Irrespective of whether you have ceased to reside in the flat as your only or main home (in which case the tenancy would cease to be a shorthold) you have a contractual right to the letting for the full period agreed. Like any other contract this cannot be varied unilaterally. Note, however, that if allowing your boyfriend to occupy the flat is in breach of some term in the tenancy agreement and the agreement also contains a provision allowing the landlord to obtain possession during the fixed term on proof of such breach, then possession might be available to him. You should read the agreement carefully to see if there is such a provision. Your landlord would, however, have to follow the correct procedure and obtain a court order (see Chapter 14).

Chapter 3

Assured tenancies

The Housing Act 1988, which applies to lettings entered into on or after 15 January 1989, introduced two new types of tenancy. One, the assured shorthold tenancy, was described in Chapter 2. This chapter looks at the other, the assured tenancy.

Lettings entered into on or after 15 January 1989 but prior to 28 February 1997 would have been assured tenancies unless the requirements for an 'old' shorthold were complied with (see Chapter 2); lettings entered into on or after 28 February 1997 are shortholds unless a notice is served by the landlord stating that it is to be an ordinary assured tenancy.

Hence, ordinary assured tenancies can arise in these two different circumstances, but the rights given to tenants will be the same.

If an assured tenancy has been created, the 1988 Act gives the tenant several rights over and above any agreed to by the landlord. In particular he is given 'security of tenure'. This means that at the end of the tenancy the tenant does not have to move out of the property: he has a legally enforceable right to remain 'in possession'.

The landlord can require the tenant to leave only if he can provide a valid reason for wanting to obtain possession. The only valid reasons for requiring possession are those set out in the Act. Known as 'grounds for possession', they include situations where the tenant has not been paying the rent regularly or the landlord wishes to occupy the house himself.

Some of the grounds for possession are mandatory. Once proved, these give the landlord an absolute right to possession. Others are discretionary, in which case the landlord will be entitled to possession only if, in addition to the ground, he can also establish that it is reasonable for him to insist on possession.

Merely having a ground for possession is not sufficient, though; with both mandatory and discretionary grounds, the landlord still has to apply to the court for a court order, following the correct procedure, before he can obtain possession.

Definition of an assured tenancy

A tenancy under which a house is let as a 'separate dwelling' will be an assured tenancy if and so long as all of the following requirements are met:

- the tenant or each of the joint tenants is an individual
- the tenant or at least one of the joint tenants occupies the dwellinghouse as his only or principal home, and
- the tenancy is not specifically excluded by other provisions of the Act.

These requirements and exceptions are identical to those for shortholds (described in Chapter 2). All lettings entered into on or after 15 January 1989 and before 28 February 1997 and complying with these conditions will be ordinary assured tenancies unless the relevant conditions for an old shorthold were complied with.

Assured tenancies today

In the case of lettings starting on or after 28 February 1997, even though the above conditions are complied with, the letting will be a shorthold, unless the landlord serves a notice on the tenant that the letting is to be an ordinary assured tenancy. This notice can be served before or after the tenancy has been entered into or can be included in the tenancy agreement itself. No prescribed form has been laid down for this notice: any form of words stating that the letting is intended to be an ordinary assured tenancy will suffice (however, the specimen tenancy agreement in Appendix III suggests a form of words).

Advantages to a landlord of an ordinary assured tenancy

As will be seen, an assured tenant has extensive security of tenure, so why would a landlord want to grant anything other than a shorthold under which he has an absolute right to obtain possession?

Some possible reasons are outlined below.

No rent challenge allowed

Assured tenancies confer no right whatever for the tenant to challenge the rent, whereas with shortholds, even if the tenant never succeeds in reducing the amount of the rent, the landlord will still have had to put time and effort into dealing with any attempt to do so. However, it has to be said that in most areas of England and Wales it is most unusual for rents to be referred to the Rent Assessment Committee.

Very short lettings

Another disadvantage of a shorthold is the fact that, although the landlord has an absolute right to possession, the court cannot order possession to be given before the expiry of six months from the grant of the first tenancy between the parties. So a landlord wishing to let for a shorter period should not use a shorthold. There is no such restriction on obtaining possession under an ordinary assured tenancy (subject to the agreed term having expired); however, as assured tenants have security of tenure, possession could be guaranteed only if one of the mandatory grounds were available.

Mandatory grounds for obtaining possession

Although assured tenants generally enjoy security of tenure, certain grounds for possession are mandatory, which means the court *must* order possession. So if a mandatory ground is available the landlord and tenant are in the same position security-wise as they would be under a shorthold. Moreover, in certain circumstances, the mandatory grounds can be made available on the grant of the tenancy, so the landlord can let secure in the knowledge that the mandatory ground will be available at the end of the tenancy.

Owner-occupiers

In particular, one ground for possession, ground 1, is specially designed to be available for landlords who rent out the house in which they have previously lived. Provided a warning notice is given to the tenant prior to the grant of the tenancy, the landlord will be able to use this ground. It is a mandatory ground, too, which means that the court must order possession. (See pages 45–6 for full details of what ground 1 comprises.)

A landlord able to use ground 1 is therefore in a better position than a landlord who lets on a shorthold. Both have an absolute right to possession (subject to the end of the contractual term), both have this right on service of two months' notice (see Chapter 14: there are different forms of notice depending on the type of tenancy), both can use a specially accelerated court procedure when they seek to obtain possession (see Chapter 14), but the shorthold landlord runs the risk of the tenant referring the rent whereas the landlord letting on an ordinary assured tenancy with a ground 1 notice does not. Similarly, the landlord with the ordinary assured tenancy can let for a period shorter than six months, should he wish to do so.

So, if you are letting the house in which you have lived for some time in the past, you should seriously consider granting an ordinary assured tenancy and thus remove the worry of the tenant referring the rent to the Rent Assessment Committee. Such rent referrals may be uncommon, but if you can avoid the risk altogether, you may well wish to do so.

Winter lets

Other mandatory grounds for possession may be available in special circumstances. Ground 3 allows landlords of property used for holiday purposes to let it on short fixed-term lettings 'out of season' and be sure of recovering possession at the end of the term. These 'winter lets' are quite common in holiday areas and shortholds are unsuitable for them; no matter how short the fixed term of a shorthold might be, the court order for possession cannot take effect until at least six months have passed since the grant of the tenancy. This could mean, therefore, that a landlord who uses a shorthold might not be able to obtain possession in time to capture the whole of the lucrative holiday trade.

Educational institutions

Educational institutions letting student accommodation during the vacation are able, in a similar way, to make use of mandatory ground 4 and let for less than six months.

Housing for ministers of religion

Church trustees who own property for housing ministers of religion can safely let it using ground 5 and thus avoid the disadvantages of the shorthold.

Granting an ordinary assured tenancy

The procedure to be adopted in granting an ordinary assured tenancy is basically the same as set out in Chapters 2 and 5 for a shorthold tenancy. There are only two differences, the first being the need to serve a notice on the tenant stating that the tenancy is to be an ordinary assured tenancy. This notice need not be in any particular form as long as it is clear to the tenant. It makes sense to include this statement in the tenancy agreement (see the specimen agreement provided in Appendix III for a suggested form of words). Even if this notice is overlooked at the time of the grant, all is not lost; the legislation allows the landlord to serve the notice even after the grant of the tenancy.

The other difference, however, is much more important. In order to rely on the mandatory grounds specified above, the landlord has to serve another notice on the tenant. This can be included in the tenancy agreement, but cannot be given after the tenancy has commenced. If the notice is not given the mandatory ground for possession will not be available (but see ground 1, below), so the landlord will not be sure of recovering possession at the end of the letting. The specimen tenancy agreement in Appendix III contains a suggested form of wording for the relevant notices.

Security of tenure for assured tenants

The landlord can bring an assured tenancy to an end only by obtaining a court order for possession. Therefore, in the case of a periodic assured tenancy, a notice to quit is of no effect. At the ending of a fixed-term assured tenancy (including a shorthold) otherwise than by an order of the court or by surrender, the tenant is entitled to remain in possession as a statutory periodic tenant.

'Surrender' consists of an agreement between landlord and tenant that the tenancy should come to an end and the tenant will leave the property. Note, however, that the tenant can in no way be required by his landlord to enter into this kind of agreement and that any agreement to terminate contained in the tenancy agreement itself will be ineffective.

This statutory periodic tenancy will be on the same terms as the previous fixed-term tenancy (although there is a little-used procedure for changing those terms under Section 6 of the Housing Act 1988).

Obtaining a court order

The landlord can obtain a court order for possession only if he follows the correct procedure and can establish one or more of the grounds for possession set out in Schedule 2 of the Housing Act 1988. Further, although some of these grounds are mandatory grounds, i.e. the court must order possession if the ground is established, many of them are discretionary, which means the court, once the ground has been proved, may order possession only if it considers it reasonable to do so. The procedure for obtaining possession, set out in detail in Chapter 14, requires the landlord to serve a notice on the tenant (a 'Section 8 notice'), in the prescribed form. The Section 8 notice must specify the ground(s) upon which the landlord intends to rely and must give two weeks' notice of the landlord's intention to commence possession proceedings. (Sometimes two months' notice has to be given: see Chapter 14.)

The proceedings must then be commenced not earlier than the date specified and not later than 12 months from the date of service of the notice. It is possible for the court to dispense with the requirement for a Section 8 notice (unless ground 8 is being relied upon), but only if it considers it 'just and equitable' to do so.

Grounds for possession

Mandatory grounds for possession

Grounds 1–8 are the 'mandatory grounds'. On proof of one of these, the landlord will be automatically entitled to an order for possession (assuming that he has followed the correct procedure). Most of these mandatory grounds require the landlord to have served a notice on the tenant at the start of the tenancy warning that the ground might be used against him.

The full wording of the various grounds is set out in Appendix I and must be included in the Section 8 notice requiring possession.

Ground 1: owner-occupier

Although this ground is often referred to as the 'owner-occupier' ground, it in fact describes two separate situations entitling the landlord to possession, only one of which requires prior occupation by the landlord.

The first part of the ground merely requires the landlord to prove that at 'some time' before the tenancy was granted he occupied the house as his only or principal home. This need not have been immediately prior to the letting; it could have been several years before. Having established this, however, he is entitled to an order for possession: he does not have to give or prove any reason as to why he might want possession.

If the second part of this ground is being relied upon, there is no need for the landlord to have resided in the property at any time in the past. In this situation, however, the landlord will be entitled to possession only if he can show that the house is required as his (or his spouse's) only or principal home. This will depend on the facts of each case. An unscrupulous person could of course buy a house subject to a tenancy, perhaps at a very low price because of this, and then use this ground to obtain possession from the tenant. This is prevented by a proviso that the ground will not be available to a landlord who has bought the house subject to a sitting tenant. The ground will be available, however, to a landlord who has inherited the house from a deceased landlord, or who obtains it by way of a gift.

For both parts of this ground it is necessary for the landlord to have given a written notice to the tenant 'not later than the beginning of the tenancy' that possession might be recovered under this ground. Such a notice would be valid if it were contained in the tenancy agreement itself, unlike the 'old' shorthold notices (see Chapter 2) which had to be served beforehand. Moreover, the notice need not be in any particular form; all it needs to do is make it clear to the tenant that ground 1 could be used against him to gain possession.

If the notice was not served, it can be dispensed with by the court, but only if the court thinks that it is 'just and equitable' to do so. This might be the case where the landlord told the tenant orally that he was an owner-occupier but omitted to give written notice as required by the ground.

This is one of the grounds for which Section 8 requires two months' notice to be given to the tenant.

Ground 2: mortgagee exercising power of sale
It is likely that an owner-occupier granting a tenancy under ground 1 will have a mortgage on the property. If a borrower does not keep

up with the payments under a mortgage, the lender's prime remedy will be to obtain possession of the house and then sell it to recover the money owed. This could pose a problem to a lender if the property were occupied by an assured tenant with security of tenure.

The position of a borrower under a mortgage granting leases is a little complex. The power to grant leases is normally excluded by the terms of the mortgage deed unless the lender's consent has been obtained. Any tenancy granted by the borrower without the consent of the lender will not be binding upon the lender. It will, however, be binding in the usual way upon the borrower. Accordingly, although the borrower/landlord would not be able to obtain possession without proving assured tenancy grounds, the lender (for example, a bank or building society) will have an absolute right to possession without the need to prove any ground. A court order would be necessary, however, to enforce this right to possession.

If the lender were to give consent to a letting during the continuance of the mortgage, it would be bound by the assured tenant's security of tenure and would not be able to obtain possession without proving assured tenancy grounds. It is likely that it would require this ground to be available to it in order to protect its position should it need to realise its security.

This ground allows a landlord's mortgagee to obtain possession in cases where the landlord has granted a tenancy under which ground 1 would be available. It is therefore dependent upon a ground 1 notice having been served and the lender's consent will be conditional upon the ground 1 notice having been served. If a ground 1 notice has not been served, it can be dispensed with by the court if the court considers it just and equitable to do so (see ground 1 above).

Many mortgagees, as a condition of giving consent to the letting, will require the borrower/landlord to give a separate notice stating that ground 2 will be available against the tenant. Although this is not necessary under the wording of the ground, giving such a notice does no harm, *provided* that a ground 1 notice is given as well; it is the service of the ground 1 notice that triggers the availability of ground 2.

As for ground 1, two months' notice of proceedings must be served.

Ground 3: out-of-season holiday accommodation
This ground is designed for use by a 'professional' landlord who lets out property for holiday purposes during part of a year – holiday

cottages or flats, for example. It may be difficult to find holiday-makers to take the property during the winter months and, in order to produce some income, the landlord may wish to make the accommodation available for ordinary residential lettings. With such lettings, however, there is a danger that the security-of-tenure legislation would prevent the landlord obtaining vacant possession when the property was once more required for holidaymakers.

This ground will be available for 'winter lets' provided that:

- written notice was served on the tenant not later than the beginning of the tenancy (possibly as part of the tenancy agreement) that this ground would be available against him. Note that unlike grounds 1 and 2 this notice may not be dispensed with by the court. If the notice is not given in writing, this ground will not be available even if there was an oral discussion of the need to vacate before the beginning of the holiday period
- the property must have been occupied for holiday purposes at some time during the 12 months prior to the granting of the tenancy. The ground is therefore not available to landlords who have not previously used the house for holiday purposes
- the letting must be for a fixed term not exceeding eight months in length. This ground will not be available for any other type of letting, such as a periodic tenancy, even if the correct notice was given.

Ground 4: out-of-term student accommodation

Many educational institutions let their halls of residence, flats and so on to non-students during vacations (for example, for conferences). This ground enables them to ensure that they can be certain of recovering possession at the end of the letting, provided that the requirements of the ground are complied with. These are that:

- written notice was served on the tenant not later than the beginning of the tenancy (possibly in the tenancy agreement) that this ground would be available against him. Note that unlike grounds 1 and 2 this notice may not be dispensed with by the court, even if the tenant had agreed orally with the landlord to vacate when the students returned
- the property was let by an educational institution to students at some time during the 12 months prior to the commencement of the tenancy

- the letting is for a fixed term not exceeding 12 months in length. This ground will not be available for any other type of letting, such as a periodic tenancy, even if the correct notice was given.

Ground 5: minister of religion's house

Many religious denominations own houses which are held for the purposes of occupation by one of their ministers. This ground enables them to let such accommodation to other tenants yet be sure of being able to recover possession should it be required in the future for occupation by a minister.

The following conditions must be complied with:

- the house must be held for the purpose of being available for occupation by a minister of religion as a residence from which to perform the duties of his office
- written notice was served on the tenant not later than the beginning of the tenancy (possibly as part of the tenancy agreement) that this ground would be available against him. Note that unlike grounds 1 and 2 this notice may not be dispensed with by the court. If the notice is not given in writing this ground will not be available even if the need to vacate the accommodation for an incoming minister had been orally discussed
- the court is satisfied that the dwellinghouse is required for occupation by a minister of religion as a residence from which to carry out his duties.

Two months' notice of proceedings is required for this ground. There are no limitations upon the type of tenancy which can be used.

Ground 6: demolition or reconstruction

While simple in its basic intent, this ground can give rise to complications stemming from the rules supporting it, which are designed to prevent unscrupulous landlords from attempting to use this ground when the circumstances do not really justify it. It is intended to apply in the event that the landlord wishes to demolish or reconstruct the house or a substantial part of it.

Unlike the previous mandatory grounds, no warning notice needs to have been served prior to the grant of the tenancy.

The ground makes it clear, however, that if the works can be carried out 'around the tenant' without possession being obtained, then the ground will not apply, unless the tenant refuses to agree to the necessary arrangements.

Further, a landlord who has purchased the house for money or money's worth since the date of the grant of the tenancy cannot use this ground. This is included for the same reason as the similar provision in ground 1.

Another 'anti-avoidance' device prevents a landlord circumventing this restriction by purchasing a property subject to a tenancy and then granting a new tenancy to the same tenant (or one of joint tenants). The purchase subject to the original tenancy again prevents this ground from being used.

Also excluded from the operation of this ground are those former Rent Act 1977 tenancies which were converted to assured tenancies following the death of the original tenant and succession of another tenant (see Chapter 7).

Two months' notice of proceedings must be served by the landlord for this ground to be applicable.

If this ground is established, the landlord must pay the tenant's reasonable removal costs.

Ground 7: death of the tenant

This ground is available following the death of the tenant when possession proceedings are begun within 12 months of that death. To deal with the possibility that the landlord may not become immediately aware of the tenant's death, the 12-month time limit can run from the date on which, in the opinion of the court, the landlord became aware of the tenant's death.

As noted in Chapter 2, in certain circumstances on the death of an assured tenant, the deceased's spouse will be entitled to succeed to the tenancy. This ground for possession will *not* be available if such a succession takes place; it will only be available if, for example, there is no spouse entitled to succeed.

Note that the ground states that the possession proceedings must comply with the conditions mentioned above. However, landlords need to be careful as the Section 8 notice still needs to have been served and to have expired before the proceedings are commenced; also, for this ground at least two months' notice must be given.

Hence, in effect, the landlord has less than 10 months from the date of death in which to serve the notice if proceedings are to be commenced within the 12-month time limit.

Ground 8: substantial rent arrears

One frequent ground for complaint by landlords of Rent Act tenants was that even if they, the landlords, brought possession proceedings and proved rent arrears they might still not obtain an order for possession; under the Rent Act, rent arrears are only a discretionary ground (see Chapter 7) and the court would often exercise its discretion and refuse to order possession. For assured tenancies, however, this ground gives a mandatory right to possession for non-payment of rent, although only in very limited circumstances.

Firstly, the arrears must be quite substantial: eight weeks' rent must be unpaid, in the case of rent payable weekly, or two months' rent if it is payable monthly. However, for the ground to be established, the rent must be eight weeks in arrears *both* at the date of the service of the Section 8 notice *and* at the date of the hearing. So a partial payment of arrears just before the hearing, so that (say) the arrears were reduced to only seven weeks, would stop the ground being proved.

It is not possible for the court to dispense with the requirement for the service of a notice under Section 8 of the Housing Act 1988 if this ground is being relied upon.

For discretionary grounds for possession based on arrears of rent, see grounds 10 and 11 (below). In case the tenant should decide to make a partial payment by the date of the hearing and thus prevent this ground being used, it would be usual for a landlord to serve a Section 8 notice and commence proceedings based on these discretionary grounds as well as ground 8.

Discretionary grounds for possession

Proof of the following grounds for possession will not inevitably result in a possession order being made against a tenant. The court can make such an order only if it considers it 'reasonable' to do so, which will depend on the facts of the case, but this proviso will enable the court to consider the respective hardship likely to be suffered by the landlord and the tenant in the event of a possession order being granted. The conduct of the parties during the tenancy will also be relevant to the question of 'reasonableness'.

Ground 9: alternative accommodation

It is a ground for possession if the landlord can show that 'suitable' alternative accommodation will be available to the tenant when the possession order takes effect.

This 'suitable' alternative accommodation need not be provided by the landlord, although the landlord must be able to prove to the court that it will be available for the tenant when the order takes effect.

If the landlord can obtain a certificate from the local housing authority confirming that it will provide alternative accommodation for the tenant, the certificate will be deemed to be conclusive evidence that the accommodation will be 'suitable' for the needs of the tenant. In practice, however, it is most unlikely that such a certificate would be forthcoming from the housing authority, in the light of other pressures on its accommodation. It may well be that, if a possession order were obtained, the housing authority would be obliged to re-house the tenant because of its responsibilities to house the homeless, but that is not to say that the authority will facilitate the making of the possession order by issuing a certificate.

Alternatively, the landlord will have to show that the proposed alternative accommodation is 'reasonably suitable' to the needs of the tenant and his family in respect of its location, size and rent. Furthermore, it must be available for letting on an assured tenancy, but not an assured shorthold, nor one to which mandatory grounds 1–5 might apply. Two months' notice of proceedings must be given.

As for mandatory ground 6, the landlord must pay the tenant's reasonable removal expenses if possession is ordered on this ground.

Ground 10: rent arrears

This is the first of the two discretionary grounds based on rent arrears (see also ground 11). The landlord must prove that 'some' rent was in arrears both at the date of service of the Section 8 notice and at the date on which the possession proceedings are commenced.

Unlike mandatory ground 8, which requires at least eight weeks' rent to be in arrears both at the date of the service of the Section 8 notice and at the date of the hearing, no minimum amount of rent needs to be outstanding for this ground. Nor need the amount outstanding at the date of the start of proceedings be the same as at the date of the Section 8 notice. Indeed, as long as *some* rent was in arrears at the date of the Section 8 notice and at the start of the possession proceedings, it does not matter whether any rent at all is still in arrears on the day of the hearing.

It therefore makes sense for a landlord to use this ground in addition to ground 8 to cover the possibility of a tenant paying off some or all of the arrears prior to the hearing date.

Even so, although it should be easier for the landlord to establish this ground rather than ground 8, it is discretionary, which means that the court can make an order for possession only if it considers it reasonable to do so. It may well not be reasonable to order possession if all the arrears have been discharged by the date of the hearing.

Ground 11: persistent delay in paying rent

For this ground, there is no need for any rent to be in arrears at all, whether at the date of service of the Section 8 notice, or when the possession proceedings are commenced, or at the date of the hearing; all that must be established is that the tenant has 'persistently delayed paying rent'. What amounts to a persistent delay will depend on the facts in each case.

Ground 12: breach of covenant

This ground will be available if the tenant has broken any express or implied obligation placed on him under the tenancy: for example, by breaking an implied obligation not to sublet or an express obligation to keep the house properly decorated.

The ground can still be established even if the breach has been remedied by the date of the hearing (although in such circumstances the court might well not consider it reasonable to order possession).

Ground 13: waste or neglect

This ground will be available if the condition of the house, or of any common parts, has deteriorated due to the acts or neglect of the tenant or anyone living with him. Often there will be an express term in the tenancy agreement to the same effect, in which case ground 12 would be available as well.

However, as will be explained in Chapter 12, it is normally the landlord who will be responsible for repairing the structural parts of the house, so 'neglect' by a tenant with regard to matters within the landlord's obligation will not cause this ground to be available.

Note that this ground also extends to the acts or neglect not just of the tenant personally but of any other person residing in the property: for example, a spouse or child or lodger. However, if the deterioration is caused by someone other than the tenant, the ground can be established only if the tenant has failed to take such steps as he could reasonably have taken to remove the lodger or subtenant. What steps would have been 'reasonable' will depend on the facts in each case. The extent of the deterioration could well be a relevant factor.

Ground 14: nuisance

This ground was substantially extended with effect from 28 February 1997 as part of the government's campaign to clamp down on anti-social behaviour by what were described as 'neighbours from Hell'. Although a landlord normally has to give at least two weeks' notice before starting possession proceedings (and some-times as much as two months' notice), in the case of ground 14 the proceedings can start immediately as long as the prescribed Section 8 notice has been served.

The ground consists of two separate circumstances that will give the landlord a right to claim possession:

- the tenant or a person residing in or visiting the house has behaved in such a way so as to cause, or to be likely to cause, a nuisance or annoyance to a person residing, visiting or otherwise engaging in a lawful activity in the neighbourhood. This part of the ground could be seen as being somewhat draconian in its implications. A tenant can be evicted not just because of his own conduct, but because of the conduct of someone living with him or even visit-ing him. However, this is a discretionary ground, so the mere fact that on one occasion a visitor to the house caused a nuisance to, say, someone taking a dog for a walk would not necessarily mean that an order for possession would be made. None the less, the ground is intended to give landlords very strong powers to deal with anti-social behaviour. The fact that the nuisance – or what-ever – can be caused to anyone engaging in a lawful activity is designed to meet the problem of obtaining witnesses to anti-social behaviour. If the behaviour is extremely bad, neighbours may be unwilling to give evidence for fear of retribution; however, if the landlord himself or his agent (such as a private detective) were to be threatened, this would be sufficient for the ground to be established without involving neighbours

- the tenant or another person living in or visiting the dwelling-house has been convicted of using or allowing the house to be used for an illegal or immoral purpose or of an arrestable offence committed in or in the locality of the house. What comprises the 'locality' of the house will depend on the facts of each case; however, it is intended to cover quite a large area – perhaps the entire estate of which the house is part, for example.

Like ground 13, ground 14 can apply even if no breach has been committed by the tenant under the terms of the tenancy; if such a breach has occurred, ground 12 will be available as well. (Note that use of the house for illegal or immoral purposes is not in itself sufficient; there has to have been a conviction. However, such usage could amount on its own to conduct causing nuisance or annoyance within the terms of the first part of this ground.)

Note also that for this ground there is no question of the tenant being in breach only if he fails to take reasonable steps to remove the offender (as for ground 13, above). The court, however, might take this into account when it considers the question of reasonableness.

Ground 14A: domestic violence
This ground is available only to registered social landlords and is identical to ground 2A for secure tenants (see page 124).

Ground 15: damage to furniture etc.
This ground is available if the condition of any furniture provided by the landlord under the terms of the tenancy has deteriorated due to the acts or neglect of the tenant or any other person living in the house. As with ground 13, in the case of damage caused by a lodger or subtenant the ground will be established only if the tenant has failed to take reasonable steps to remove the offender.

If there is an express term in the tenancy prohibiting damage, ground 12 will also be available.

Ground 16: former employee

This ground will be available where the house was originally let to the tenant in consequence of his employment by the landlord and that employment has now ceased. It does not matter why the employment has ended – for example, whether or not it was the landlord or the tenant who ended it. Nor is it necessary for the landlord to prove that he requires the accommodation to house a new employee. This, however, may well be a relevant factor when the court decides whether it is reasonable to order possession.

Note, finally, that not all employees housed by their employers will have tenancies. If it is essential for the employee to occupy the house in order for him to carry out the terms of his employment, then he will be a 'service occupant', a mere licensee, and therefore the arrangement could not amount to an assured tenancy. The landlord would have an absolute right to possession on termination of the employment.

Ground 17: false statement by tenant

This ground applies where the landlord alleges that he was induced to grant the tenancy by a false statement made knowingly or recklessly by the tenant or someone acting at his instigation. 'Knowingly' means that the tenant actually knew that the statement was untrue; 'recklessly' means that the tenant made the statement not caring whether it was true or not.

Sometimes tenants are so desperate to obtain accommodation that they are less than truthful in the statements they make to landlords. A prospective tenant might, for example, tell a landlord that he is in employment when he is not, in order to deceive a landlord who, had he been told the truth, would not have granted the tenancy. However, when the landlord discovers the truth he can try to obtain possession using this ground.

Note that the ground covers not only statements made by the tenant personally, but also by other people at his instigation. This would include, for example, false statements made in a reference supplied by a friend.

As this is a discretionary ground, the court would be able to take into account both the nature of the false statement made and the reaction of the landlord when he discovered the truth. A landlord who discovers the untrue statement but then waits for six months before commencing possession proceedings might not be allowed to rely on the ground.

Other issues to do with assured tenancies

Amount of rent charged by the landlord

There is no restriction on the amount of rent which can initially be charged on the grant of an assured tenancy. (This is so even if there is an existing registration of a fair rent for the purposes of the Rent Act 1977: see Chapter 7.) The amount of the rent under an assured tenancy is fixed by agreement between landlord and tenant. Market forces will therefore prevail. Assured tenants do not have the right, as shorthold tenants do, to refer the rent to the Rent Assessment Committee. Once the tenant has entered into the agreement, he is stuck with the amount of rent agreed, even though he may subsequently realise that it is excessive.

However, should the landlord subsequently wish to *increase* the rent, he may not be able to do so unless he follows the correct procedure. This is the same as set out for shorthold tenancies in Chapter 2.

Subletting, or transfer of the tenancy by the tenant

The position for assured tenants is the same as set out for shorthold tenants in Chapter 2.

Death of the tenant

Again the position is the same as that for shorthold tenants (see Chapter 2). However, it should be noted that on the death of a periodic assured tenant, if there is no succession under the provisions of the Act, the landlord can make use of one of the mandatory grounds in order to obtain possession, should he wish to do so (see ground 7, page 50).

Legal position of subtenants

The position of subtenants is dealt with in Chapter 2. Note, in particular, that a head tenant who has a shorthold can validly grant a subtenancy that will be an ordinary assured tenancy and that in some circumstances this will be binding upon the owner of the freehold.

Resident landlords

If the landlord lives in the part of the same building as the tenant, the 'resident landlord exception' applies (see also pages 32–4), and is of particular significance to an ordinary assured tenant. The loss of the security of tenure which goes with his status as an assured tenant will place him in a much worse position than a shorthold tenant who has a resident landlord.

Q *I have a monthly tenancy. My landlord tells me that he will be increasing the rent next week. I cannot afford the extra but he says that I've got to pay. Do I have to? I can't afford to pay but I don't want to lose my flat.*

A Check the tenancy agreement: unless it allows him to, a landlord cannot unilaterally change the amount of the rent originally agreed unless he follows the procedure prescribed in the 1988 Act (outlined in Chapter 2), which requires the landlord to serve a notice on the tenant in the form laid down by the Act. If he does not follow the correct procedure, you do not have to pay the increased amount.

If you refuse to pay, there is no risk of your losing your flat. Rent arrears are a ground for possession (see grounds 8, 10 and 11) only where the rent is 'lawfully due'. As the landlord was never entitled to increase the rent, it will not be lawfully due and therefore cannot be used as the basis of possession proceedings.

Once you have stated your legal rights, simply refusing to pay and virtually challenging the landlord to take you to court is not likely to create good relations between you. It would be better to try to have a friendly chat with your landlord and explain that he is not adopting the right procedure. Try to reach a compromise. Ask, or check, when the rent was last increased: if it has been unchanged for several years it may well be possible, and fair, to agree a modest increase in line with inflation. In the long term it might be preferable to reach an amicable settlement rather than insisting on your strict legal rights.

Q *I have a monthly tenancy. I have become pregnant and my landlord says that as he doesn't allow children I must leave my flat before the baby comes. I have nowhere else to go. Can he make me leave?*

A In the short term, no, but it all depends upon the terms of the agreement you signed. Many tenancy agreements do prohibit children (and animals), but such a provision will not be implied into a tenancy. So unless children are expressly prohibited by your tenancy agreement, the landlord has no legal ground for objecting to your baby. In the absence of any ground for possession against you, you are fully protected in your continued occupation of the flat.

If children are prohibited by the terms of your agreement, the landlord may well try to obtain possession against you. However, as an assured tenant you have security of tenure so he must follow the correct procedure: see Chapter 14. Breach of a term of the tenancy agreement is a ground for possession (ground 12), but it is a discretionary ground. This means that even though you have broken a term of the lease, the court will order you to leave only if it considers it reasonable to do so. The hardship that you and your baby would suffer would certainly be taken into account by the judge when considering whether to make a possession order or not. You should also claim that the term is void as being unfair under the Unfair Terms in Consumer Contracts Regulations (see Chapter 5).

Q *I am landlord of a small terraced house which is let on a monthly tenancy. Owing to financial problems I am having to sell the house in which I live and so I urgently need somewhere to live. Can I get possession of this house? (The tenant has always been a good tenant and paid his rent on time.)*

A In order to obtain possession you will need to go to court, following the correct procedure (see Chapter 14). You will then need to prove a ground for possession. The second part of ground 1 (a mandatory ground) allows a landlord to obtain possession where the house is required as the only or principal home for the landlord. It is not necessary for the landlord to have lived in the house before the letting where this part of the ground is being relied upon. However, ground 1 will be available only if notice was given to the tenant no later than the beginning of the tenancy that this ground might be available. If, as is likely, this notice was not given, the ground might still be available if the court thinks it just and equitable to dispense with the notice. The question of whether it would be 'just and equitable' will be looked at from the *tenant's* point of view and may not help you. If this is the only ground applicable to you in your situation, you would probably have difficulty in obtaining an order for possession.

Q *I inherited a small house from my grandmother last year. It was let on a weekly tenancy to friends of hers. I have just discovered that the tenants moved out a few months ago and the house is now occupied by their nephew. I was happy for my grandmother's friends to live in the house but the nephew is not paying the rent regularly and is holding wild all-night parties. I am worried about complaints from the neighbours and that the police may be called. Can I obtain possession?*

A In order to obtain possession you will need to go to court, following the correct procedure, and prove one of the grounds for possession laid down by the Act. One of the grounds (ground 12) is breach of the terms of the tenancy agreement by the tenant. Assuming that there is nothing to the contrary in the tenancy agreement (and no premium was charged at the start of the tenancy), it is an implied term of the agreement that the tenants cannot transfer the tenancy without the landlord's consent (see above), so this ground should be available to you. If the noisy parties have been causing annoyance to the neighbours, you might be able to establish ground 14 as well. The snag is that both of these grounds are discretionary – that is, the court does not have to order possession even on proof of the ground. It can only make an order for possession if it considers it reasonable to do so, which will depend upon the court's view of the circumstances of the case. The fact that you have been accepting rent from the nephew for some time now may well be taken into account in deciding whether it is reasonable to make an order under ground 12.

Q *When my grandmother was ill I moved into her house and lived with her in order to look after her. I had to give up my own flat to do this. I lived with her for nearly two years before she died, last month. The landlord now says that I must leave the house. Do I have to go?*

A The tenancy did not end on your grandmother's death. In the absence of a surviving spouse who would be entitled to succeed to the tenancy under the terms of the 1988 Housing Act, it would pass under her will or according to the rules of intestacy. Therefore, it may well not have passed to you. Even if it has, the landlord has a mandatory right to possession under ground 7. However, he must follow the correct procedure (serving a Section 8 notice and commencing proceedings within 12 months from when he learned of the death). Your only hope is that the landlord does not commence proceedings within this 12-month time limit, which would render any claim under ground 7 unsuccessful.

Chapter 4

Finding a tenant

One of the first decisions landlords need to make is how they will find their tenants. One option would be to use a letting agent.

Letting agents

A letting agent will market your property, find a suitable tenant, obtain references, prepare a tenancy agreement and obtain the signatures of the parties to it. In the case of furnished lets, the agent will also, if required to do so, prepare an inventory of the contents and obtain the tenant's agreement to the contents and its condition if items are worn or damaged. Agents will also collect the rent, if required, and many offer a 'full management service', which includes collecting the rent as well as arranging for any necessary repairs and maintenance to be carried out.

Agents' charges vary. Ten per cent of the rental over the term of letting is typical for finding a tenant and dealing with the grant of the tenancy. If an inventory is to be prepared, this is likely to be extra, as are rent collection and the provision of a full management service (the latter typically 15 per cent of the rental).

If the rent is not paid regularly, extra charges may be incurred for chasing up rent arrears.

Most agencies will take up references for potential tenants (from employers, previous landlords, banks and so on) to help ensure that a tenant can pay the rent and is of good character. Most operate on a 'no let, no fee' basis, but a few charge a fee to include a property on their list, redeemable against the full fee applied when a tenant is found.

Finding a letting agent

Just as the market for rental property grew enormously during the 1990s, so did the number of letting agents. Every town, large or small, has a plethora of agents vying for business. Some specialise in lettings while others are offshoots of established estate agency businesses.

The quality of service varies, and the best way to find a good agent is probably personal recommendation. This is all very well if you know someone who lets property, but not much help if you do not.

Agents are often judged by the quality of the tenants they find: ones that pay the rent regularly, on time, look after the property and its contents, and do not upset the neighbours. Even with careful checking of references, it is impossible to know in advance that your tenants will fulfil these criteria and certainly no agent can guarantee the reliability or good conduct of the tenants on its books. Even a tenant in comfortable financial circumstances can be a bad payer, or could do a 'moonlight flit' leaving extensive arrears. Misfortunes such as these do not make the agent a 'bad' agent – they are just some of the day-to-day risks of letting property.

Equally, it can be unwise to make your choice purely on the basis of the lowest charges. The old maxim that 'you get what you pay for' could apply, and whilst competition certainly encourages agents to keep their charges as low as possible, a firm charging much below the average for the area might only be able to do so because it is not providing as good a service as the others.

Before picking an agent, you could try visiting a few as a prospective tenant. This will enable you to see the quality of the service provided first-hand and to compare different methods of presenting the rental properties. You can also judge the attitude to taking up references from the tenant's viewpoint. Some agents might treat references as a mere formality, while others will stress to prospective tenants the importance of being able to provide good references.

It makes sense to choose an agent who is a member of one of the recognised professional bodies. This shows a commitment to the profession and should guarantee both a reasonable standard of competence and a right to appeal to a third party should a dispute arise.

Membership of the Royal Institution of Chartered Surveyors (RICS),★ or the National Association of Estate Agents (NAEA)★ should also help to ensure a professional and efficient service. The Association of Residential Letting Agents (ARLA)★ is the only professional body dedicated to the residential lettings market. It sets criteria for membership, operates a code of practice, provides training for members, and aims to promote high standards throughout its 1,300 member offices; its bonding scheme protects clients' money (such as rental deposits held by an agent) in the event of fraud or dishonesty on the part of the agent (for more on rental deposits, see page 85).

Finding a tenant without using an agency

Some landlords operate on a do-it-yourself basis, preferring to rely on their own judgement as to who will make a suitable tenant, rather than being presented with a tenant by a third party.

One way to find a tenant is to advertise in the local press or in a shop window. Sometimes a friend or other personal contact – perhaps through your place of work – will know of someone looking for accommodation. Whichever way you find a tenant, it is essential to obtain (and check) references. No matter how plausible the tenant seems, or how well you seem to get on with him, and no matter how good a judge of character you think you are, take up the references and do all you can to ensure that they are genuine. Regrettably, there are people who prey on unsuspecting landlords, happily taking on a six-month tenancy on payment of a month's rent in advance and a similar amount as a deposit, then paying nothing else. The landlord eventually commences court proceedings for possession and the rent arrears, then, just before the court order is to be made, the tenant disappears. The landlord is left with four or five months' rent unpaid plus the cost of the court proceedings – and often, to add insult to injury, damage to the property.

While some landlords prefer the rent to be paid in cash, owing to the risk of cheques bouncing, the tenant who runs a bank account has at least been required to provide some proof of identity, and might well have his wages paid directly into it: these would suggest some degree of financial stability. A preference for paying the rent in cash, on the other hand, might smack of fly-by-night tendencies, as mentioned above.

In the first instance, the landlord should wait for the cheque to clear before granting the tenancy; he can also insist on the rent being paid by a standing order.

Unless the landlord intends to specialise in letting to people on housing benefit (see Chapter 9) he should insist on proof that the prospective tenant is in regular employment: either the last two months' pay slips, or a letter from the employer. It is best to write to the employer yourself, rather than accept a letter proffered by the tenant (forgery of references is not unknown). It is also worth obtaining a character reference from someone who has known the prospective tenant for some time and can testify as to his honesty and good character.

But even with the best references in the world there is no guarantee that the tenant will prove to be honest and trustworthy and look after the property. Some references leave a lot to be desired, too, saying only something vague and meaningless such as 'I know nothing to cast doubt on his honesty' or 'I know nothing against him'. In a way these are perhaps more reassuring, and more likely to be an honest opinion, than a gushing reference – perhaps from a drinking companion – which describes the tenant as being the property market's version of Mother Teresa.

In any event, it is unlikely that a person giving a reference could be held liable if the tenant turned out to be untrustworthy (unless a deliberate untruth could be proved), but a prospective tenant who is unable to provide any references, or perhaps does not want you to write to his employer, is best avoided.

Advantages and disadvantages of using an agent

There is no guarantee of success in letting property, whether you use an agent or do it yourself. Even the most experienced of landlords can make a misjudgement, or simply have the bad luck to find themselves saddled with a bad tenant who does not pay the rent and/or trashes the property.

However, an established letting agent should be more used to taking up references than a novice landlord and may well have tenants on its books to whom it has let property before. The letting agent should also be more skilled in matters such as the grant of the tenancy and the preparation of any necessary inventory. Companies looking for temporary accommodation for staff (perhaps people they have re-located from one site to another) often use letting agents, which gives them access to a tenant who is likely to be reliable and whose rent is probably being paid by a company.

The disadvantage of using an agent is the cost, whether you opt for tenant-finding only or a fuller service. Virtually everything else that the do-it-yourself landlord would do for nothing will be chargeable. But of course, the advantage of using an agent is convenience. While you could draw up an inventory of the property, it would take you a long time (certainly longer than an agent would take). You could place advertisements in the paper to find a tenant yourself, set aside time in which to show the property, take up references for a likely tenant, and so on, but, again, it will all take time. Do you want/are you able to spend so much time in finding a tenant?

Similarly, if you decide against a full management service, you could collect the rent – ideally, have it paid directly into your chosen bank account – without too much trouble. But what if the house needs repairing, or a pipe bursts? Are you going to want the hassle of finding a plumber at short notice? On the other hand, the agent will charge you for sending the plumber round, and you may suspect that you could have found a plumber who would have charged less, but what you would be paying for is the convenience of having someone else deal with these matters, taking the hassle off your shoulders.

The impact of housing benefit

Housing benefit is a means-tested social security benefit available to tenants who have insufficient resources to meet their rental payments in full. It is administered by the district council, or its equivalent. If the tenant is in receipt of income support, entitlement is automatic, and the full amount of benefit will be payable. People on a low wage will also be entitled to this benefit, subject to a means test. However, the amount of benefit payable may not be the full amount of the rent, even in cases where a tenant is in receipt of income support. (See also Chapter 9.)

Some landlords specialise in taking tenants who are in receipt of income support. Often, the rent is paid in full and so the landlord can be reasonably sure that the rent will be paid regularly. The benefit can be paid directly to the landlord, provided the tenant agrees, and it is common to include a term in the tenancy agreement to this effect. It could be great advantage to a landlord to have the rent paid directly by the state.

But there are disadvantages. In the case of claimants claiming for the first time after 6 October 1996, the benefit is payable in arrears and where it is paid directly to the landlord it will be payable every four weeks in arrears, i.e. the tenant will be in occupation for four weeks before the landlord receives the rent for that four weeks. Landlords normally prefer rent to be paid in advance.

Tenants can also be taken off benefit. Also, it is not unknown for an overpayment of benefit to be made – for example, because the tenant did not disclose his full circumstances when making a claim, or disclose a subsequent change of circumstances. In such a situation, where the benefit has been paid directly to the landlord, the local authority can require repayment from the landlord. The landlord could then, of course, request that the tenant reimburse him, but runs the risk that the tenant, assuming he is still around, may not have the money.

Every advantage has a corresponding disadvantage; whether you deliberately plan to take tenants who are on benefit or not, your tenancy agreement should contain provisions dealing with the possibility that the tenant might be on benefit. Any tenant could find himself unemployed and in receipt of benefit. See Chapter 5 as to the provisions which should be included.

Sureties from the tenant

As mentioned above, it is essential that landlords ask for references from prospective tenants – and then take them up. Even so, references cannot tell you everything about a person. Sometimes, too, there may be perfectly good reasons why a person cannot supply a reference. For example, if a reference has been requested from a previous landlord but the prospective tenant has never rented property before, obviously no reference will be forthcoming.

The most important reference, however, is probably that from the tenant's current employer, which at least provides some assurance that the tenant will be able to pay the rent. Sometimes, it is clear that the tenant will not be able to afford it – if the tenant is a student, for example, or a trainee on a low rate of pay – no matter how good his references. In that kind of situation, it is advisable to ask the tenant to provide a surety, or guarantor, who will enter into an agreement with the landlord on the basis that if the tenant fails to pay the rent or fails to comply with any of the other terms of the letting agreement, he will be liable for the landlord's loss.

The guarantor is someone else for the landlord to claim against should he be faced with a defaulting tenant. The guarantor could well be the tenant's parent or other close relation – whom, it may be assumed, the tenant will not want to let down. The tenant might therefore be expected to make every effort to pay in order to avoid his guarantor becoming liable.

However, it is always wise to make some elementary checks on the prospective guarantor. It is no use having a guarantor who does not have the money to meet his or her obligations.

A sample guarantee agreement is set out in Appendix V.

The Property Misdescriptions Act 1991

As a landlord, you must ensure when you advertise your property, or give information to the letting agent for that purpose, that any statements you make about the house are true. Equally, when showing prospective tenants around the house, or negotiating the terms of the letting, you must be completely truthful in what you say.

If you *do* make untruthful statements, when the tenant discovers the truth he will have remedies against you for 'misrepresentation' – an untrue statement of fact which induced him to enter into the tenancy. The tenant would then be entitled to rescind the tenancy agreement – that is, treat it as though it had never been entered into, and possibly also claim damages from you.

In addition, untrue statements can also give rise to criminal sanctions under the 1991 Property Misdescriptions Act. The Act mainly affects estate agents, including letting agents. If an untrue statement is made about 'specified matters' (as defined) in the course of estate agency business, the agent has committed a criminal offence. It is likely when you instruct a letting agent that he will require you, as landlord, to undertake that anything you tell him about the house is correct, and also that if he should be penalised as a result of such statements you will reimburse him.

The Act applies not only to agents but to anyone carrying on a property development business. This is widely defined and includes someone who converts or refurbishes a building with the object of letting it for profit. Therefore, if you have converted an old house into flats, or carried out improvement work prior to letting, you could also fall within the scope of the Act and be liable to criminal sanctions in relation to any untrue statements made about the 'specified matters'.

The 'specified matters', set out in the Property Misdescriptions (Specified Matters) Order of 1992, comprise 33 items in relation to which the liability arises. These include:

- location, aspect and environment of the property
- proximity to services and facilities
- size of accommodation
- amount of council tax payable
- fixtures and fittings.

It is therefore worth taking particular care to be accurate in respect of all these issues.

Chapter 5

Granting a shorthold tenancy

This chapter deals with the terms of the tenancy agreement and various preliminary matters landlords and tenants need to consider.

From the landlord's point of view it is good sense to choose an arrangement that ensures that he can be certain of recovering possession when the letting ends. Although permanent security of tenure offers great benefits to tenants, it can be a great problem to landlords. If their assets are tied up in a property of which they cannot get vacant possession, they cannot realise their investment. The market for tenanted property is very small and commands a far lower price than property offered with vacant possession. The situation can be particularly frustrating if the property needs to be sold in order that the landlord can finance the purchase of a house for his own use.

Fortunately, from the landlord's point of view, there is little private property available to let with security of tenure, so his wish to let without security will not unduly depress the amount of rent which he can expect to receive. Most landlords let on a shorthold basis, which is what this chapter deals with in the main. However, if you are letting the house in which you have lived yourself at some time in the past (not necessarily recently) you should first read the first part of Chapter 3, which deals with ordinary assured tenancies. Although these normally give the tenant full security of tenure, a mandatory ground for possession is available and there are some advantages in using an ordinary assured over a shorthold if you have previously lived in the house. Similarly, you should read Chapter 3 if you are seeking to let property used during the rest of the year for holiday purposes and consider using an ordinary assured tenancy coupled with mandatory ground 3.

For tenants looking for permanent security, the marketplace is not in their favour. Some landlords, including charities and some individuals concerned about their public image, will let on ordinary assured tenancies, but these are very much the exception.

Permission to grant a tenancy

Landlords intending to grant a tenancy may need to obtain consent in certain circumstances.

Lender's consent to letting

If the rental property is mortgaged, the consent of the lender must be obtained. If there is more than one mortgage on the property, the consent of all the lenders will be required. It will be a term of the mortgage that you may not let the property without the consent of the lender. If you grant a tenancy without consent, you will be in breach of the terms of the loan and the lender will be within its rights to require repayment of the full amount of the loan. If the repayment was not made, the lender could take possession of the property and sell it in order to recover its money.

Lenders' attitudes to giving consent differ. Some local offices seem not to want to know and (unofficially) have been known to say, 'Just let it – as long as you keep up the repayments everything will be OK'. However, as a landlord you should request consent in writing for your own protection; it will normally be forthcoming provided that the tenant is not being granted security of tenure, which would make it necessary to evict before the lender could take possession and sell the property in order to recover the loan.

Some lenders, however, give consent only subject to an increase in the interest rate on the loan. This is sometimes an extra ¼ per cent, sometimes an extra ½ per cent. Some lenders will charge a one-off fee for considering the application and giving consent. Such factors need to be considered at an early stage in case they undermine the financial viability of the letting.

Insurer's consent to letting

The consent of the property's insurers should also be obtained prior to granting a tenancy. If the house is being let furnished, the consent of the contents insurers (if different from the insurers of the building) will be needed. The fact that the house is to be let will, in the eyes of the insurers, increase the risk to them, and so it is likely that they will charge a larger premium to cover this.

If you were not to inform the insurers, and a claim was made, the insurance company would be within its rights to treat the insurance policy as void owing to your deception. The company could therefore refuse to meet the claim. This could prove rather expensive if, say, thousands of pounds' worth of damage were done to the house. By not informing your insurers, you would also be in breach of the terms of your mortgage.

Permission for subletting

If you yourself are a tenant, whether under a long or a short-term lease, you should check the terms of the lease under which you own the property before you sublet. If a tenant grants a lease to allow someone else to occupy the property, this is called a sublease. Most short leases prohibit the granting of a sublease or allow a sublease only if the head tenant's landlord consents. Some long leases also contain restrictions on granting subleases. Sometimes the head tenant is required merely to give notice to the landlord of the sublet: whatever the provisions of your lease, as a head tenant intending to sublet, you should comply with them.

If you do not obtain your landlord's consent when required to do so, or fail to comply with the provisions of your own lease in some other way, the landlord would almost certainly be entitled to seek to terminate the lease and obtain possession against you.

Planning permission

Planning permission is not normally required for letting residential property, unless some degree of 'development' is proposed. This includes building works and a material change of use. Assuming that you are letting a house that has previously been occupied by a single family and that you are letting it for the same use, no change of use is being made and hence there is no need for planning consent.

If, however, you are converting a house into several flats, planning consent may well be required for the building works and will definitely be required for the change of use from occupation by one family to occupation by several tenants.

Where building works are being carried out, you will also need to contact the Building Control department of the local authority. You must also ensure that the building works comply with the building regulations currently in force, which govern the methods and materials used.

If you are not converting the house into flats, but letting it to a group of people (for example, students) rather than as a family home, this could also constitute a material change of use. You should seek the advice of your local planning officer at an early stage. If you have such an arrangement in mind, you should also read Chapter 8 of this book to see whether you need to register the property as a house in multiple occupation (HMO) and to comply with any special provisions.

If you do not obtain planning permission when it is required, the local authority could serve an enforcement notice on you requiring you to remedy the breach within a specified period. If you then failed to do so, you could be liable to criminal sanctions.

The granting of the tenancy

Unless the tenancy complies with all of the following:

- it takes effect on the day it is granted
- is for a term not exceeding three years, and
- is at the best rent which can reasonably be obtained without a premium (a capital sum charged for the grant of a lease) being taken

it must be created by a deed: a written agreement which complies with various formalities (see below). However, if all the conditions are complied with, no formalities are required and the tenancy could therefore be granted orally. As most residential lettings are for less than three years, and lettings are normally granted at the 'best' rent, a deed may not be legally essential in many cases, but it is none the less highly desirable to have a written tenancy agreement, for the avoidance of disputes over the terms of the letting or, indeed, any claim that a legal lease has not been granted.

The agreement itself no longer has to be 'sealed' as a deed, as was formerly the case, but it should say at the end 'Signed as a deed'. It is preferable that two identical copies of the tenancy agreement are drawn up. The landlord will then sign one, and the tenant the other. This will then enable each party to have a copy of the agreement signed by the other and so facilitate enforcement of each other's obligations, should the need arise. The copy signed by the tenant is often referred to as the 'counterpart', the copy signed by the landlord being the actual lease. (A sample tenancy agreement is provided in Appendix II.)

Fixed-term or periodic tenancy?

At an early stage, the landlord needs to decide how long he wishes the letting to last. Most shorthold tenancies are for a fixed term, often six or 12 months.

If you wish to let for a longer period, you should bear in mind that under a shorthold tenancy the tenant can have the rent determined by the Rent Assessment Committee, and if so determined it will remain the same for the rest of the tenancy, despite any provisions for increase in the agreement (see Chapter 2). It is best, therefore, not to let for longer than (say) 12 months, to avoid the risk of being stuck with a tenant paying a rent which has been seriously eroded in value by inflation.

If you wish to let for a shorter period, such as three months, remember that under a shorthold the courts cannot order possession to take effect within six months of the start of the tenancy.

If you want the house back by a particular date so that you can sell it, or occupy it yourself (or for any other reason), you should be aware that, although a shorthold tenancy has no security of tenure, sometimes tenants do not leave voluntarily at the end of the letting. You would then have to obtain a court order for possession. Although this is only a formality, it will take time. So to be on the safe side you should allow two months for court proceedings between the end of the letting and the time by which you must have possession.

Alternatively, if you have no fixed date in mind by which you require possession, you can let on a periodic tenancy. This can be either weekly or monthly and will go on from week to week or month to month unless or until either the landlord or the tenant serves notice to bring it to an end (see Chapter 14). This has the added advantage that, if the tenant does not apply for the rent to be fixed by the Rent Assessment Committee within the first six months, you can allow the letting to continue for several years – provided that the agreement allows you to increase the rent. If the tenant does refer the rent, you can then terminate the tenancy when the rent needs to be increased. With a fixed term, on the other hand, you will be stuck with the same rent until the end of the fixed term.

Terms of the agreement

Many residential lettings are entered into quite informally, but this can be a recipe for disaster. A written agreement sets out the rights and responsibilities of the parties. Landlords should realise that when they let their property, the law will normally allow the tenant to do more or less what he or she likes with the premises. If any particular activity is to be prohibited then this must be written into the agreement.

The appendices of this book contain model agreements covering three types of tenancy, which should serve the needs of most landlords.

- Appendix II contains an agreement for an assured shorthold tenancy
- Appendix III contains an agreement for an ordinary assured tenancy (see Chapter 3)
- Appendix IV contains an agreement for a tenancy which is not an assured or a shorthold (because, for example, there is a resident landlord: see Chapter 2)
- Appendix V contains a guarantee agreement.

Each agreement should be read in conjunction with the following notes.

Impact of the Unfair Terms in Consumer Contracts Regulations 1999

These regulations, implemented by an EU Directive, apply to all consumer contracts including all residential lettings between a landlord and a private individual, but not to company lets.

The regulations declare that any terms in the tenancy agreement which have not been individually negotiated and which are 'unfair' to the tenant will be void. The rest of the agreement would, however, remain valid.

A term is deemed to be 'unfair' if it tips the contract against the consumer (tenant) and in favour of the business (landlord, in this case).

The following types of clause could be open to challenge under the regulations:

- clauses requiring the tenant to pay an excessive deposit: letting agreements do not currently contain a similar provision requiring the landlord to pay a deposit to secure the performance of his obligations under the agreement (for example, repairs to the property), hence there may be a 'significant imbalance in the parties' rights'
- forfeiture clauses
- landlords' break clauses: unless a similar right is given to the tenant, there may again be an imbalance in the parties' rights
- provisions allowing landlords to increase the rent arbitrarily.

The Office of Fair Trading has published Guidance on Unfair Terms in Tenancy Agreements. The agreements provided in this book attempt to provide a fair balance between landlord and tenant, taking into account this guidance, but ultimately it would be for the courts to decide on the facts of a particular case as to whether a specific clause was or was not 'unfair' to a tenant.

Description of the property
This should be clearly defined, including, for example, the number or precise location of the flat, should this be appropriate. Particular care is needed with a letting of part of a building: see Appendix IV.

Inventory of contents
If the house is being let furnished, a detailed inventory of all the contents should be drawn up and attached to the tenancy agreement (see also 'Inventories' on page 87).

Payment of rent
Express provision should be made for payment of rent in advance. If it is not, the common law implication is that rent is payable in arrears. The intervals for payment must also be stated. If weekly intervals are chosen the landlord must provide the tenant with a rent book. The intervals should be weekly, fortnightly, monthly, quarterly or yearly. If any other intervals are chosen (for example, six-monthly), assured tenancy mandatory ground 8 (see Chapter 3) may not be available to the landlord. (See also 'Collecting the rent' on page 87.)

Interest on arrears

In the case of arrears of rent, the law will not allow the landlord to claim interest unless and until he commences court proceedings. It is advisable, therefore, to overcome this problem by including an express term in the agreement allowing the landlord to add interest to any arrears at a specified, reasonable rate.

Council tax

Council tax is payable on 'dwellings' – i.e. houses or self-contained units such as flats. Liability for the tax generally falls on the person in occupation – the tenant. However, if the property is in multiple occupation (see Chapter 8) it is the landlord who will be responsible. The definition of multiple occupation includes any dwelling inhabited by persons who do not constitute a single household all of whom either have the right to occupy only part of the house or who are mere licensees paying no rent. In sharing arrangements it will therefore be necessary for the landlord to pay the council tax. The rental figure charged should reflect this fact and a provision should be inserted allowing the landlord to increase the rent to take into account any increase in council tax during the tenancy.

In other cases, the tenancy agreement should contain provisions stating that the rent is exclusive of council tax and requiring the tenant either to pay it to the local authority or to reimburse the landlord should he become responsible for payment.

Water charges

Provision should be made for the payment of water charges. The implication in the absence of express provision is that the tenant must pay them. Often in short-term lettings the landlord will accept responsibility for them. If so, there should be some provision in the agreement allowing the landlord to increase the rent to take account of any increase in water charges during the continuance of the tenancy.

Repairs and decoration

It is likely that Section 11 of the Landlord and Tenant Act 1985 will apply to the letting. This imposes an obligation on the landlord to repair, for example, the structure and exterior of the property where the tenancy is for a term of less than seven years (see Chapter 12).

However, a provision needs to be included to allocate responsibility for non-structural internal repairs and decoration, which is not covered by the landlord's implied obligation. Without such a provision neither landlord or tenant would be under an obligation to attend to such matters.

In a long-term tenancy (say, one for more than 12 months) it would be reasonable to impose the liability for these matters on to the tenant. However, in a shorter letting, it would not be reasonable to expect a tenant to decorate the house or to carry out even non-structural repairs — unless, of course, they were caused by his acts or neglect. The tenancy agreements provided in the appendices contain alternative clauses to deal with these options.

If the property includes a garden, it is wise to include an obligation on the tenant to maintain the garden or, at the very least, to cut the grass.

Alterations

Although the law prohibits tenants from deliberately damaging the property, tenants could legally make 'improvements' to it. But the tenant's idea of an improvement might not be the landlord's and it is essential, therefore, to prohibit any alterations being made to the house.

Use

Despite the fact that the letting is of a house, by the landlord to the tenant, the law will allow the tenant to use the property for whatever purpose he chooses unless the tenancy agreement provides otherwise. It is usual, therefore, to restrict the use of the property to that of a single private dwelling and also to impose obligations on the tenant not to cause nuisance or annoyance to the neighbouring occupiers and not to damage the house or contents in any way.

Insurance

In a short lease, the landlord will normally insure the premises as he has the most valuable interest in the house. However, as the activities of the tenant could affect the validity of the insurance policy or the amount of premium payable by the landlord, terms should be included obliging the tenant not to do or omit to do anything which might affect the insurance.

Assignment

It is essential that the landlord retains control over who occupies his house. There is no point in a landlord carefully vetting a potential tenant only to find that the tenancy has subsequently been transferred to a person who is unacceptable as a tenant. Under common law, however, a tenant can freely transfer the tenancy to whomsoever he wishes. For this reason, it is advisable to include an express provision in the tenancy agreement prohibiting transfer of the tenancy. Although there is an implied term in most periodic assured tenancies prohibiting assignment without consent (see Chapter 2), this should not be relied upon. It is not always implied and will not be implied in fixed-term lettings.

It may well be that an absolute prohibition on letting would be declared 'unfair' on the tenant and therefore void under the Unfair Terms in Consumer Contracts Regulations 1999 (see page 75). So a provision that the assignment is permitted only with the landlord's prior consent would be preferable. Although the landlord cannot then withhold his consent unreasonably (see page 28), it would of course be quite acceptable for him to refuse consent if a transfer was proposed to a person who could not provide acceptable references or who in any other way would be an unsuitable tenant.

Subletting

In the case of a shorthold tenancy, there is a danger that if the tenant is allowed to sublet, he might grant an ordinary assured tenancy which would give the subtenant – as opposed to the head tenant – full security of tenure. The statutorily implied prohibition applies only to periodic tenancies and so an express provision is needed. As in the case of assignments (see above), it is likely that an absolute prohibition would be declared void under the Unfair Terms etc. Regulations — at least in the case of the subletting of the whole of the house. The agreements provided with this book contain an absolute prohibition on the subletting of part of the house, together with the requirement that the landlord's consent be obtained prior to any other subletting. A landlord would be able to refuse consent to a person who would make an unacceptable tenant or who was to be given the full security of an assured tenancy.

Address for service

Under Section 48 of the Landlord and Tenant Act 1987 no rent is lawfully due from a tenant unless and until the landlord has given to the tenant notice in writing of an address in England and Wales at which notices (including notices in proceedings) can be served upon him.

Hence, the tenancy agreement should clearly state the landlord's address for service (as the model agreements in this book do). This will avoid the need for service of a separate notice and the possible problems of proving such service. The address given need not be the landlord's residence and can be the address of an agent – for example, the landlord's solicitors or letting agent.

Deposit

The agreements make provision for payment of a deposit (see 'Deposits' on page 85).

Rent increases

In a tenancy of any length it is essential to include a provision allowing the landlord to increase the rent to take account of the effects of inflation. Without such a provision an increase in rent will not be possible without the tenant's agreement. Remember, however, that if your tenancy is a shorthold, the tenant has the right to refer the rent to the Rent Assessment Committee during the first six months of the term. If he does, then the rent fixed by the Committee will prevail throughout the remainder of the lease, notwithstanding a provision for increase.

Shortholds in excess of 12 months in length should therefore be avoided. Provisions which allow the landlord to increase the rent arbitrarily may well be regarded as unfair under the Unfair Terms etc. Regulations. The agreements provided in this book attempt to maintain a fair balance between the landlord and the tenant by allowing the landlord to increase the rent, but not within 12 months of the beginning of the term or a prior increase, and limiting the amount of any increase to 5 per cent of the original rent. The tenant is also given the right to terminate the tenancy after a rent increase, so that he is not 'locked in' to a lengthy agreement at a rent he cannot afford.

Break clauses

A break clause is a term in a lease which allows the party specified to bring the lease to an end before it has run its full length. In the case of fixed-term tenancies (including shortholds) a break clause in favour of either the landlord or the tenant, or both, may be appropriate.

A landlord's break clause is included in the sample tenancy agreements allowing the landlord to terminate if he, or a member of his family, wishes to occupy the house or he wants to sell with vacant possession. Provision is also included for termination if the landlord dies and his personal representatives need to obtain possession.

If a periodic tenancy is granted, there is no need for a break clause, as either party can terminate the tenancy at any time by giving the appropriate notice.

It is possible that giving the landlord, but not the tenant, the right to terminate the letting prematurely might be regarded as 'unfair' under the Unfair Terms etc. Regulations. Where a landlord's break clause is included, therefore, the circumstances under which it is available should be limited, and it may be preferable to include a tenant's break clause too.

Children and pets

If these are to be prohibited, an express provision will be required. It may well be, however, that too onerous a provision would be regarded as being unfair to the tenant under the Unfair Terms etc. Regulations and so void. The sample agreements in the appendices allow pets, provided that they are kept in secure cages. Dogs and cats are thus not allowed. It is thought that this is fair as such animals might cause damage to the house, particularly if left unattended. It would always be open to a landlord to permit a particular tenant to keep a particular dog or cat in the house. It should also be noted, however, that it would be unlawful to prevent a blind or deaf person from keeping their guide or 'hearing' dog in the house.

Forfeiture

A forfeiture clause allows a landlord to terminate a fixed-term lease prior to the expiry of the fixed term if the tenant fails to comply with his obligations under the tenancy (for example, by not paying the rent). Although it is not possible to forfeit an assured tenancy –

it can only be terminated as laid down by the Housing Act 1988 – a forfeiture clause is still essential in any fixed-term assured tenancy of any length, including a shorthold.

The tenancy may at some time cease to be assured, in which case the forfeiture clause could be operated to terminate the tenancy. More importantly, some of the assured tenancy grounds for possession may be exercised during the fixed term, even in the case of a shorthold tenancy. However, this will be possible only if the tenancy agreement makes specific provision for this.

As this provision can take any form the forfeiture clause should make it clear that termination can be made using grounds 2 or 8 of the mandatory grounds and grounds 10–15 of the discretionary grounds. This will allow the landlord to terminate the tenancy during the fixed term in the case of rent arrears or other breach of the terms of the tenancy. For details of the assured tenancy grounds, see Chapter 3.

Although it is possible that a forfeiture clause may be regarded as 'unfair', the specimen tenancy agreements provided do contain one, for the reasons explained. It is thought that this will not be regarded as being 'unfair' to a tenant as the agreements also give the tenant the right to terminate the letting prematurely.

Stamp duty

This tax, so called because payment is recorded by a means of a stamp on the document, is payable on the tenancy agreement. If it is required that this be paid by the tenant, a provision to this effect should be included in the tenancy agreement. The amount varies according to the amount of rent payable. The completed agreement should be sent to the nearest Inland Revenue Stamp Office for the duty to be assessed and paid.

At the time of writing, if the tenancy is granted for seven years or fewer, as it usually will be, then no stamp duty is payable, provided that the annual rent does not exceed £5,000. If the rent exceeds £5,000 per annum, duty is chargeable of 1 per cent of the average annual rent throughout the term.

It is not unknown for short-term tenancy agreements to remain unstamped, but this practice is not to be recommended. If a tenancy agreement does not bear the correct amount of stamp duty, this does not invalidate the agreement, but the document cannot be produced as evidence in any court proceedings – for example, to obtain possession or non-payment of rent.

Setting the rent

One of the first decisions you need to make as a potential landlord is the amount of rent you want to charge. If you are putting the property in the hands of letting agents (see Chapter 4), they will advise on this. Otherwise, check in the local newspaper and letting agents' offices for properties similar to yours in the same locality and ascertain what rent is being charged for them, to ascertain what the current market rent for your type of property seems to be. This is essentially what a professional valuer would do – look at the rents being achieved for similar properties, then adjust that figure according to the property's precise location, state of repair and so on.

Safety regulations

Before entering into any tenancy agreement, you should ensure that the property complies with all the relevant safety regulations, and continue to comply with them throughout the tenancy.

Gas safety

The various Gas Safety (Installation and Use) Regulations apply to leases of less than seven years and to licences of residential property. The regulations apply to gas supplied in tanks or cylinders (LPG, or liquefied petroleum gas) as well as mains gas. If the property contains a gas appliance (other than one belonging to the tenant), the landlord must ensure that it, and any flue or pipe serving it, is maintained in a safe condition. The appliance must be inspected at least every 12 months by a CORGI-registered plumber and a record of these inspections, and any remedial work, kept and made available to the tenant on request.

The landlord must also produce this record to the tenant on the grant of the tenancy and within 28 days of each annual inspection. The record must be kept for a minimum of two years from the date of the check and must contain the following information:

* the date of the check
* the address of the installation
* the name and address of the landlord or his agent

- a description of the location of each appliance etc. checked
- any remedial action taken
- confirmation that the check complies with the rules laid down in the regulations
- name and signature of the individual who carried out the check and his company's registration number with the Health & Safety Executive.

These regulations were brought into being following a spate of tragic accidents in which tenants died from carbon monoxide poisoning caused by defective gas appliances.

As the record of inspections has to be produced on the grant of the tenancy, an inspection should be arranged before a tenant is found, allowing sufficient time for any defects to be remedied. Landlords who fail to comply with these regulations can be held criminally liable (to say nothing of the insurance policy for the property potentially being invalidated): in April 1999, the Court of Appeal upheld a verdict of manslaughter imposed on a landlord following a tragedy caused by non-compliance with the regulations.

Electrical safety

Landlords are also responsible for ensuring that any electrical appliances and the electrical supply system are maintained in a safe condition. Although there is no legal requirement to do so, it would be advisable to have the electrical system and any appliances inspected for safety purposes by a qualified electrician prior to the letting.

Soft furnishings safety

If the property is being let furnished, upholstery and soft furnishings such as cushions and mattresses must comply with various flammability criteria. Older upholstered furniture that has no swing ticket or safety label stating its compliance to the regulations is now illegal.

Fire safety

Unless your house is a house in multiple occupation (HMO) (see Chapter 8), there are no specific fire regulations you need to comply with when letting a house. However, it makes sense to discuss fire safety with your local fire brigade and follow any advice it may give. As a minimum, you should get rid of any outdated heaters and fit smoke alarms, ensuring that the batteries are regularly changed.

Responsibility for repairs

Landlords are obliged to keep rental property in good repair. Under the Landlord and Tenant Act 1985 (see Chapter 12) landlords are responsible for the repair of the structure and exterior of the property together with the installations for supply of gas, electricity and water and for sanitation. If the property is not in a good state of repair at the commencement of the tenancy, the tenant will immediately be able to insist that repairs are carried out. If the premises were in a serious state of disrepair, the tenant would be entitled to treat the letting as being at an end because of the landlord's breach of his obligations. The tenant could walk away from the property without any notice whether it was a fixed-term or periodic tenancy. (Chapter 12 also details the powers of the local authority to require landlords to repair property which does not comply with various standards.)

Deposits

Landlords usually require a deposit from the tenant on the grant of a tenancy in addition to the payment of rent in advance. The amount is normally equivalent to one or two months' rent. The deposit provides some degree of security to the landlord in respect of non-payment of rent (in the light of which, the landlord need not immediately go to the trouble and expense of commencing court proceedings) or damage to the property or removal/breakage of items provided in furnished property.

More disputes arise between landlord and tenant over deposits than almost anything else, so the tenancy agreement should deal very clearly and precisely with the following:

- circumstances under which the landlord may retain part or all of the deposit: for non-payment of rent, damage to the property, etc.
- if recourse is had to the deposit during the tenancy, can the landlord insist on the tenant making up the deposit to the former amount? If not, the landlord has lost his security in relation to any future default made by the tenant
- when the landlord should return the deposit to the tenant: immediately on the ending of the tenancy, or within a certain period following that date

- arrangements regarding any interest earned on the deposit whilst the landlord is holding it. Unless the agreement makes express provision to the contrary, it is likely that the landlord would have to repay the deposit with interest, even if he did not keep it in an interest-earning account
- whether the tenant may withhold any rent or other sums due from him because the landlord is holding an equivalent (or greater) amount as deposit. Normally, the tenant would be able to withhold such an amount unless the agreement provided to the contrary. The agreement should make a contrary provision, otherwise the landlord will have lost the security provided by the deposit in relation to any potential future default by the tenant.

If the deposit is to be held by a letting agent, there is a danger that the money would be at risk if the agent became insolvent. Both landlord and tenant should therefore ensure that the agent holds the deposit in a separate bank account held on trust for clients. You should also ensure that the deposit money is covered by some form of bonding scheme (e.g. the one operated by the Association of Residential Letting Agents, ARLA★) to protect against any fraud or dishonesty by the agent or its employees.

The Tenancy Deposit Scheme

In an effort to deal with the frequent problems caused by deposits, the government has introduced a Tenancy Deposit Scheme, overseen by the Independent Housing Ombudsman. If there is a dispute over the repayment of a deposit (e.g. there is a dispute as to damage allegedly caused by the tenant), the Ombudsman will resolve the dispute within ten working days of receiving the necessary information. The Ombudsman's decision is final. There are special provisions to ensure that the deposit is repaid without any delay after the Ombudsman's decision. The deposit will either be held in a special Nationwide Building Society account, payment out being made on receipt of the Ombudsman's decision, or the landlord will have to take out insurance to guarantee repayment should the Ombudsman so order. The scheme is supported by ARLA and the Royal Institute of Chartered Surveyors (RICS),★ but you do not need to use an agent to take advantage of it. Information can be obtained from the Independent Housing

Ombudsman website.★ At present the scheme is available only in the following areas:

- Brent and Camden
- Birmingham and the West Midlands
- Brighton and Hove
- Merseyside and West Lancashire
- Norwich and Norfolk.

It is expected to be extended to other areas shortly.

The specimen tenancy agreement provided in the appendices to this book contains provisions dealing with the matters to consider when tailoring an agreement to your own requirements.

Requirements for tenants to pay excessive rental deposits may be challenged in the courts under the Unfair Terms in Consumer Contracts Regulations.

Collecting the rent

If the rent is to be payable weekly, the landlord is legally obliged to provide a rent book. Many landlords now prefer rent to be paid by standing order directly into their bank account, and it makes sense for the rent to be payable monthly as most people are paid monthly (and mortgage repayments are made monthly), quite apart from the fact that under this arrangement there is no need to provide a rent book as well. (If you are using letting agents, they will, if you wish and for a consideration, collect the rent for you: see Chapter 4.)

Inventories

If the landlord is letting the property furnished, he will need to provide an inventory of the contents of the property at the time of the letting. The tenant will be responsible for the contents under the terms of the agreement and he will have either to replace or to compensate the landlord for any items lost or damaged during the tenancy.

Landlord and tenant should both sign the inventory to agree the house contents and any existing defects. At the end of the tenancy, they should again meet in the house and go through the contents to ensure that all are still present and in similar condition. If it is not possible for both parties to be present, the landlord should do this on his own as soon as possible to check that all is in order. If it is not, he will be entitled to withhold repayment of an equivalent part of the deposit to compensate for the loss or damage. However, it is always best for the tenant to be present when the examination is made in order to avoid, as far as possible, the risk of dispute.

Chapter 6

Granting non-shorthold tenancies

Lettings which cannot be shortholds include those where the landlord is resident in another part of the same house, new lettings to existing Rent Act tenants and lettings where the rent is in excess of £25,000 per year (see also Chapter 2). In addition, if you are letting the house in which you have previously lived, you may choose to let on an ordinary assured tenancy rather than a shorthold (see pages 41–3 for the pros and cons of ordinary assured and shorthold tenancies). This chapter deals with the procedure for letting in such cases.

Procedure and formalities

The basic procedure is similar whatever the type of tenancy, because the same considerations regarding consents, landlord's obligation to repair, safety regulations and so on (see Chapter 5) apply to non-shortholds.

Terms of the agreement

Although the tenancy agreement for non-shortholds is very similar to that used for shortholds, it will need a few modifications, which are included in the model ordinary assured tenancy agreement in Appendix III. This includes the appropriate notices for the various mandatory grounds for possession which are available to landlords letting under an ordinary assured tenancy (see Chapter 3).

Appendix IV contains a model tenancy agreement for a letting of part of a property where there is a resident landlord. If you are letting the whole of a property on a non-assured tenancy in other circumstances you will need to amend this agreement to delete the references to letting part of the property.

Chapter 7

Lettings prior to 28 February 1997

The law relating to lettings entered into prior to 28 February 1997 differs depending upon whether the letting started before or on or after 15 January 1989. For lettings before 15 January 1989, the provisions of the Rent Act 1977 still apply; for lettings on or after that date, the Housing Act 1988 will apply, but the rules are different from those described in Chapter 2.

Rent Act 1977: lettings prior to 15 January 1989

Tenancies originally entered into prior to 15 January 1989 are still governed by the provisions of the Rent Act 1977. The Housing Act 1988 changed the law for tenancies created on or after 15 January 1989, but basically did not alter the position with regard to those tenancies already in existence on that date.

Note that if you had a Rent Act tenancy on 15 January 1989 but were granted a new tenancy by your landlord after that date, that new tenancy will also be a Rent Act tenancy. This will be the case whether or not the tenancy is of the same premises. Hence, if you had a tenancy of no. 1 Coronation Street, and the landlord were later to grant you a new tenancy of no. 8 Coronation Street, that new letting would still be a Rent Act tenancy even though it was entered into today. For this rule to apply, however, there can be no gap between the end of the original Rent Act tenancy and the grant of the new one; if there is, the new tenancy will be governed by the 1988 Housing Act.

There are still many thousands of Rent Act tenancies in existence today, although their numbers are likely to decline as the years go by and tenants leave.

Rent Act tenants are given wide-ranging security of tenure, in many ways similar to that given to assured tenants. This means that, as in assured tenancies, a landlord will be able to obtain possession of the property only if he goes to court and establishes one of the grounds for possession laid down in the Rent Act.

The main difference between Rent Act tenancies and assured tenancies is that the former are subject to rent control, the 'fair rent' system which tends to keep rents below those which would prevail in the open market.

On the death of a Rent Act tenant, succession rights also tend to be more generous than those applying to assured tenancies. Sometimes, however, the new tenant will lose his Rent Act protection and become an assured tenant under the Housing Act 1988 (see pages 102–3).

Protected tenancies

Protection under the Rent Act is given to 'protected tenancies' and 'statutory tenancies', as described below.

A protected tenancy exists where a dwellinghouse was 'let as a separate dwelling' (see page 19, where the similarly worded requirement for an assured tenancy under the Housing Act 1988 is discussed).

Note, however, that in contrast to the Housing Act's requirements for an assured tenancy there is no need for the letting to be to an individual, nor does the house need to be the tenant's only or principal home. Therefore a letting to a limited company, or a letting of a 'second home', can be a protected tenancy.

The various exceptions are generally very similar to those for assured tenancies: for example, lettings by resident landlords, holiday lettings and tenancies at a low rent. Also excluded from the definition are lettings where the rent includes payment for board or attendance, including those where meals are provided or the landlord cleans the rooms. There is no similar exclusion for assured tenancies.

Protected tenancies can be either periodic tenancies or for a fixed term – of any duration. Tenants have rent control and succession rights, but not necessarily security of tenure. To have security of tenure, the Rent Act tenant must qualify as a 'statutory tenant' on the ending of the protected tenancy. During the tenancy the tenant is protected by the terms of the contract. The landlord cannot obtain possession without ending the tenancy – for example, by notice to quit. Only at the end of the tenancy can the question of security of tenure arise.

Statutory tenancies

A statutory tenancy is the device by which security of tenure is given. At the end of the protected tenancy, the tenant will become a statutory tenant only 'if and so long as he occupies the dwelling-house as his residence'. So although occupation as a residence is not necessary for the letting to qualify as a protected tenancy, it is necessary for the tenant to be given security of tenure. Whilst he satisfies this definition of a statutory tenant, the tenant continues to have the benefit of rent control and succession rights; he will also have security of tenure and can be evicted only once the landlord has been to court and established one of the grounds for possession laid down by the Rent Act.

Only an individual can occupy a property as a residence: a company tenant can therefore be a protected tenant but not a statutory tenant, even if one of the directors or employees of the company is living in the property.

There is no requirement that the dwellinghouse should be occupied as the tenant's only or main residence as there is under the Housing Act 1988; for Rent Act purposes it is accepted that a person can have two homes and that there can be a statutory tenancy of either or both of them.

As a statutory tenancy can arise only on the ending of a protected tenancy, it means that in order to obtain possession against a protected tenant, the landlord must first terminate that protected tenancy – for example, by serving notice to quit. If the tenant does not qualify as a statutory tenant (say, because the tenant is a company), the landlord will be immediately entitled to a court order for possession. If a statutory tenancy does arise, the landlord will be entitled to possession only if he goes to court and can establish one (or more) of the grounds for possession. As with assured tenancies, some of these are mandatory, in which case the court must order possession on proof of the ground; but many are discretionary, which means the court can order possession only if it considers it reasonable to do so. Many of the assured tenancy grounds for possession were based on Rent Act grounds and reference should be made to the equivalent assured tenancy ground where relevant. The Rent Act 1977 grounds are called 'Cases' and are set out in the 15th Schedule to the Act.

Discretionary grounds for possession

Case 1

Where any rent lawfully due from the tenant has not been paid, or any obligation of the protected or statutory tenancy ... has been broken or not performed.

This case should be compared with grounds 8, 10, 11 and 12 for assured tenancies. Note, in particular, that non-payment of rent is only a discretionary ground, no matter how great the amount of the arrears. If you are a landlord seeking possession from a Rent Act tenant because of rent arrears, note that even if you establish the arrears you may still not obtain a possession order as the court may well not consider it reasonable to make such an order. In deciding what is reasonable, the court will consider the amount and frequency of the arrears and the hardship to the tenant in the event of a possession order being made. The impact of the arrears on the landlord is also a relevant factor. Even if a possession order is made, it may well be suspended on condition that the tenant pays off the arrears in a prescribed manner, such as £X per week. This means that as long as the tenant makes these payments, the landlord will not be able to obtain possession.

Case 2

Where the tenant or any person residing or lodging with him or any subtenant of his has been guilty of conduct which is a nuisance or annoyance to adjoining occupiers, or has been convicted of using the dwellinghouse or allowing the dwellinghouse to be used for immoral or illegal purposes.

This case is identical in effect to the original version of assured tenancy ground 14. It has not been extended to cover the other types of anti-social behaviour now covered by ground 14, so it is only nuisance or annoyance to adjoining occupiers which will give a right to possession.

Case 3

Where the condition of the dwellinghouse has, in the opinion of the court, deteriorated owing to acts of waste by, or the neglect or default of, the tenant or any person residing or lodging with him or any subtenant of his and, in the case of any act of waste by, or the neglect or default of, a person lodging with the tenant or a subtenant of his, where the court is satisfied that the tenant has not, before the making of the order in question, taken such steps as he ought reasonably to have taken for the removal of the lodger or subtenant, as the case may be.

This is virtually the same as assured tenancy ground 13 and shares its problems. Unlike ground 13, though, it does not extend to damage etc. caused to the common parts of the building.

Case 4

Where the condition of any furniture provided for use under the tenancy has, in the opinion of the court, deteriorated owing to ill-treatment by the tenant or any person residing or lodging with him or any subtenant of his, and in the case of any ill-treatment by any person lodging with the tenant or a subtenant of his, where the court is satisfied that the tenant has not, before the making of the order in question, taken such steps as he ought reasonably to have taken for the removal of the lodger or subtenant, as the case may be.

See assured tenancy ground 15.

Case 5

Where the tenant has given notice to quit and, in consequence of that notice, the landlord has contracted to sell or let the dwellinghouse or has taken any other steps as the result of which he would, in the opinion of the court, be seriously prejudiced if he could not obtain possession.

This ground has no equivalent under assured tenancies. It is necessary for Rent Act tenancies because a statutory tenancy, with security of tenure, arises on the ending of the protected tenancy no matter how it may have ended. So if a tenant gives notice to quit, a statutory tenancy will still arise and the landlord will not be entitled to possession unless he can prove one of the grounds laid down by the Act. This could place him in difficulty if, thinking that the tenant is about to vacate the property, he enters into a contract to sell with vacant possession – or to let the house to another tenant.

Without this case, the landlord would have no right to possession if the tenant should subsequently change his mind and decide not to vacate after all. If the tenant were to decide not to go, the landlord would be in breach of his contract to sell or re-let and could find himself having to pay substantial damages for breach of that contract.

This case will apply only if the landlord has actually entered into a contract to sell/let or would otherwise be seriously prejudiced. If the landlord has merely incurred expense in trying to find a buyer or new tenant, the ground will not be available.

There is no need for an equivalent ground for assured tenancies, as the Housing Act 1988 makes it clear that if an assured tenancy comes to an end by virtue of a tenant's notice to quit, there is no security of tenure for the tenant and the landlord will have an absolute right to possession without further proof.

Case 6

Where, without the consent of the landlord, the tenant has … assigned or sublet the whole of the dwellinghouse.

This case will apply whether or not there is any express prohibition on assignment (i.e. transferring the tenancy) in the tenancy agreement. Note that the ground will not apply to a subletting of part only of the house, or where the tenant takes in a lodger. However, if taking lodgers was prohibited by the terms of the tenancy agreement, the tenant would be liable to an order being obtained under case 1.

This ground has no direct equivalent in assured tenancies, but it is an implied term of every periodic assured tenancy that the tenant will not assign without consent. A breach of this implied term would then render the tenant liable to possession being ordered against him under ground 12 (breach of the terms of the tenancy).

Case 7

This has been repealed and is therefore no longer applicable.

Case 8

Where the dwellinghouse is reasonably required by the landlord for occupation as a residence for some person engaged in his whole-time employment, or in the whole-time employment of some tenant from whom or with whom, conditional on housing being provided, a contract for such employment has been entered into, and the tenant was in the employment of the landlord or a former landlord, and the dwellinghouse was let to him in consequence of that employment and he has ceased to be in that employment.

This is similar to assured tenancy ground 16. For this ground to apply, the landlord needs to establish that the property was let to the tenant because of his employment by the landlord. Unlike assured tenancy ground 16, however, the landlord also has to prove that he reasonably requires the house for accommodation by another employee. Whether he 'reasonably' requires possession will depend upon the facts of the case.

Case 9
Where the dwellinghouse is reasonably required by the landlord for occupation as a residence for: (a) himself; (b) any son or daughter of his over 18 years of age: (c) his father or mother; (d) the father or mother of the landlord's wife or husband, and the landlord did not become landlord by purchasing the dwellinghouse or any interest therein.

It should also be noted that a court cannot order possession under this case if, considering all the circumstances, it appears that greater hardship would be caused by granting the order than by refusing to grant it. Obviously, the question of hardship will depend upon the facts of the case, but factors such as the availability of alternative accommodation to the respective parties and their respective financial circumstances will be relevant. The court is required to compare the relative hardship to landlord and tenant.

This case will be available to a landlord whether or not he has resided in the property prior to the letting and there is no need for any warning notice to have been served on the tenant prior to the letting (*cf* case 11 and assured tenancy ground 1). Remember also that, unlike those grounds, it is only a discretionary ground for possession. This means that even if the landlord proves the ground and overcomes the 'greater hardship' test, the court will order possession only if it considers it reasonable to do so.

Note also that the ground will not apply if the landlord became landlord by purchasing the property – hence, a landlord who buys a house with a sitting tenant will not be able to use this ground. This is to prevent landlords buying up property with sitting tenants and then using this ground to gain possession. The ground will be available to a landlord who bought a property (with or without a tenant) and then granted a new tenancy to a new tenant.

Case 10

This allows possession to be claimed if the tenant has sublet part of the house at a rent greater than legally permitted. This principle ties in with the fair rent system, which fixes the maximum rent which can lawfully be charged on a Rent Act letting, and is little used.

Suitable alternative accommodation

Although not allocated a case number, the Rent Act 1977 also allows the court to order possession on this ground, but again only if it considers it reasonable to do so. See assured tenancy ground 9 (page 52) for what constitutes 'suitable alternative accommodation'.

Mandatory grounds for possession

If the landlord can establish one of these 'mandatory' grounds , the court has no discretion and must order possession, notwithstanding whether it is reasonable to do so or whether any hardship will be caused to the tenant.

Case 11

Where a person who occupied the dwellinghouse as his residence (in this case referred to as 'the owner-occupier') let it ... and

(a) *not later than [the date of the commencement of the tenancy] the landlord gave notice in writing to the tenant that possession might be recovered under this case; and*

(b) *the dwellinghouse has not ... been let by the owner-occupier on a protected tenancy with respect to which the condition mentioned in paragraph (a) above was not satisfied; and*

(c) *the court is of the opinion that ... one of the following conditions has been satisfied:*

(1) *the dwellinghouse is required as a residence for the owner or any member of his family who resided with the owner when he last occupied the dwellinghouse as a residence*

97

(2) the owner has died and the dwellinghouse is required as a residence for a member of his family who was residing with him at the time of his death

(3) the owner has died and the dwellinghouse is required by a successor in title as his residence or for the purpose of disposing of it with vacant possession

(4) the dwellinghouse is subject to a mortgage, made by deed and granted before the tenancy, and the mortgagee is entitled to exercise a power of sale and requires possession of the dwellinghouse for the purpose of disposing of it with vacant possession

(5) the dwellinghouse is not reasonably suited to the needs of the owner, having regard to his place of work, and he requires it for the purpose of disposing of it with vacant possession so that he can use the proceeds to purchase another house as his residence which would be more suited to his needs.

This case must be distinguished from the superficially similar case 9. Unlike case 9, it is dependent upon the service of a warning notice prior to the letting and the landlord must have resided in the house at some time prior to the letting. There is no requirement for this written notice to be in any particular form: it could have been included as a term of the tenancy agreement, or it could have been in a letter from the landlord to the prospective tenant. However, if the court is of the opinion that it is just and equitable to make an order for possession, it has the power to dispense with the notice requirement. This might be the case where, for example, a landlord made it clear to a tenant before the letting that the house was his home and that he might want it back at some future date, but did not actually put this in writing.

While the basic ground is that the landlord requires possession from the tenant so that the house can be used as a residence for himself or a member of his family, for the ground to be established in the case of a family member he or she must have lived in the house with the landlord the last time he resided in the property.

This case also deals with the possibility that possession might be required after the death of the owner, either for sale or as a residence. Possession is also recoverable to enable a sale with vacant possession to take place either by a mortgagee or if the landlord has changed his place of work.

Case 12

This allows possession to be claimed by a landlord who has purchased a house as a prospective retirement home, but lets it in the meantime. There is no need for prior residence (*cf* case 11), but the availability of the case is again dependent upon a warning notice having been given no later than the commencement of the tenancy. This notice can, however, be dispensed with in the same circumstances as in case 11. The landlord will then be entitled to possession on retirement or in the circumstances set out in points 2–4 of case 11 above.

Cases 13 and 14
These are now obsolete and need not be considered.

Case 15
This case refers to the letting of houses kept for occupation by ministers of religion and is identical with assured tenancy ground 5.

Cases 16, 17 and 18
These relate to lettings of farmhouses and lettings of houses to persons employed in agriculture where the house is required for occupation by a new employee.

Case 19
This is now obsolete.

Case 20
This case allows members of the armed forces who acquired and let houses during their service to obtain possession in similar circumstances to owner-occupiers under case 11. Although a warning notice needs to have been served on the tenant no later than the commencement of the tenancy, there is no need for the landlord to have occupied the house prior to the letting. The warning notice can be dispensed with in the same circumstances as under case 11.

The fair rent system

With protected and statutory tenancies, the amount of rent the landlord may charge is subject to control. The Rent Act 1977 set up a register of 'fair rents' for dwellinghouses: once a rent has been registered in relation to a property, that becomes the maximum chargeable under any present or future protected or statutory tenancy of the property.

(The existence of a registered fair rent does *not* limit the amount of rent chargeable under an assured or assured shorthold tenancy.)

The rent is assessed by the rent officer, a local authority official, in accordance with criteria laid down by the Act. These are designed to exclude any scarcity element from the calculation of the rent. Under normal market forces and the principles of supply and demand, a high demand for rented property and a small supply would tend to push up commercial rents. For years the scarcity of letting accommodation in Britain and resulting high levels of rent put many properties beyond the means of a lot of people. As the rent officer is required to assume that there is no shortage of accommodation to let (even though there might be), the rent he assesses is often considerably lower than it would otherwise be.

The existence of the fair rent system is a valuable asset for Rent Act tenants, but is viewed less favourably by landlords, who consider that it prevents them from receiving an adequate return on their investment.

Applying for a fair rent

Assuming that no fair rent is registered in respect of the property, on the grant of a tenancy the landlord could charge whatever rent the market would bear. However, at any time during the continuance of the tenancy the tenant can apply for a fair rent to be assessed. The landlord cannot prevent an application being made. Once assessed, the rent then becomes the maximum payable, despite the existence of a higher agreed figure in the tenancy agreement.

The only way in which the landlord can increase the rent is by applying on his own behalf to the rent officer for the assessment of a higher fair rent. However, he cannot make such an application within two years of a fair rent having been assessed unless there has been a material change in the condition of the dwelling or the terms of the tenancy.

On the fixing of a fair rent, therefore, a tenant is usually assured of a minimum period of two years before an increase in rent can take place. Even if council tax is increased during the two-year period and the landlord is responsible for paying it, he will still have to wait until the end of the two years before he can increase the rent.

However, if a landlord carries out improvements to the property, he can then apply for a new fair rent within the two-year period; otherwise, if the landlord had to wait until the end of two years before he could increase the rent, this would be unfair on him, as well as being a disincentive to landlords to spend money on improving their property.

Process for increasing a registered fair rent

Once a fair rent has been registered. the only way in which the landlord can increase the rent is by obtaining the registration of a higher fair rent. However, even if the landlord succeeds in this, he cannot immediately claim the increase. To become entitled to the increased amount, he must first of all give to the tenant a 'notice of increase' in the form laid down by Parliament. When it is given, payment of the increased amount of rent can be backdated, but not for more than four weeks and not to a date prior to the registration of the new amount.

Restrictions on the amount of the rent increase

In many areas of Britain, there is no longer a shortage of property to let. This has meant that, as there is no scarcity element to ignore, some fair rents have been increased virtually to open market levels. In relation to applications made on or after 1 February 1999, there is now a limit on how much the rent can be increased at any one time. It is based on a complex formula which involves taking the percentage increase in the Retail Price Index (RPI) for the period between the registration of the initial rent and the present determination. The maximum rent increase is then dependent on whether this is the first application for a determination since 1 February 1999. If it is the first, the rent cannot increase by more than the percentage increase in the RPI plus a further 7.5 per cent. In the case of a second or subsequent application, the increase cannot be more than 5 per cent above the increase in the RPI.

Hence, if the original registered rent were £40 and over the period since it was registered the RPI had increased by 5 per cent, the maximum increase will be 12.5 per cent (i.e. the 5 per cent increase plus 7.5 per cent) of £40, which is £5. Note that there is no guarantee that the rent will go up by this amount: all that the law states is that this is the maximum by which it can be increased.

Where the result of the calculation would be to reduce the existing registered rent, then the maximum fair rent which can be registered is the existing registered rent.

These provisions do not apply if, because of a change in the condition of the house as a result of repairs or improvements, the new rent exceeds by at least 15 per cent the rent previously registered. In the case of repairs and improvements, there is no restriction on the amount of the increase if the new rent exceeds the old by 15 per cent; if it exceeds the old by less than that amount, the restrictions on the increase will still apply.

Over-payment of rent

Any rent over and above the amount permitted by the Rent Act under the above provisions is 'irrecoverable' by the landlord. This means that the tenant does not have to pay it and that the landlord cannot bring court proceedings to claim it or bring possession proceedings based on non-payment. Indeed, any sums already paid can be recovered from the landlord by the tenant but only for a maximum period of two years.

Succession to Rent Act tenancies

On the death of a statutory or a protected tenant, that person's spouse (or partner of opposite sex, living with the tenant as husband or wife) will become the statutory tenant, entitled to all the associated benefits of security of tenure and rent control.

If there is no surviving spouse (or opposite-sex partner who has lived with the tenant as husband or wife), in the case of deaths that occurred prior to 15 January 1989, any member of the deceased's family who had lived with the deceased at the time of death and for at least six months prior to death would have become a statutory tenant. In the case of deaths that occurred on or after 15 January 1989, for a family member to succeed he or she would need to have been living with the deceased for at least two years prior to death.

However, when such deaths occur the family member will become entitled only to an assured tenancy, not a statutory tenancy. The main effect of this is that, although the tenant will still have wide-ranging security of tenure, he will lose the benefit of the fair rent system. This means that the rent could be increased quite substantially to bring it up to the level of open-market rents chargeable under assured tenancies. As with other assured periodic tenancies, if the tenant does not accept the landlord's suggested increase, he has the right to ask the Rent Assessment Committee to assess a fair market rent (see page 25).

In the case of deaths prior to 15 January 1989, two successions were permitted. On the death of the first successor, the same succession rules would apply in favour of that person's spouse or family member. However, in the case of the death of a first successor after 15 January 1989, a second transmission is possible only in very limited circumstances. An individual is entitled to a second succession only if he was *both* a member of the original tenant's family *and* a member of the first successor's family *and also* if he had resided with the first successor for at least two years prior to the first successor's death. Note that there is no requirement for this second successor to have lived with the original tenant at all; it is sufficient for him to be a member of the original tenant's family, although often, of course, he will have resided with the original tenant.

This complicated formula is designed to cover a situation where the original tenant was, say, a man living in the house with his wife and child. On his death, a first transmission will occur in favour of his wife; on her death, a second transmission is then possible in favour of the child, provided that the child satisfies the residence requirement. Note that this second successor will always take the tenancy as assured tenant.

Protected shorthold tenancies

These were introduced by the Housing Act 1980 but few remain in existence today.

They were the precursors of the assured shorthold and shared some of its characteristics. Hence, they had to be for a fixed period and be preceded by the serving of a warning notice on the tenant. Unlike assured shortholds they had to be for at least 12 months. At the end of the fixed term the landlord had a mandatory right to possession under Rent Act case 19. However, the procedure for obtaining possession was very complex and had to be approached with care if the landlord was to be successful.

The effect of the Housing Act 1988 was to phase out these protected shorthold tenancies. It provided that any new letting on or after 15 January 1989 to a protected shorthold tenant would be an assured shorthold (whether or not the normal assured shorthold requirements were complied with). It is this provision, coupled with the short duration of most protected shortholds, that ensured their rapid demise after the implementation of the 1988 Act.

Tenancies entered into on or after 15 January 1989 but before 28 February 1997

As explained in Chapter 2, lettings entered into on or after 15 January 1989 but prior to 28 February 1997 would have been ordinary assured tenancies (with full security of tenure) unless the conditions for a shorthold were satisfied. There are still many tenancies in existence which began prior to 28 February 1997, so these conditions are still of some significance, particularly as any lettings to an existing assured tenant on or after 28 February 1997 will still be an assured tenancy, not a shorthold. So, if a tenant was granted a purported shorthold in 1996 and, in fact, the requisite shorthold conditions were not complied with, that 1996 tenancy would be an ordinary assured tenancy with full security of tenure, as would any further tenancy granted to the tenant by the same landlord, even if made today.

Old shortholds (granted before 28 February 1997)

An 'old' shorthold is subject to the same requirements as a 'new' shorthold: hence, it must be a letting of a house as a separate dwelling, and so on, as set out in Chapter 2. Also, the exceptions set out in Chapter 2 will apply. But in addition to these the tenancy must:

(1) be for a fixed term of not less than six months
(2) contain no power for the landlord to terminate it during the first six months, and
(3) have been preceded by the giving to the tenant of the prescribed shorthold notice.

Minimum six-month fixed term
The initial grant of an old shorthold could not be for a periodic tenancy, i.e. a weekly or monthly tenancy. It must be for a fixed term and

for a minimum duration of six months. There is, however, no maximum length, despite the use of the term 'shorthold'. It is legally possible to have a shorthold granted for, say, 21 years or more.

Where shortholds were granted for a minimum six-month period care must be taken to ensure that the tenant was given a right to occupy for the full duration of the minimum period. The six-month period runs from the date that the tenancy is entered into and cannot be backdated. So a tenancy granted 'from and including 1 January 1997 until 30 June 1997' but not actually entered into until 15 January 1997 would not give the tenant the necessary six months' occupation from the date of grant and so could not be a shorthold. It would therefore be an ordinary assured tenancy with full security of tenure.

No termination by landlord during first six months
Even if a minimum period of six months was granted, any power, however expressed, which would or might allow the landlord to terminate the tenancy within the first six months of the tenancy will prevent the tenancy from amounting to a shorthold. Again, an ordinary assured tenancy will be created giving the tenant full security of tenure.

A term allowing the *tenant* to terminate during the first six months could be validly included.

Prescribed shorthold notice
As the tenant under an assured shorthold would have no security of tenure, it was thought necessary for him to be given a notice prior to the grant of the tenancy warning him of this fact. This notice must be in writing and in the prescribed form, i.e. it must conform precisely to the layout and content required by the law. An oral 'notice' is not sufficient. Note, however, that the content of the necessary form has changed twice since the introduction of assured shortholds on January 15 1989 and care must be taken to ensure that the shorthold notice served was the correct one as at the date of service.

If the correct version of the form was not given to the tenant, the letting will not amount to a shorthold and the landlord will not be entitled to possession unless he can establish ordinary assured tenancy grounds.

The prescribed notice had to be given to the tenant before the tenancy agreement was entered into and therefore could not be included in the tenancy agreement itself, or given at the same time as the tenancy agreement was signed. In the case of joint tenants, all of the prospective tenants should have been given the notice.

If the notice requirements are not correctly complied with, the tenancy will almost certainly amount to an ordinary assured tenancy giving the tenant full security of tenure. Chapter 3 describes the protections given to ordinary assured tenancies.

Rent control for old shortholds

As for new shortholds, the tenant has the right to refer the rent to the Rent Assessment Committee (see Chapter 2). The main difference is that an old shorthold tenant can apply at *any time* during the first shorthold granted to him; no application can be made, however, during any subsequent letting, even if no application was made during the first shorthold. Once the rent has been determined it becomes the maximum amount chargeable throughout that tenancy, despite any provisions in the tenancy agreement for increase.

However, it will not restrict the amount of rent chargeable under a subsequent tenancy of the same premises. Further, if at the end of a shorthold the landlord does not obtain possession immediately, the tenant will be allowed to remain in occupation as a statutory periodic tenant. The landlord will then be able to increase the rent by following the procedure described on page 25.

If a new tenancy is granted

If the parties are the same, a new tenancy of the same (or substantially the same) property will be deemed to be a shorthold unless the landlord serves notice on the tenant that the new letting is not to be a shorthold.

The effect of this 'deeming' provision is that any new tenancy following an old shorthold would be a shorthold even though it did not comply with the normal shorthold requirements. So no shorthold notice need be served, the letting need not be for a fixed term (hence, a periodic shorthold is permissible), and any fixed term need not be for a minimum period of six months.

A further feature of these deemed shortholds is that there is no right to refer the rent to the Rent Assessment Committee. This is the case whether or not an application was made to the Committee during the initial shorthold term. If a rent was determined by the Committee during the initial term this would not limit the amount of rent chargeable by the landlord under the new tenancy agreement.

Old ordinary assured tenancies

All tenancies entered into on or after 15 January 1989 but before 28 February 1997 will be ordinary assured tenancies unless the conditions set out above for an old shorthold apply. (Note that the letting must also satisfy the requirements – letting a house as a separate dwelling, and so on – as set out in Chapter 2).

An ordinary shorthold tenant has extensive security of tenure: hence, the landlord cannot obtain possession, even though the term agreed between the parties has expired, unless and until he can establish one of the grounds for possession laid down in the Act. The full details of the security given and the grounds are set out in Chapter 3.

Any new letting to an existing ordinary assured tenant will remain an ordinary assured tenancy whenever granted (even if this was after 28 February 1997). However, on such a re-letting it is possible for the tenant to serve a notice on the landlord, in the form prescribed, stating that he wants the new tenancy to be a shorthold. By so electing, the tenant would, of course, have a tenancy with no security of tenure.

The question arises as to *why* a tenant with full security would elect to have a shorthold tenancy. When the legislation was going through Parliament, it was stated that this was intended to cover a situation where the landlord had a ground for possession available against an ordinary assured tenant. Due to the discretion given to the court, neither landlord nor tenant could be sure as to who would win. The availability of this option to elect that a new tenancy would be a shorthold might provide an effective way of compromising the possession action. Hence, the landlord would discontinue the action in return for the tenant accepting a new letting that was going to be a shorthold. The landlord would therefore be sure of possession at the end of the shorthold and the tenant would have avoided the risk of having to give up possession immediately.

The arrangement is not limited to such circumstances and there is therefore a danger that it could be exploited by unscrupulous landlords.

Q *I moved into my flat in 1988. The rent has always been quite reasonable, but a new landlord has now taken over and has put the rent up so much that now I cannot afford to pay it. What can I do?*

A Your tenancy is still governed by the Rent Act 1977. As such you have the right at any time to apply for a 'fair rent' to be assessed by the rent officer according to criteria laid down by the Act. Once a fair rent has been assessed it becomes the maximum payable for the flat. You should contact your county or unitary council's rent officer (look under the council's entry in the phone book or *Yellow Pages*) as soon as possible for advice as to how to apply for a fair rent.

Q *I took a weekly tenancy of a house in 1987. In 1997 I was granted a new tenancy of the same house at a higher rent. The landlord now wants me to leave the house. Do I have to go?*

A You are still a fully protected Rent Act tenant. Although the new tenancy in 1997 was created after the Housing Act 1988 came into operation, as an existing Rent Act tenant you remain protected by that Act. The landlord can obtain possession only by going to court and only then if he can establish one of the Rent Act grounds.

Q *I have looked after my aged mother for many years. She has been a tenant of her house since the tenancy was granted in about 1985. She died a few weeks ago and the landlord has now said that he wants me to leave. He has said that he does not want to be unreasonable and has given me two months to find somewhere else to live. Do I have to go? The house is my home.*

A Your mother was a Rent Act tenant. As you lived with her for more than two years prior to her death, you are entitled to succeed to her tenancy. You will take over as an assured tenant. This means that you inherit her security of tenure and the landlord will be able to obtain possession only if he can prove one of the grounds laid down in the Housing Act 1988. You should write to the landlord to inform him of your status. However, under an assured tenancy, the fair rent system will no longer apply and it may therefore be possible for the landlord to increase the rent. He must do so in the way laid down for assured periodic tenancies. If you do not agree with his proposals you will have the right to refer the rent to the Rent Assessment Committee for the proper market rent to be fixed.

Chapter 8

Houses in multiple occupation

This chapter looks at houses in multiple occupation (HMOs), what this expression means in law and the various consequences of letting such houses. If a house is divided into 'bedsits', for example, it may be more vulnerable to the risk of fire than one occupied by a single family. Most houses in multiple occupation have shared facilities – bathroom, kitchen, staircases and so on – which must be properly maintained and managed. Health and safety issues have given rise to special rules for these types of houses.

The legal definition of a house in multiple occupation is one which is occupied by 'persons who do not form a single household'. But the 'house' need not be a house in the conventional sense: it could be any residential unit. For example, a self-contained flat is a house for the purposes of the HMO regulations: the key factor is that the property is in 'multiple occupation' and multiple occupation implies, broadly, unrelated people occupying separate units under the same roof. (A property occupied by just one person or by a couple living together with or without children would obviously be excluded.) Examples of 'houses in multiple occupation' include:

- bedsits or flatlets
- non-self-contained flats where facilities such as bathroom or kitchen are shared
- student accommodation
- hostels and refuges
- guesthouses or B&Bs where one or more of the residents has no other accommodation.

This list is not comprehensive, so do seek legal advice, or contact the local authority, if in doubt about the definition of a property.

HMOs usually have to be registered with the local authority, which has a duty to run a registration scheme. The requirements of such schemes vary from area to area, so it is advisable to check the situation locally.

HMO regulations

In addition to his obligations under the tenancy agreement or terms implied by law (see Chapter 12), the landlord of an HMO must:

- maintain the water supply and drainage in proper working order
- not unreasonably interrupt the supply of gas and electricity
- keep in proper working order installations in common use (that is, shared facilities such as baths, refrigerators and so on)
- ensure that the living accommodation is in a clean condition at the beginning of each resident's occupation
- keep the windows and ventilation facilities in good repair
- take adequate precautions to ensure that the premises are safe
- ensure that all fire escapes are in good repair and free from obstruction
- ensure that the common parts of the house such as staircases, passageways, landings and balconies are kept free from obstruction so as not to block a means of escape in the case of fire or other emergency
- maintain any outbuildings and yards that form part of the HMO
- provide adequate rubbish bins and ensure that rubbish is removed regularly
- display a notice giving the name, address and telephone number of the manager of the house
- provide the local authority with details of the occupiers and any changes in occupancy.

A breach of these regulations could lead to the landlord being prosecuted and fined.

The tenants also have responsibilities: to co-operate with the landlord in order that these regulations can be followed, including allowing access to their rooms at all reasonable times by the manager. Moreover, if the tenants cause damage to the property this will constitute a breach of their tenancy agreement or licence to occupy and could form the basis of an action for eviction.

Registration schemes

Each local authority must have a registration scheme for HMOs, details of which are available from the local authority's housing department. Subject to certain exceptions (for example, houses with not more than four occupants), landlords must register HMOs, pay the appropriate registration fee and comply with the scheme's regulations.

Broadly, each scheme:

- requires the landlord to register the house and provide details of the occupants and changes in occupancy
- sets out fire escape requirements
- ensures the proper management of the house by a named manager (who can, of course, be the landlord)
- sets out detailed standards for the running of HMOs.

How to register an HMO

To register an HMO, the landlord must complete a form, available from the local authority, and pay a fee. The form requires the name and address of the landlord and the address of the house in question, plus:

- names of (a) owner (b) lessee and (c) mortgagee
- name of person having control of or managing the house
- number of storeys, total number of rooms in the house, number of households and number of persons occupying the house
- details of kitchens, bathrooms, washing facilities and toilets.

Breaches of HMO regulations

Most of the regulatory powers are vested in the local authority, which can usually:

- make landlords carry out any necessary repairs and, in extreme cases, take over control of the house for up to five years or make a compulsory purchase order
- insist that the landlord provides facilities such as fire escapes and adequate amenities
- if the house is overcrowded, require the landlord to reduce the number of occupants to an acceptable level
- insist on access for the purposes of ensuring compliance with the regulations

- prosecute defaulting landlords (which can result in a fine)
- carry out essential work itself and recover cost from the landlord.

General legislation affecting HMOs

Apart from the rules cited above which relate specifically to HMOs, the law places the following obligations on property-owners:

- **planning permission** If a house is currently being used as a single private dwellinghouse, that is, occupied by one family only, turning it into an HMO requires planning permission owing to the change of use, even if no physical alterations are involved
- **building regulations** If physical alterations are required to convert a house into, say, bedsitters or flats, the Building Regulations must be complied with and the plans and specifications approved by the local authority
- **insurance** If a house is to be converted into an HMO, a different insurance policy for buildings and contents will be required
- **nuisance** A change of use to an HMO may result in nuisance or annoyance to the neighbours. Sometimes title deeds contain restrictive covenants forbidding nuisance or annoyance which could be breached if, for example, noise or accumulation of rubbish were to increase to a level that became actionable. Even if there are no restrictive covenants a substantial increase in noise or rubbish levels could constitute the tort of nuisance, as long as the neighbours can show serious detriment. Although such a charge would be aimed primarily at the occupiers of the property rather than the landlord, it is not impossible that the landlord could be held responsible
- **problems with fluctuating tenants** If a house is let to several unrelated people, such as students, it is likely that from time to time some will leave and others will come in. If the landlord or agent is consulted on such changes (as he should be) the situation can be supervised, but if, as sometimes happens, the landlord is not told, the property is no longer under legal control. This can present problems if there are rent arrears or if the landlord needs to take possession proceedings against the occupiers at any stage (see Chapter 14)
- **council tax** The landlord is liable for this. The rent charged should reflect this and the tenancy agreement should allow for increases in council tax occurring during the tenancy.

Chapter 9

Housing benefit and council tax

Housing benefit is a means-tested payment available to tenants who cannot pay their rent. It is available whether or not the applicant is in employment. Unlike most means-tested benefits which are administered by the Department of Social Security, housing benefit is administered by the district, metropolitan or unitary local authority. However, the local council is itself reimbursed by funds from central government. Payment of benefit is governed by the Housing Benefit Regulations (as periodically amended).

This chapter is a general introduction to housing benefit for those involved in letting residential property. It is not a guide to eligibility. For the latter, consult the relevant DSS manual or the annual guide to means-tested benefits published by the Child Poverty Action Group.*

The method of payment of the benefit differs according to whether the tenant has a private landlord or a local authority landlord. If the tenant is in the private sector, a 'rent allowance' is paid to the tenant, who then pays the landlord. Local authority tenants, on the other hand, receive a 'rent rebate' – that is, the amount of rent they pay will be reduced by the amount of the benefit.

It is estimated that over 800,000 households in England and Wales are currently in receipt of housing benefit, including about half of all tenants with private landlords. To combat the potential for unscrupulous landlords to charge tenants excessively high rents, knowing that the payments would be met by housing benefit, rent officers have been given wide powers to limit the amount of rent charged.

Entitlement

The rules for entitlement differ according to whether or not the claimant is in receipt of income support. In the case of an income support recipient, entitlement is automatic and the maximum allowable benefit will be payable without a further means test. For other claimants, entitlement is means-tested in accordance with the current version of the regulations, which change from time to time. A complex calculation is applied which, depending upon the applicant's resources, will sometimes result in sufficient benefit being paid to cover all of the eligible rent and sometimes only part of it, the rest being payable by the applicant personally. Note that it is not only the claimant's income which is relevant: capital over a certain amount will be deemed to be income-producing (whether or not it actually is), and if the claimant's capital is considerable the claimant will be disentitled to benefit altogether.

The claimant must occupy the dwellinghouse as his/her home, although temporary absence will be ignored. Normally, benefit will be payable only for one home.

Entitlement is based on the amount of the 'eligible' rent. This means that items such as heating, lighting and water charges which may be included in the rental payment made to the landlord are excluded from the calculation of the amount of the benefit. This means that no benefit will be payable in respect of those elements of the rent.

Restrictions on the amount of benefit

As mentioned above, the benefit payable will not necessarily be the full amount of the eligible rent: this is to discourage claims in respect of excessively large rents and excessively large properties.

The rules governing the amount paid differ depending upon whether the applicant first became entitled to benefit before 2 January 1996 or afterwards.

Previously, private-sector rents were referred to the rent officer to determine whether or not they were a 'reasonable market rent'. The rent officer had to decide whether the rent was significantly higher than the rent which the landlord might reasonably be expected to obtain, having regard to rents for similar tenancies of similar properties in the locality. This no longer happens.

In determining this reasonable market rent the rent officer will also apply the size criteria, which are laid down. If the rented accommodation is significantly larger than the tenant and his family reasonably need according to the regulations, the rent officer can set a lower figure. Although some local authorities automatically limit the amount of benefit to this lower figure, they should take into account the requirements of the tenant and his family. If there is illness or disability within the family, for example, a tenant might reasonably be considered to need larger accommodation. The local authority should also consider whether any alternative, smaller accommodation is in fact available.

The size criteria are:

(1) one bedroom for each of the following category of occupiers (each occupier falling within the first category for which he is eligible):
   • a married or unmarried couple
   • a person who is not a child
   • two children of the same sex
   • two children who are less than 10 years old
   • a child (a person under 16).
(2) the number of rooms (excluding any allowed as a bedroom) suitable for living in:
   • for fewer than four occupants, one
   • for more than three but fewer than seven occupants, two
   • in any other case, three.

For claimants who first became eligible to benefit on or after 1 January 1996, the maximum rent up to which benefit will be paid may be less than under the above provisions.

Local authorities are required to ask the rent officer to fix a 'local reference rent' for the area. This is the average rent which the rent officer would expect a landlord to be able to obtain on a letting of a house of that size in that locality to a tenant not claiming benefit. If the house is larger than that needed by the tenant according to the size criteria, the local reference rent will be gauged in relation to a house of the size appropriate for that size of family. In no case can a claimant's eligible rent exceed the 'maximum rent' for that house. If a local reference rent has been assessed, the maximum rent is not to exceed twice that figure.

However, in many cases the local authority asks the rent officer to fix a 'property-specific' rent, i.e. a rent for the house in question. This will be the rent which it would be reasonable for the landlord to charge for that particular house. Where a property-specific rent has been assessed, the maximum rent will be the property-specific rent if that is lower than the local reference rent. If the local reference rent is lower than the property-specific rent, the maximum rent will be the local reference rent plus one half of the difference.

In cases where the eligible rent for benefit is less than that set out in the tenancy agreement, this will not affect the right of the landlord to claim the excess from the tenant. The tenant will be obliged to make up the deficit out of his own funds: whether he is able to so is another matter.

Payment of benefit

Benefit is calculated on a weekly basis and is normally paid directly to the claimant (with the exception of public-sector tenants who receive the benefit by means of a reduction in the amount of the rent). However, in certain circumstances benefit can be payable directly to the landlord. Direct payments can be made if the tenant requests this. It might therefore be wise for the landlord to include a term in the tenancy agreement that the tenant agrees to the benefit being paid direct. For a suggested form of wording, see the sample agreements at the back of this book.

Direct payment may seem very attractive to the landlord as a means of ensuring regular payments, but there are disadvantages. Should it be subsequently discovered that there has been an overpayment of benefit, for example, because the claimant omitted to inform the local authority of a change in his circumstances, the overpayment will be recoverable from the landlord. The benefit is, of course, also recoverable from the claimant and normally local authorities will seek repayment from that source. However, there is a risk that the local authority will seek repayment from the landlord – in the case, for example, of a tenant disappearing from the local authority's records and the property. It is necessary, therefore, for the landlord to insert a provision in the tenancy agreement allowing the landlord to retain the deposit until it is clear that there has been no overpayment or that no claim for repayment will be made against the landlord. It must be borne in mind, however, that it is in precisely this kind of situation that the landlord may need to make use of the deposit for other reasons, such as damage to the property, so there is no certainty that the deposit will be sufficient.

In the case of individuals claiming housing benefit for the first time on or after 6 October 1996, rent allowance is payable in arrears. When it is paid direct to the landlord it is payable four-weekly in arrears.

Council tax and council tax benefit

Council tax is payable by occupiers of residential property. All such properties in England and Wales have been 'banded', or rated, according to their value. The amount of tax payable varies according to the band in which the house has been placed, higher-value properties being liable for more tax than lower-value ones.

Council tax is a daily charge, new occupiers becoming liable from the date of their occupation.

Generally, when property is let, the liability to pay the tax falls on the tenant, not the landlord. However, when the property is in multiple occupation, it is the landlord who is responsible. The definition of multiple occupation for council tax purposes includes any dwelling inhabited by persons who do not constitute a single household, all of whom either have the right to occupy only part of the house or are licensees not paying rent. It is sometimes difficult to decide whether a group of people sharing a house do so as a single household. In cases of doubt, the landlord should include a provision in the tenancy agreement allowing him to increase the rent by the amount of any council tax he may be required to bear.

Certain types of property and certain types of occupier are exempt from council tax. Exemptions include properties empty for less than six months and full-time students.

Discounts of 25 per cent are available, irrespective of income, if the property is occupied by only one person aged 18 or over. Reductions are also available for households which contain a person with specified disabilities.

Council tax benefit (assessed on similar principles to housing benefit) is available to tenants in the private sector to assist with council tax liability. In the case of houses in multiple occupation, where the landlord rather than the tenant is liable to pay the council tax, council tax benefit is not available to the tenant. However, the council tax element of the rent is treated as rent and therefore is eligible for housing benefit in the usual way.

Chapter 10

Public-sector tenancies

Lettings of property by local authorities and some housing associations are specifically excluded from being assured tenancies under the Housing Act 1988 or protected tenancies under the Rent Act 1977.

Such lettings have their own system of protection under the Housing Act 1985. If a tenancy is a 'secure tenancy', as defined, the tenant has extensive security of tenure but no rent control. There are also succession rights on the death of a secure tenant and a 'right to buy' the house or flat at a discount on the open market price.

This chapter looks at the position of local authority tenants. The position of tenants from housing associations (or registered social landlords) is considered in Chapter 11, including situations where local authorities have transferred their housing stock to housing associations.

Secure tenancies

A secure tenancy is a tenancy or licence of a dwellinghouse let as a separate dwelling at any time when both 'the landlord condition' and the 'tenant condition' are satisfied. (For the significance of the term 'let as a separate dwelling' see page 19.)

The definition of secure tenancy expressly includes a licence to occupy, unlike the definition of assured and protected tenancies. However, the legal distinction between a licence and a tenancy is still significant, as a licence can amount to a secure tenancy only if it confers the right to exclusive possession on the occupier. So a licence which does not confer the right to exclusive possession cannot amount to a secure tenancy and will have no protection.

The use of the phrase 'at any time when' shows that the status of a tenancy can change during its term depending upon whether the landlord condition and the tenant condition are satisfied. If either condition ceases to apply during the tenancy, it will cease to be secure. Note also that there is no requirement for any rent to be paid, nor any exemption for low-rental tenancies.

The 'landlord condition' denotes that the interest of the landlord belongs to one of a specified list of bodies, which include a local authority, a new town corporation, an urban development corporation and the Development Board for Rural Wales.

If you have a secure tenancy, it is most likely that you are a tenant of a district council.

The 'tenant condition' denotes that the tenant is an individual who occupies the dwellinghouse as his only or principal home. In the case of joint tenants, all of them must be individuals but only one need occupy as his only or principal home.

Even though the landlord condition and the tenant condition might be satisfied, there are 12 exceptions where there will not be a secure tenancy. These include:

(1) fixed-term leases exceeding 21 years. (A periodic tenancy, i.e. a weekly or monthly tenancy which may be or has already been in existence for 21 years or more, will *not* be excluded under this provision. It is not a fixed-term lease at all and will therefore still be capable of being a secure tenancy)

(2) premises occupied by an employee of the landlord where the employee's contract of employment requires him to occupy the house for the better performance of his duties – for example, a school caretaker. Many lettings to police officers and firefighters are also excluded

(3) tenancies granted to homeless persons

(4) dwellinghouses comprised in agricultural holdings, as defined by the Agricultural Holdings Act 1986. This provision excludes from being a secure tenancy the letting of a farm which includes a farmhouse in which the tenant lives

(5) dwellinghouses comprised in lettings to which Part II of the Landlord and Tenant Act 1954 applies, i.e. tenancies occupied for the purpose of a business

(6) lettings to students

(7) licences to occupy almshouses.

Security of tenure

A secure tenancy cannot be brought to an end by the landlord otherwise than by obtaining a court order for possession. A notice to quit is therefore of no effect and on the ending of a fixed-term secure tenancy a periodic secure tenancy will arise. Note that this rule does not prevent a *tenant* terminating a periodic tenancy by the usual notice to quit.

In order to obtain an order for possession the landlord must both follow the correct procedure and establish one (or more) of the grounds for possession laid down by the Act. Unlike assured tenancies under the Housing Act 1988 and protected tenancies under the Rent Act 1977, no mandatory grounds are available. So even if the ground is established, there is no guarantee that possession will be ordered.

Obtaining a court order

Before the court will allow the commencement of proceedings seeking possession the landlord must have given notice to the tenant in accordance with Section 83 of the Housing Act 1985 and in the form laid down by the legislation, giving particulars of the ground for possession in sufficiently clear terms for the tenant to understand precisely what is alleged against him. If the ground is not stated with sufficient clarity, the tenant may himself have grounds for claiming that the notice is invalid. If he makes such a claim, it is possible that any ensuing possession proceedings could fail. For details of how to defend possession proceedings, see Chapter 15.

In addition, if the tenancy is a periodic tenancy, as most council tenancies are, the notice must also specify the earliest date upon which possession proceedings can be commenced. This cannot be earlier than the date on which the landlord could have brought the tenancy to an end by giving the tenant notice to quit. So in the case of a weekly tenancy this date will be at least four weeks after the notice is given to the tenant; in the case of a monthly tenancy, it will be at least one month afterwards.

Look very carefully at the Section 83 notice, as the rules governing notices to quit are complicated. For a notice to quit to be valid, as well as being of the correct length, it has to expire on the day of the week or month corresponding to the one on which the tenancy commenced. So in the case of a weekly tenancy commencing on a Monday, the notice must expire on either a Monday or a Sunday (technically it is midnight between the two, but either day can be stated). Similarly with a monthly tenancy commencing on the 10th of the month, the notice must expire on the 9th or 10th of a subsequent month. Tenants with security of tenure should note that this does not mean that the landlord must serve a notice to quit.

If you receive one of these notices of intention to start possession proceedings, the next step the landlord is entitled to take is to commence court proceedings against you claiming possession. You will not receive a notice to quit as well.

The possession proceedings must commence after this date but within 12 months thereafter. However, where ground 2 is being alleged, whether alone or with other grounds, the landlord can commence possession proceedings as soon as the notice has been served.

Orders for possession

There are 17 grounds for possession, but no mandatory grounds. So even if the landlord can establish one of the grounds (and he has followed the correct procedure), there is no certainty that the court will order possession. The nature of the discretion given to the court differs according to the ground proven.

The court cannot make an order for possession on grounds 1–8 unless it considers it reasonable to do so. Nor can it make an order for possession on grounds 9–11 unless it is satisfied that suitable alternative accommodation will be available to the tenant when the order takes effect, or on grounds 12–16 unless it both considers it reasonable to make an order and is satisfied that suitable alternative accommodation will be available when the order takes effect.

Grounds for possession

Ground 1
Rent lawfully due from the tenant has not been paid or some other obligation under the tenancy has not been complied with.

While there is no minimum amount of rent which must be due before this ground can be used, it is likely that the amount and frequency of arrears would be taken into account by the court in considering whether it was reasonable to order possession.

As to the requirement that the rent must be 'lawfully due', note that the provisions of Section 48 of the Landlord and Tenant Act 1987, which require landlords to provide their tenants with an address (in England or Wales) at which documents can be served on them, also apply to local authority landlords.

Ground 2

The tenant or a person residing at or visiting the house has been guilty of conduct which is, or is likely to be, a nuisance or annoyance to anyone residing, visiting or otherwise undertaking a lawful activity in the neighbourhood; or has been convicted of using the house for an illegal or immoral purpose or of an arrestable offence committed in the locality.

This ground is identical to assured tenancy ground 14 and, like that ground, was rewritten as part of a clampdown on anti-social behaviour by tenants. Some local authorities have made extensive use of it in an attempt to 'clean up' housing estates. Local authority landlords can also obtain injunctions to restrain such behaviour (see below).

It is not sufficient to show that the house is being used for illegal or immoral purposes: a conviction is necessary. However, mere use for these purposes may well be a nuisance or annoyance to neighbours and be sufficient for possession purposes.

Ground 2A

This ground was introduced in order to provide additional help in cases of domestic violence. It applies where the house was occupied by a married couple or two people living as husband and wife but the tenancy was in only one of their names. It is a ground for possession if one of the occupants has been forced to leave the house due to violence or threats of violence by the other and it is unlikely that the person forced to leave will return. It does not matter whether the person forced to leave was the tenant or not. The ground enables the landlord to obtain possession against the violent partner and thus provide a safe home for the other partner.

Ground 3

The condition of the house has deteriorated due to the acts or neglect of the tenant or someone residing in the house. In the case of acts/neglect by a person other than the tenant it is also necessary to show that the tenant has not taken such steps to remove that person from the house as he ought reasonably to have taken.

Ground 4

The condition of the furniture provided by the landlord has deteriorated due to ill-treatment by the tenant or a person residing in the house. In the case of ill-treatment by a person other than the tenant it is also necessary to show that the tenant has not taken such steps to remove that person from the house as he ought reasonably to have taken. It would be a question for the court to decide as to whether a tenant should, for example, have taken steps to have removed his own child from the house in the event of the child being the culprit

Ground 5

The landlord was induced to grant the tenancy by a false statement made knowingly or recklessly by the tenant, or by a person acting at the tenant's instigation. This ground is the same as assured tenancy ground 17.

Ground 6

The tenancy was assigned to the tenant and a premium was paid in connection with that assignment.

Ground 7

The house forms part of, or is within the curtilage of, a building which is used mainly for non-housing purposes and the house was let to the tenant by reason of his employment and the tenant or a person residing with him has been guilty of conduct such that, having regard to the purpose for which the building is used, it would not be right for him to continue in occupation of the house.

Ground 8

The house was made available to the tenant whilst his previous house was repaired and the latter is now once more available for occupation.

Ground 9
The dwellinghouse is overcrowded to such a degree as to render the occupier guilty of an offence under the Housing Act 1985. The definition of overcrowding is complex, but includes situations such as two or more people of different sexes over the age of 10 sharing a room (unless they are living together as husband and wife).

Ground 10
The landlord intends to demolish or reconstruct the house and cannot reasonably do so without having obtained possession.

Ground 10A
The house is within the area of a redevelopment scheme approved by the Secretary of State or the Housing Corporation and the landlord intends to dispose of the house in accordance with the scheme.

Ground 11
The landlord is a charity and the tenant's continued occupation of the house would conflict with the aims and objectives of the charity.

Ground 12
The house forms part of, or is within the curtilage of, a building which is used mainly for non-housing purposes, the house was let to the tenant by reason of his employment and the landlord reasonably requires the house for occupation by another person in his employment.

Ground 13
The house contains features designed to make it suitable for physically disabled persons, there is no longer such a person living in the house and the landlord requires possession for occupation by such a person.

Ground 14
The landlord is a housing association or trust which lets property to persons whose circumstances (other than financial) make it difficult for them to secure housing, there is no longer such a person living in the house and the landlord requires possession for occupation by such a person.

Ground 15

The house is one of a group of houses let for occupation by persons with special needs, there is no longer such a person living in the house and the landlord requires possession for occupation by such a person.

Ground 16

The accommodation in the house is more extensive than is reasonably required by the tenant and the tenancy vested in the tenant on the death of the previous tenant, who was not his spouse, and the notice of the proceedings for possession was served more than six months but not more than 12 months after the date of the previous tenant's death.

Succession on the death of a tenant

The tenancy does not end with the death of a secure tenant. If there is a spouse, he or she will succeed to the secure tenancy, provided that he/she was occupying the house as his/her only or principal home at the time of the tenant's death.

If there is no 'spouse', a member of the tenant's family who has resided in the house with the tenant *for at least 12 months* prior to the tenant's death will succeed to the tenancy. Note that there is no 12-month residence requirement in the case of a spouse, only in the case of a family member.

The definition of 'spouse' includes a person living with the tenant as 'husband or wife'. Thus the survivor of an unmarried heterosexual couple will have succession rights. The courts have held that the survivor of a same-sex couple cannot succeed, as he or she does not live with the tenant as 'husband or wife', but this ruling may be subject to challenge under the Human Rights Act.

However, the courts have also held that if there is a long-standing same-sex relationship, then the survivor may be able to succeed as a member of the deceased tenant's family.

Only one succession is permitted, so on the death of a secure tenant who himself succeeded to the tenancy, either under this provision or because he was the survivor of joint tenants, there can be no further succession.

In cases where there is no succession, the tenancy will pass on the death in the same way as the rest of the deceased's property, i.e.

either by the deceased's will or otherwise according to the rules of intestacy. However, it will cease to be a secure tenancy, so the landlord will be entitled to possession on the termination of the tenancy. Termination will take place under normal common law rules – for example, by notice to quit in the case of a periodic tenancy. Possession proceedings can then be brought without the need to comply with the secure tenancy procedure, but a court order will still be necessary to enforce the landlord's right to possession.

Assignment of secure tenancies

Secure tenancies are generally incapable of assignment. If a purported assignment takes place, then the tenancy will cease to be a secure tenancy. As exceptions to this general rule, assignments are permitted:

(1) by way of exchange with another secure tenant
(2) in pursuance of a property adjustment order made in matrimonial proceedings
(3) to a person who, if the tenant died, would be entitled to succeed to the secure tenancy under the succession provisions above.

Lodgers and subletting

A secure tenant may take in lodgers but may not part with possession or sublet the whole or part of the house without the landlord's written consent. Such consent cannot be unreasonably withheld.

If a secure tenant parts with possession or sublets the whole house, the tenancy will cease to be secure. This means that on the termination of the tenancy the landlord will be entitled to possession without the need to follow the secure tenancy procedure or prove secure tenancy grounds.

Rent control

There is no limit on the amount of rent chargeable by a landlord on the grant of a secure tenancy. However, once a tenancy has been granted, the landlord can subsequently increase the rent only if there is a provision in the tenancy agreement permitting such increase – or if no such provision, in accordance with the procedure laid down by the Act. This applies only to periodic tenancies and the increase can take effect only if a notice of variation is served on the tenant at least four weeks – or the equivalent of the rental period, whichever is the longer – beforehand.

Tenants' improvements

It is an implied term of every secure tenancy that a tenant cannot carry out any improvement, alteration or addition to the property without the landlord's consent. The landlord's consent may not be unreasonably withheld; if it is, the tenant can proceed as if consent had been given.

It is a little-known feature of this requirement that the landlord's consent is necessary for the erection of a television aerial or satellite dish, a provision much honoured in the breach. Breach of this term of the tenancy would, in theory at least, leave the tenant open to possession proceedings based on ground 1, although whether it would ever be reasonable to order possession in such a situation must be open to question.

Repairs

Repairs to council houses and other secure tenancies are governed by the same provisions that apply to other tenancies (see Chapter 12). In the vast majority of cases, therefore, this will mean that the landlord is responsible for the repairs to the structure and exterior of the property and for keeping in repair and proper working order the facilities in the house for the supply of gas and electricity, space and water heating and sanitation.

Under the Secure Tenants of Local Housing Authorities (Right to Repair) Regulations 1994 secure tenants have the right to compensation if certain types of repair are not carried out within a prescribed period. The regulations are complex, and apply only to repairs costing no more than £250. The maximum compensation payable is £50.

Introductory tenancies

The 1996 Housing Act allowed local housing authorities to elect to set up an introductory tenancy scheme – an election that can be revoked at any time. If an election is in force, any periodic tenancy or licence that would otherwise be a secure tenancy will take effect as an introductory tenancy, under which the tenant undergoes a trial period before being given permanent security of tenure. (However, if a tenant already has a secure tenancy at the time of the grant, he will immediately become a fully protected secure tenant. This existing secure tenancy need not be of the same house or have been granted by the local authority.)

Under an introductory tenancy, the tenant is on trial for one year with no security of tenure. If he proves not to be a suitable tenant, the local authority can obtain possession from him without having to prove any of the usual secure tenancy grounds. A court order will still be required (the judge must order possession) and the proceedings must be commenced during the trial period. If the tenant proves to be suitable, neither landlord nor tenant need take any action: the tenancy will automatically become a secure tenancy at the end of the trial period.

Obtaining possession

The only way in which the landlord can bring an introductory tenancy to an end is by obtaining a court order for possession. However, provided the landlord follows the correct procedure, the court has no discretion: it must order possession.

The landlord must first serve a notice on the tenant stating that the court will be asked to order possession. The notice must state the earliest date on which the proceedings can be commenced. This cannot be earlier than the date on which a notice to quit served on the same date would have expired. See 'Obtaining a court order' (on page 122) as to the date on which a notice to quit would have expired. The notice must also contain the landlord's reasons for requiring possession. Note, however, that there are no formal grounds for possession – just the requirement to give a reason.

The notice must also inform the tenant of his right to request a review of the landlord's decision to apply for possession. This must be sought within 14 days of service of the notice. In a review, the tenant may challenge the reasons given for possession.

The review must be carried out, and the tenant notified of the result, before the date specified as the earliest on which the landlord could apply to the court. There is, however, no further right of appeal if the review confirms the landlord's decision to apply for possession.

Injunctions against anti-social behaviour

The emphasis in the Housing Act 1996 on preventing/penalising anti-social behaviour by tenants, as demonstrated by the extension to ground 2 (and also the similarly worded ground 14 for assured tenancies), is taken one step further by Sections 153–8 of the 1996 Act. The provisions apply only to premises held under secure or introductory tenancies and allow the local authority to apply to the county court for an order prohibiting a person from:

- engaging in or threatening to engage in conduct causing or likely to cause a nuisance or annoyance to a person residing in or visiting such premises or engaging in a lawful activity in the vicinity of such premises
- using or threatening to use such premises for immoral or illegal purposes, or
- entering such premises or being found in the vicinity of such premises.

However, the court can make an order only if the person in question has used or threatened violence and there is a significant risk of harm if the injunction is not granted.

The availability of this order is therefore an alternative to trying to obtain a possession order, which in any event may not be granted due to the court's discretion. A court would be much more likely to grant possession if an injunction had first been obtained and then not complied with.

However, these provisions do not only allow injunctions to be obtained against tenants: they can be obtained against any person engaging in the behaviour specified.

If an order is obtained against a tenant, the court may attach a power of arrest to the injunction. The effect of this is that a police officer may arrest without a warrant any person whom he has reasonable cause to believe is in breach of such an injunction.

The right to buy

Perhaps the most valuable right enjoyed by a secure tenant is the right to buy the freehold in his house, or, in the case of a flat, to acquire a 125-year lease of it. However, in order to claim this right he must, as well as being a secure tenant, satisfy a residence qualification.

The right to buy has been enormously popular since its introduction in 1980 and has been exercised by over 1.1 million public-sector tenants.

Residence qualification

The tenant (or the tenant's spouse) must have resided in public-sector accommodation for at least two years. Note that the tenant need not have been resident as a secure tenant, nor indeed in the same premises, nor in the premises which he now wishes to purchase.

Cost of purchase

The price is to be the open-market value of the property, but this price is subject to a substantial discount in recognition of the length of time that the tenant has occupied public-sector accommodation.

To encourage tenants of flats, in particular, to buy, a greater discount is available for flat purchases than for the purchase of houses.

Every house purchase is subject to a minimum discount of 32 per cent on the open-market value, plus a further discount of 1 per cent for every complete year for which the residence qualification has been satisfied, up to a maximum of 60 per cent. A flat purchase is subject to a minimum discount of 44 per cent plus a further 2 per cent for each complete year of residence, with a maximum discount of 70 per cent. Remember that this discount is based on the period of residence as a public-sector tenant and is not necessarily the length of residence in the property which is to be bought.

However, the discount to be given cannot reduce the price below the level specified by the Secretary of State. The maximum discount varies between £24,000 in Wales and £38,000 in London.

Fixing the price

Initially the local authority will specify what it considers to be the market value. If, as tenant, you disagree with this, you can appeal to the District Valuer. This must be done within three months, and the decision then made will be final.

Repaying the discount

If the purchasing tenant sells the property within three years of buying it, he must repay some or all of the discount to the landlord.

The objective behind the right to buy is to enable tenants to buy their own homes, not to enable them to obtain large profits on reselling. So if the tenant resells within 1 year, he must repay 100 per cent of the discount; if he resells between 1 and 2 years after purchase, he must repay 66 per cent of the discount; and if he sells between 2 and 3 years after purchase, he must repay 33 per cent of it. Once three years have passed, no repayment of discount is required. Also, even within the three years, a gift can be made of the property to certain family members, or it can pass on death, without the need for a repayment of discount.

Q *I have a tenancy of a council house. My house needed a lot of work doing to it so the council put me in another house temporarily. This is in a much nicer area. Where we were before there was a lot of drug-taking and my 5-year-old child frequently found discarded needles in the garden. Do I have to go back to the old house?*

A Possibly. Otherwise, the council could try to get a possession order against you, using ground 8. However, the court can order possession only if it thinks it reasonable to do so. You would have to try to argue that, in the circumstances described, it was not. In the event of an order for possession being made against you, it is unlikely that you would be made homeless, as your local authority would be obliged to find you accommodation. As you have a young child, you would be classed as a priority case, and the most likely outcome is that you would be rehoused in your former home. You should discuss your worries with the housing department and your local councillor without delay.

Q *I have a council flat. Am I allowed to keep a dog?*

A There is nothing in the Housing Act 1985 dealing with this matter: it depends upon the terms of your tenancy agreement. Tenancy agreements for flats frequently prohibit the keeping of dogs and if yours does you would put yourself in breach of your tenancy agreement if you were to do so, which would entitle the council to bring eviction proceedings against you. If there is no such prohibition in your tenancy agreement you may keep a dog.

Q *I have a council house and am short of cash. Can I take in a student from the nearby college to bring in some extra money?*

A Yes. Notwithstanding the terms of your tenancy agreement, you have the right to take in a lodger. What you must not do, however, is let off all or part of your house. This would be in breach of the terms of your tenancy and the council would be entitled to bring possession proceedings against you.

Chapter 11

Housing associations and registered social landlords

A housing association is a non-profit-making body established to provide affordable accommodation. Such organisations have existed in one form or another since the mid-nineteenth century, but their number has grown considerably since the introduction of state-funded housing associations in the 1960s. Most local authorities, housing advice centres and Citizens Advice Bureaux will provide a list of properties available locally.

Housing associations are now one of the major providers of state-funded housing. Some of them are registered with the Housing Corporation or with Housing for Wales and are called registered social landlords. (The Housing Corporation has responsibility for England; Housing for Wales is the government body responsible in the principality.) Some housing associations (but by no means all) are also registered as charities and must therefore operate within their own charitable rules as well. Other housing associations are run on a co-operative basis where the tenants themselves own and manage the houses they live in.

Under policies adopted by the Conservative government in the 1990s, registered social landlords have become the main providers of new social housing in England and Wales in place of local authorities. Indeed, many local authorities have transferred some or all of their housing stock to registered social landlords. Such transfers require the consent of the Secretary of State and a local authority contemplating such a disposal must carry out a consultation exercise with the tenants affected. Several hundred thousand dwellings have been transferred in this way.

The law relating to security of tenure and rent control will depend not only on the type of housing association, but also on the date when the tenancy was granted: tenancies entered into before 15 January 1989 are dealt with differently from tenancies granted on or after that date.

Registered social landlords

Tenancies granted on or after 15 January 1989

The Housing Act 1988 brought registered social landlord tenancies into the private sector. Therefore, these tenants will have either an assured tenancy or an assured shorthold tenancy under the Act (see Chapters 2 and 3). Most of these will be ordinary assured tenancies rather than assured shorthold tenancies, although there is no legal rule prohibiting a housing association from granting an assured shorthold tenancy if it sees fit to do so.

Assured tenants have security of tenure in that the landlord must prove a statutory ground for possession under the 1988 Act if it wishes to evict one of its tenants (see pages 44–57). Tenants should be aware, however, that there is no legal control over rent increases even though one of the reasons for having a housing association is to create lettings at affordable rents. Registered social landlords should provide their tenants with a written agreement specifying the level of rents to be charged and the conditions of the tenancy. Tenants also have the benefit of a 'tenant's guarantee', which is an assurance from the landlord of good standards of management. Although not legally binding, the guarantee specifies the minimum contractual rights a tenant should be given in his tenancy agreement with regard to taking in lodgers, carrying out improvements, etc.

It also contains information on:

- the association's policies for selecting tenants and allocating homes
- rents (which should be kept within the reach of people in low-paid or no employment)
- management, maintenance and tenant participation.

Housing ombudsman service

Local authority tenants who are dissatisfied with the service they are receiving can complain to the authority's housing department or bring the complaint through a local councillor. Use may also be made of the commissioners for local administration (usually referred to as the 'local government ombudsmen'), who have juris-diction to investigate complaints of maladministration by an authority. A significant proportion of such complaints are over housing matters. However, the local government ombudsmen can-not investigate complaints by tenants of registered social landlords.

The Housing Act 1996 now makes provision for an independent housing ombudsman service for tenants of registered social land-lords. All social landlords must be a member of a scheme approved by the Secretary of State. The housing ombudsman must investi-gate any complaint made to him and not withdrawn. He may also investigate any complaint made but later withdrawn.

The ombudsman has wide powers. He may in his determination order the landlord to pay compensation to the complainant, and order that the landlord or the complainant must not exercise or require the performance of any of the contractual or other obliga-tions or rights existing between them. If the landlord fails to com-ply with the determination within a reasonable time, the housing ombudsman may order the landlord to publish in such manner as the ombudsman sees fit that the landlord has failed to comply with the ombudsman's determination. If the landlord fails to publish notice of his refusal, the ombudsman has power to do so himself. The idea of this is that fear of adverse publicity will make the land-lord comply with the ombudsman's decision.

Tenancies resulting from a transfer from a local authority

Former tenants of public landlords where the property has been transferred to a registered housing association on or after 15 January 1989 will normally become assured tenants under the Housing Act 1988 (see Chapter 3). However, such tenants retain their right to buy (see pages 132–3) and this is enforceable against the new land-lord. This is known as 'the preserved right to buy'.

Tenancies granted before 15 January 1989

Before 15 January 1989, housing association tenancies were treated, in the main, as being in the public sector and therefore the rules relating to secure tenancies apply, including the right to buy. Unlike public-sector tenancies, however, the fair rent system also applies (see pages 99–101).

Unregistered housing associations

An unregistered housing association is one that has not registered with the Housing Corporation or Housing for Wales. This means it does not qualify for state funding and is not supervised by a government body. Some housing associations have deliberately chosen not to be registered but prefer to act independently so that the members can set up shared-ownership schemes, not possible with a registered association.

Tenancies granted on or after 15 January 1989
These tenancies will be assured tenancies or assured shorthold tenancies under the Housing Act 1988. They are governed by the same rules regarding security of tenure and rent control as private-sector tenancies. They do not, however, have the benefit of the 'tenant's guarantee' (see above).

Tenancies granted before 15 January 1989
Unregistered housing association tenancies granted before this date will come under the protection of the Rent Act 1977 as regards both security of tenure and rent control (see Chapter 7).

Co-operative housing associations

Tenancies granted before 15 January 1989
Co-operative housing association tenancies granted prior to this date enjoy no statutory security of tenure. The security therefore depends on the terms of the tenancy agreement. However, since the tenants are in effect their own landlords, with their own co-operative constitution, they should be reasonably protected.

The fair rent system applies (see pages 99–101) and therefore a registered rent is the maximum that can be charged.

Tenancies granted on or after 15 January 1989
A fully mutual housing association is exempt from the Housing Act 1988 and therefore the tenant will have no statutory protection apart from what is stated in the tenancy agreement. However, the tenant's guarantee applies (see page 136), which gives the tenant some measure of protection.

Registered social landlord tenants' right to buy

Under the Housing Act 1996 most tenants of registered social land-lords have the right to buy their homes on the same terms as council tenants (see Chapter 10) provided the property was built or purchased with public money and has remained in the social rented sector ever since. As for council tenants, there is a residence qualification of a minimum of two years.

Q *I was a council tenant for many years but in 1993 the ownership of my flat was transferred to a registered housing association. Has this affected my legal rights?*

A You are now an assured rather than a secure tenant, and your landlord should have informed you of how this change would affect you before it took place. In fact, your new status should have very little effect on your rights, as the landlord is still unable to evict you without proving a ground for possession, you still have no protection against rent increases, and you retain the right to buy your home.

Q *I am a tenant of a housing association. I am worried that the landlord never gets round to doing any repairs. What is my legal position on this?*

A Your landlord has exactly the same repairing obligations as any private landlord. If you have a periodic tenancy or a fixed-term tenancy of less than seven years, you should enforce these obligations without delay (see Chapter 12).

Q *Is there any legal limit on the amount of rent which a housing association can charge?*

A In the case of housing association tenancies granted before 15 January 1989 the 'fair rent' system, whereby a maximum is fixed by a rent officer, will apply. Tenancies granted after this date will usually be governed by the Housing Act 1988 and rental values are not controlled by law. However, registered housing associations have a 'tenant's guarantee' which, although not legally binding, states that rents should be kept within reach of people in low-paid employment.

Chapter 12

Repair and maintenance of rented property

One of the major issues relating to the renting or letting of property is that of maintenance and repair. Who is to be responsible if the roof starts leaking, the central heating system breaks down, or someone is injured after tripping on a broken path or garden steps? Even if the landlord and tenant have a comprehensive tenancy agreement that covers these matters in full (which is rare in any event), various Acts of Parliament often overrule what the parties have actually agreed. To make matters worse, the law is not contained in any one single statute: it is a mixture of common law (judge–made law) and various statutory provisions designed to deal with diverse matters.

EXAMPLE

Bleak House is a large Victorian house divided into two flats. The ground-floor flat is occupied by tenant A, the top-floor flat by tenant B. The ground-floor flat is let on a five-year lease but under the terms of the lease the tenant has an option to renew for a further five years. The top-floor flat is let on a monthly periodic tenancy. Both tenants have undertaken to keep the property in a good state of repair.

The large attic is retained by the landlord and used for storage purposes. There is a shared front door and the staircase is used by tenant B to gain access to the top-floor flat and by the landlord to gain access to the attic. There is a communal boiler in the basement (retained by the landlord) which supplies hot water and central heating to both flats; it often breaks down. There is rising damp in the ground-floor flat because there is no damp-proof course, and penetrating damp in the top-floor flat because the gutters and downspouts are defective and the brickwork needs repointing. Both flats are affected by condensation because of the lack of ventilation and their wallpaper is peeling. The window frames are rotten and could do with replacing. The roof is also in a poor condition.

Who is liable for these defects?

An overview of the law

In common law landlord/tenant liability for repairs is governed by the tenancy agreement. The tenancy between the landlord and the tenant is a form of contract. The terms of that contract may be set out expressly (express terms) or may be implied by law (implied terms). Some of these implied terms are implied by common law, others by Acts of Parliament known as statutory implied terms. The common law implied terms can be overridden by express terms of the tenancy agreement but the statutory implied terms cannot generally be ousted by the tenancy agreement, which makes the statutory implied terms extremely important.

It is therefore necessary to look at:

- the express terms of the tenancy agreement
- the common law implied terms (but bearing in mind that these can be excluded if the tenancy agreement says otherwise)
- the statutory implied terms (bearing in mind that these cannot normally be excluded and will therefore operate despite the terms of the tenancy agreement).

Breach of these express or implied terms is a breach of contract and can be enforced by the parties to the contract, i.e. the landlord or the tenant as the case may be. They cannot be enforced by third parties, such as members of the tenant's family, any visitors to the property or the local authority unless the agreement says that they can or it implicitly confers benefits on specified third parties and does not exclude them from enforcing these rights.

However, quite apart from the express or implied terms of the tenancy, the Environmental Protection Act 1990 gives the local authority wide powers of intervention to deal with premises which create a 'statutory nuisance' – for example, where the premises are a danger to health (see page 151). Enforcement of the Environmental Protection Act is in the hands of the local authority which, if necessary, may bring a prosecution in the magistrates' court. In certain circumstances, such as where the landlord is itself a local authority, the tenant can take direct action under the Act. Local authorities also have wide additional powers to deal with 'unfit houses' under the Housing Act 1985.

Finally, if someone is injured as a result of defective premises the injured party may be able to bring an action for damages for breach of the Occupiers' Liability Act 1957 or the Defective Premises Act 1972. In such a case, the claim would be for negligence and a claim for monetary compensation could be pursued through the civil courts. This is of course not a direct method of getting the defects put right.

These matters are examined in more detail below, in the context of the problems facing tenants A and B at Bleak House.

The tenancy agreement

The tenancy agreement may set out clauses which stipulate who is liable for what repair. If the landlord has undertaken to do all the repairs the tenant can enforce these obligations – through the courts if necessary. The landlord's liability will depend upon the precise wording of the relevant clauses. However, even if the tenancy agreement says that the landlord is liable for repairs it does not necessarily follow that the landlord will be liable for *all* the matters about which the tenant complains.

'Repair' must be distinguished from 'improvement'. The word 'repair' is confined to the renewal or replacement of subsidiary parts of the building; improvement is adding things to the property that do not already exist. The law does not impose an obligation on the landlord to effect improvements unless (and this would be most unusual) he has expressly agreed to do so.

The dampness at Bleak House caused by leaking gutters and brickwork that needs repointing would be classed as repairs and the landlord would be liable to do this work if he has undertaken to carry out repairs. However, putting in an entirely new damp course (Bleak House does not have one to repair) would probably be classed as an improvement. Similarly, curing the condensation may involve putting in new windows or a new type of heating system, which, again, would probably be considered an improvement, not a repair.

If the terms of the tenancy agreement place the repairing obligation on the tenants the question of whether or not this would be enforceable depends on the length of the tenancy and the type of repairs. If a tenant has a periodic tenancy (like tenant B at Bleak House) or a fixed-term tenancy for less than seven years, most of the major repairing obligations will be placed on the landlord by virtue of Section 11 of the Landlord and Tenant Act 1985 (see page 144). Tenant A at Bleak House is not covered by Section 11 as his five-year lease contains a five-year renewal option, thus exceeding the seven-year limit.

The tenancy agreement may stipulate that the tenant is liable for internal decorative repairs. Quite often, however, the tenancy agreement is silent on this matter, in which case one must look to the implied terms arising either at common law or under statute.

Common law implied terms

Unfortunately, the common law is of little assistance in the vast majority of cases: if the tenancy agreement is silent, the general rule is that there is no implication that the premises are fit for human habitation or that either party will be responsible for repairs. In other words, the common law is largely neutral. However, there are some minor exceptions which are explained below.

Furnished lettings

In the case of a furnished letting the landlord warrants (by implication) that the property is fit for habitation at the date when the tenancy commences. Therefore, if a furnished house is uninhabitable because it is infested with bugs the tenant can, at the start of the tenancy, immediately repudiate the tenancy, recover any deposit or rent that he has paid and sue the landlord for any damage or loss suffered. However, the tenant must act quickly since this implied term arises only at the commencement of the tenancy. The landlord cannot be compelled to make the property habitable. The tenant's remedy is simply to cancel the agreement and recover his losses. There is no continuing obligation on the part of the landlord to keep the furnished premises fit for habitation.

Tenant's duty to use the property in a tenant-like manner

There is no implied term in any tenancy agreement, whether of a furnished or unfurnished property, that the tenant is to be responsible for repairs. However, the tenant must use the property in a 'tenant-like manner'. This means that he must take proper care of the property by doing the little jobs which can reasonably be expected of him, such as unblocking drains, having chimneys swept, mending fuses, and so on.

Common parts

In certain circumstances where a tenancy agreement is signed but is incomplete, the court may imply a term, at common law, that the landlord will take reasonable care of common parts – for example, staircases and other facilities which are shared between various tenants. If the premises consist of a large tower block containing lifts, staircases and other common parts and the tenancy agreements of the individual flats do not oblige either tenant or landlord to maintain the common parts, the court may hold that, since the agreement is incomplete and the premises cannot function without such common parts being maintained, the landlord must have taken responsibility by implication to keep them in a reasonable condition. This could help tenants A and B if, for example, the shared staircase became dangerous to use. However, the tenants would probably be better advised to look to the statutory implied terms.

Statutory implied terms

These are to be found in the Landlord and Tenant Act 1985. The most important provisions are contained in Section 11, but if the lease or tenancy is at a very low rent the tenant may also find assistance in Section 8 (see page 147).

Section 11 of the Landlord and Tenant Act 1985

Section 11 applies to leases or tenancies granted on or after 24 October 1961 for less than seven years. The expression 'for less than seven years' can, however, be misleading, since Section 11 applies to *all* periodic tenancies even if the tenant is there for longer than seven years, but if the lease is for a fixed term of seven years or longer, Section 11 will not apply. Moreover, Section 11 will not apply if the fixed term was originally granted for less than seven years and the tenant was also granted an option to extend the lease which, if exercised, would take the lease beyond the seven-year limit (as with tenant A at Bleak House).

The vast majority of residential tenancies are, however, periodic or for terms of less than seven years, therefore Section 11 will apply in most cases, including that of tenant B.

The landlord's implied obligations under Section 11 are:

• to keep in repair the structure and exterior of the dwelling (including drains, gutters and external pipes)
• to keep in repair and proper working order the installations in the dwelling for the supply of water, gas, electricity and sanitation (including basins, sinks, baths and sanitary conveniences)
• to keep in repair and proper working order the installations in the dwelling for room and water heating.

'Structure and exterior' in the first point are not defined by the Act. However, 'structure' clearly includes the main fabric of the dwelling such as the main walls, foundations and roof timbers (including window frames) as distinct from decorations and fittings, while 'exterior' has been held by the courts to include paths or steps which form an essential means of access to the dwelling but not paving in the backyard or a footpath at the rear of the house.

The words 'structure' and 'exterior' can cause particular problems where a property is divided into flats. The courts have held that the landlord's implied obligation extends only to the particular flat in question and not to the entire building. Therefore, it would not extend to the roof or common parts which do not physically form part of one or other of the flats. On this interpretation, tenants A and B of Bleak House would have great difficulty in arguing that the roof or the staircase forms part of their individual flats. New legislation was brought in by the Housing Act 1988 but only in respect of leases or tenancies granted on or after 15 January 1989. Under this legislation the landlord's obligations under Section 11 are deemed to include parts of the building belonging to the same landlord or which are under the landlord's control. However, this extended obligation will apply only where the disrepair affects the tenant's enjoyment of the flat or common parts in question.

For tenant B of Bleak House the extension of the legislation is a welcome improvement. It means the landlord can be held liable for repairs to the roof if it is the cause of damp in the flat. The same applies to the gutters and drains.

The condensation, however, remains a problem, as the landlord is only obliged to carry out 'repairs'. If the condensation has caused damage to the main fabric of the property, such as the plasterwork, the landlord could be made to repair the plasterwork, but this will not cure the condensation; it will simply repair the *consequences* of condensation. If the condensation cannot be cured by 'repair' but can be eradicated only by 'improvements', the landlord is not liable under Section 11 to remedy the problem. To get rid of the condensation tenants A and B may well have to invoke the Environmental Protection Act 1990 (see pages 150–2).

The landlord's obligations to repair and keep in proper working order the installations for the supply of water, gas, electricity, sanitation, room and water heating merely require him to maintain and repair the facilities that exist at the *start* of the tenancy. If the dwelling does not have these facilities to begin with, then there is no obligation on the part of the landlord to provide the necessary installations.

Originally, the legislation was confined to installations which were actually within the four walls of the dwelling. If, as at Bleak House, there is a communal central heating boiler in the basement serving both flats the landlord would not, originally, have been liable under Section 11 to repair that boiler since it was not within either flat. However, if the tenancy was granted on or after 15 January 1989 the landlord would be liable for the boiler irrespective of where it was located.

The landlord is liable for these matters even if the problem is a manufacturing defect – for example, if the boiler was defective when it was supplied and fitted. He has to put the problem right even if it was not his fault: this is known as strict liability (the landlord may none the less have rights under the Sale of Goods Act 1979 or the Supply of Goods and Services Act 1982 in respect of the faulty boiler). The only exception would be where the defect is due to some fault on the part of the tenants, who must use the property in a 'tenant-like manner' (see page 144). So if the problems arise because the tenants have not used the property in a tenant-like manner, the landlord is not liable for repairs to the items in question.

Standards of repair

Section 11 provides that in determining the standards of repair to the property the courts must have regard to the character and prospective lifespan of the property and the locality in which it is situated. Therefore, if the house is in a poor condition at the start of the tenancy and in an area of very poor-quality housing the landlord will not have to carry out comprehensive repairs under Section 11, nor will he be obliged to carry out improvements. Patching repairs may satisfy the requirements of Section 11, depending upon the circumstances of the case.

Exceptions to Section 11

Some specific situations are *not* covered by Section 11. These are:

- repairs for which the tenant is liable by virtue of his duty to use the premises in a tenant-like manner (see above)
- re-building or reinstating the premises in case of damage or destruction by fire, tempest or other accident
- keeping in repair or maintaining anything that the tenant is entitled to remove from the dwelling when he leaves (tenant's fixtures).

The requirement for notice

The landlord is not liable under Section 11 (or indeed under any of the express or implied obligations) unless the tenant has given him notice of the need for repair. So, if a tenant is injured as a result of a defect, the landlord will not be liable for his injuries if he had not been notified of the need to repair the defect. Tenants should, therefore, inform their landlord as soon as they are aware that a problem exists. The notice does not have to be in any particular form, nor does it necessarily have to come from the tenant. A letter from the local authority, from a surveyor or from the landlord's agent would also be sufficient to put the landlord on notice.

Section 8 of the Landlord and Tenant Act 1985

If the dwelling has been let at a very low rent, not exceeding £80 in London or £52 per annum elsewhere, the landlord has an additional obligation: namely, that the house is fit for human habitation at the start of the tenancy and will be kept in that condition throughout the tenancy. (Few properties fall into this category, for obvious reasons.)

Landlord's right of access to carry out repairs

Normally the tenancy agreement will expressly allow the landlord to enter the property for the purpose of inspection and carrying out repairs. If not, the landlord also has a right of entry if the tenancy is governed by the Rent Act 1977 (see Chapter 7) or the Housing Act 1988 (see Chapter 3). In any event, where the landlord is obliged to carry out repairs under Section 11 of the Landlord and Tenant Act 1985 he may, on giving 24 hours' notice in writing, enter the property to inspect its condition and state of repair.

Remedies for breaches of the landlord's repairing obligations

The repairing obligations mentioned above are part of the express or implied terms of the tenancy contract, and therefore the tenant can enforce them; third parties can enforce them only if the agreement confers benefits upon them expressly or implicitly. If the landlord fails to meet his obligations, the tenant has a number of remedies available to him, outlined below:

- he could sue the landlord through the courts for an order known as 'specific performance', which compels the landlord to carry out the specified repairs
- if he has already done the repairs he could recover the cost by making a claim for damages. Damages could also be claimed for the cost of finding alternative accommodation while the repairs were being carried out, assuming that the property was unfit for habitation during this period
- he could opt for a 'self-help' scheme whereby notice of the need for repairs is given to the landlord and he is allowed a reasonable time in which to carry them out.

The problem with the first option – the order known as 'specific performance' – is that this is a discretionary remedy and can be obtained only through litigation. The 'self-help' scheme is therefore preferable wherever possible.

Under this scheme, it is possible in certain circumstances for the tenant to have the work done and to deduct the cost of the work from rent due to the landlord or from future rent. This option will be feasible only if the cost of repairs is within the tenant's own means and the rent is sufficiently high for the tenant to be able to recoup the amount spent over a reasonable period. It is advisable for the tenant to obtain at least three estimates for the cost of the work and to submit copies of these estimates to the landlord together with a letter informing him that if he does not carry out the work by a certain date (which must give the landlord reasonable time), the tenant proposes to have the work done and to deduct the cost from the rent which would otherwise be due.

The self-help remedy should be used only if the landlord is clearly in breach and the repairs are clearly the landlord's responsibility: if there is any doubt about the matter the tenant should not pursue this option, since the erroneous withholding of rent by the tenant could render him liable to being sued by the landlord for possession on the grounds of rent arrears.

In the Bleak House example one of the clear breaches by the landlord was his failure to mend the leaking gutters. If the landlord, having been given notice, fails to repair these gutters within a reasonable time, it would be appropriate for the tenants to obtain estimates for the work themselves, forward them to the landlord and tell him that they propose to have the work done if the landlord fails to carry out the work within, say, four weeks. The tenants could then deduct the cost by withholding rent.

This self-help scheme is available to all residential tenants whose landlord is clearly in breach of a landlord's repairing obligation. Secure tenants in the public sector have a special scheme, described below.

Secure Tenancies (Right-to-Repair Scheme) Regulations 1985

Since 1 January 1986 public-sector secure tenants (with the exception of tenants of co-operative housing associations) have been able to use a special statutory procedure, set out in the right-to-repair scheme regulations. The scheme is limited to 'qualifying repairs', which means any repairs for which the landlord is responsible other than repairs to the structure and exterior of a flat. Under the scheme, the tenant must first serve notice on the landlord describing the proposed works, why they are needed and the materials to be used. The landlord must then reply within 21 days, either granting or refusing the tenant's repair claim. The landlord *may* refuse the claim in the following circumstances:

- where the landlord's costs would be more than £200
- where the landlord intends to carry out the work within 28 days of the claim
- where the works are not reasonably necessary for the personal comfort or safety of the tenant and those living with him and the landlord intends to carry them out within one year as part of a planned programme of repair
- where the works would infringe the terms of any guarantee of which the landlord has the benefit
- where the tenant has unreasonably failed to provide the landlord with access for inspection.

The landlord *must* refuse the claim in the following circumstances:

- where the landlord's costs would be less than £20
- where works do not constitute qualifying repairs
- where the works, if carried out using the materials specified, would not in the landlord's opinion satisfactorily remedy the problem.

Because of these conditions many tenants choose not to use the statutory scheme but to reply upon the common law rules mentioned earlier (page 148).

The Environmental Protection Act 1990

As an alternative to suing privately to make the landlord do the repairs a tenant may enlist the assistance of the local authority under Sections 79–82 of the Environmental Protection Act 1990. This legislation is concerned primarily with public health and is designed to prevent what is termed 'statutory nuisance'. This is defined in Section 79 to include, amongst other things, 'any premises in such a state as to be prejudicial to health or a nuisance'.

If a local authority is satisfied that a statutory nuisance exists, it must serve an abatement notice on the appropriate person (usually the landlord) requiring work to be carried out to 'abate the nuisance'. Not complying with an abatement notice is an offence, for which the landlord could be prosecuted in the magistrates' court. If the prosecution is successful, the tenant may be eligible to apply for a compensation order against the landlord for loss or damage arising from the offence committed.

Prejudicial to health
A statutory nuisance arises if the premises are, owing to disrepair or for some other reason, injurious or likely to cause injury to health. Therefore, if it can be shown that the premises are in such a condition that a person living there who is normally in good health is likely to become ill or that a sick person's health is likely to deteriorate further because of the condition of the premises, a statutory nuisance exists.

Damp, condensation, defective plasterwork, broken glass, dangerous gas and electrical installations may all constitute statutory nuisances, but the evidence of an environmental health officer who has inspected the premises will be required as grounds for an abatement notice.

A nuisance
A 'nuisance' means either a public nuisance or a private nuisance at common law. Public nuisance consists of an act or omission which adversely affects the comfort and quality of life for the public generally or a particular class of citizen. Public nuisance is unlikely to be relevant in the context of tenancies. Private nuisance is a substantial interference by the owner or occupier of a property with the use or enjoyment of neighbouring property. So if a landlord retains common parts or adjoining or neighbouring premises and the common parts or the neighbouring premises are in disrepair and this leads to interference with the tenanted property, such as water penetration, this may constitute a statutory nuisance for the purposes of the Act.

Tenants can therefore ask the local authority to intervene if the condition of the property makes it prejudicial to the occupants' health or a nuisance exists caused by defects in other premises owned by the landlord. If the local authority is satisfied that a statutory nuisance exists, it must serve an abatement notice requiring work to be carried out to prevent the nuisance occurring or recurring. The notice will specify what work has to be done. If the notice is not complied with the local authority may bring a prosecution, but this would be a criminal proceeding, in which the case against the landlord must be proved beyond reasonable doubt.

If the local authority is also the landlord and the tenant wishes to use the Environmental Protection Act, the procedure described above is clearly inappropriate as the local authority cannot take proceedings against itself. The tenant may therefore use an alternative procedure laid down in Section 82 of the Act. This requires the tenant to make a complaint to a local magistrates' court, which, if satisfied that a statutory nuisance exists, may require the local authority to abate the nuisance within a specified time and, failing compliance, to impose a fine. It should be noted that legal aid is not available for proceedings under the Environmental Protection Act.

Houses unfit for human habitation: Housing Act 1985

If the property is in such bad condition that it is unfit for human habitation, the local authority has wide powers to deal with the situation under Part VI of the Housing Act 1985.

The Act defines fitness for habitation in negative terms: a house is deemed to be fit for human habitation *unless*, in the opinion of the local authority, it fails to meet certain criteria such as:

- it is structurally stable
- it is free from serious disrepair
- it is free from damp that is prejudicial to the health of the occupants
- it has adequate provision for lighting, heating and ventilation
- it has an adequate pipe supply of good-quality water
- it contains satisfactory facilities for food preparation including a sink with hot and cold running water
- it has suitable WC facilities
- it has a suitable fixed bath or shower and hand basin and a satisfactory supply of hot and cold running water
- it has an effective drainage system.

If a house does not meet the above criteria it may be judged unfit for human habitation.

Local authorities have a duty to consider what action should be taken regarding housing in their area. Normally, a visit from an environmental health officer would be a prerequisite for any action taken under the 1985 Act. Possible courses of action are listed below.

Repair notice

The first option is to carry out repairs and improvements to render the property fit for human habitation. In this case, the local authority must serve a notice on the landlord or managing agent (normally) requiring certain work to be carried out. The recipient has the right to appeal against the notice within 21 days. Subject to an appeal, if the notice is not complied with the local authority may enter and carry out the work itself (but it cannot be compelled to do so) and may charge the cost to the landlord (or managing agent); otherwise, it may institute criminal proceedings against the landlord.

Closing order

The second option is a closing order. This means that the property may not be used for habitation whilst the order remains in force.

Demolition order

The third option is a demolition order requiring the owner to demolish the property and clear the site. If the order is not complied with the local authority has powers to act in default. Again, there is a right of appeal.

Clearance area

If the whole area comprises unfit houses the local authority may declare a clearance area. The result will be the compulsory acquisition of all the relevant properties and the rehousing of the tenants.

Fit houses in need of repair (Section 190, Housing Act 1985)

If a house is fit for human habitation but is in need of substantial repairs to bring it up to a reasonable standard, the local authority may serve a repairs notice on the landlord requiring specified work to be done. This also applies where the condition of the premises is such as to interfere materially with the personal comfort of the tenant. If the notice is not complied with the local authority may do the work itself or commence criminal proceedings.

Gas safety regulations

These stipulate that landlords must maintain all gas appliances, flues and installation pipework in the property they let to tenants, and that the appliances must be inspected at least once a year by an approved inspector. The landlord must also keep a proper record of maintenance/inspections which is available to tenants or prospective tenants for inspection (see page 82).

The record must be made available to all such tenants/licensees. A copy must be given to tenants/licensees within 28 days and to new tenants/licensees before they move in, although if the letting is to be for less than 28 days it may, alternatively, be prominently displayed on the premises instead. Any landlord convicted of breaching the regulations faces potentially heavy penalties under criminal law. Landlords should arrange for a registered CORGI member to check gas appliances and installations.

Other safety requirements

Landlords must ensure that electrical installations and appliances are safe. It is a criminal offence to supply unsafe electrical equipment. Soft furnishings in furnished property must conform to the current flammability criteria. For further details on these issues and fire safety in general see page 83.

Q *I rent a house from a private landlord on a monthly tenancy. The property is old and in need of repair but my landlord refuses to do any work. It needs a new damp-proof course since the existing one does not work and the wallpaper in the front room is peeling off. What are my rights?*

A Assuming your tenancy was granted on or after 24 October 1961, your periodic tenancy is covered by Section 11 of the Landlord and Tenant Act 1985. Your landlord is therefore legally responsible for maintaining the structure and mending the damp-proof course. You should write to your landlord telling him that if he does not carry out the work you will sue him for damages or for an order compelling him to carry out the work (or both). Damages would include the cost of repapering the room (and repair to any plasterwork) and also general damages for the inconvenience you have suffered.

Alternatively, if you can afford to have the work done yourself, you should obtain three estimates for the work and send these to your landlord telling him that if he does not do the work, you will. You can then recover the cost by withholding rent.

Another possible course of action is to contract your local authority's environmental health department; it will intervene if the damp is so bad that your health is likely to be affected.

Q *I am a council tenant and want to know how I can insist that the landlord carries out essential repairs. Despite my letters of complaint, no action has been taken.*

A If the repairs relate to the structure and exterior of the property you could use Section 11 of the Landlord and Tenant Act 1985 (legal aid may be available for this). If the house is unhealthy to live in you could threaten to take the local authority to court under the Environmental Protection Act 1990. To do this, however, you will need the evidence of an independent environmental health consultant (legal aid is not available for this). Depending on how much the repairs will cost, you could use one of the 'self-help' schemes (provided you obtain estimates first and give the landlord notice of your intentions) described in 'Remedies for breaches' on page 148.

Q *My son was injured after tripping on a broken staircase leading to my rented flat. Can he claim compensation?*

A Your son (assuming he is not the tenant or joint tenant) cannot himself sue the landlord for breach of the tenancy agreement but you may be able to sue on his behalf. However, under the Contracts (Rights of Third Parties) Act 1999, he may be able to argue that the tenancy confers a benefit on him directly, in which case he can sue for breaches of it. In addition, if negligence by the landlord can be established, your son may be able to make a claim for his injuries regardless of the tenancy. If you want to force the landlord to repair the staircase, you may need to take court proceedings for 'specific performance' of his obligations under the express or implied terms of the tenancy agreement.

Q *I am a landlord and recently granted an assured shorthold tenancy for six months. The tenant has given me a letter demanding that I sort out the* *condensation problem in the house. This is a long-standing problem which dates back to the construction of the house in the 1960s. It is not my fault and can be solved only by virtually rebuilding the place. Am I liable?*

A The tenancy is covered by Section 11 of the Landlord and Tenant Act 1988 and therefore you have responsibility for structural 'repairs'; if the condensation is not caused by disrepair you may not be directly liable to rectify the problem. However, if the condensation has caused damage to the fabric of the property you may be liable for this. If the tenant enlists the help of the local authority under the Environmental Protection Act 1990 and it is found that the condensation poses a health risk, you could be made liable or face a fine.

Chapter 13

Harassment and unlawful eviction

Among the most traumatic experiences that a residential tenant or licensee may have to face are harassment and peremptory eviction. Landlords sometimes resort to threats and violence because they see these as cheaper, easier and quicker methods of eviction than taking court proceedings for possession with no guarantee of success.

Tenants who suffer at the hands of their landlords in this way may have civil remedies as well as criminal sanctions available to them.

The tenant's basic remedies are damages, i.e. compensation for the loss suffered, or an injunction, i.e. a court order compelling the landlord to refrain from such actions in the future and to restore the dispossessed tenant to the property. These statutory protections apply not only to tenants but also to licensees, although there is a category of licences and tenancies for which protection is more limited. Apart from these excluded tenancies (see page 161), the protections will apply whether or not the tenant has security of tenure.

Criminal sanctions

The Protection from Eviction Act 1977

This Act imposes criminal penalties in cases of harassment and unlawful eviction. Criminal proceedings may result in the landlord being imprisoned or fined; compensation for the tenant may also be available. Details of offences under the Act are outlined below.

Protection from eviction

It is an offence to evict a residential occupier without a court order unless it is reasonably believed that he no longer lives in the premises.

A residential occupier is defined as someone who occupies the premises as a residence and includes all tenants, whether they are protected tenants under the Rent Act 1977, assured or assured shorthold tenants under the Housing Act 1988, or whether they have no statutory protection at all. Contractual licensees are also included within the definition.

Protection from harassment

Actions by a landlord which would amount to harassment include removing doors and windows, disconnecting services and acts and threats of violence.

There are two offences of harassment: one requires intent on the part of the offender and is set out in Section 1(3); the other is contained in Section 1(3A) and requires only knowledge or belief.

Section 1(3) harassment

It is an offence to commit acts likely to interfere with the peace or comfort of a residential occupier or to withhold services reasonably required for the occupation of the premises with intent to cause the residential occupier to give up the occupation of the premises. The need to *prove* that the landlord intended to cause the occupier to leave can cause problems. What if the landlord says he never intended that to happen? Generally, intent can be presumed only if the particular result was foreseeable as a natural consequence of the actions in question.

Section 1(3A) harassment

It is an offence for a landlord to commit acts likely to interfere with the peace and comfort of a residential occupier, or to withhold services reasonably required for the occupation of the premises, if he knows or has reasonable cause to believe that such conduct is likely to cause the residential occupier to give up the occupation of the premises.

As no proof of specific intention is required for this offence it may well be easier to establish than Section 1(3): this was certainly the intention of the legislature.

The Criminal Law Act 1977

Under Section 6(2) of the Criminal Law Act 1977 it is an offence for anyone 'without lawful authority' to use, or threaten to use, violence to secure entry to premises if there is someone on those premises at the time who is opposed to the entry.

The police are responsible for prosecutions against a landlord under the Criminal Law Act, whereas the local authority will normally bring proceedings under the Protection from Eviction Act. A private prosecution is also possible if the responsible authority refuses to bring proceedings.

Compensation in criminal proceedings

Under Section 35 of the Powers of the Criminal Courts Act 1973, magistrates have the power to order compensation for personal injury, loss or damage resulting from an offence. Compensation is available in relation to all the above offences regardless of who brings the prosecution. If compensation is awarded, however, it will be deducted from any damages subsequently awarded in civil proceedings.

If criminal proceedings are being brought, this provision provides an easy and cost-free method by which a tenant can obtain compensation. However, amounts awarded by the magistrates' court under this provision tend to be less than the civil courts would award and therefore might not prove adequate compensation for the loss suffered. Furthermore, the criminal courts are not empowered to order a landlord to restore a dispossessed tenant to a property.

Civil proceedings

As has been shown above, criminal sanctions are often an inadequate remedy for a dispossessed or threatened occupier. The occupier may well need an injunction to restrain the landlord or to regain possession of the property. Damages and injunctions are available only in civil proceedings in the county court and often provide a more effective and speedy remedy; if need be, emergency procedures can be followed in order to obtain immediate relief (see pages 165–8). It is a popular fallacy that the law is incapable of moving swiftly in an emergency.

Causes of action

In order to bring civil proceedings in court a 'cause of action' is necessary. This means that the landlord must be shown to have broken some rule of law by his actions *and* to have caused the tenant to suffer loss or harm because of this.

Various causes of action are available to dispossessed or harassed tenants, some statutory and some based upon the common law, depending upon the facts of the particular case. It is advisable for the tenant to allege as many causes of action as is reasonably possible. Actions based both on contract law (i.e. the tenancy agreement) and the law of torts (civil wrongdoing) may be possible.

Actions for breach of contract

(1) Breach of the covenant for quiet enjoyment

It is an implied term of every tenancy that the landlord will allow his tenant 'quiet enjoyment' of the premises. Quiet is used here in the sense of 'peace', not absence of noise. Unlawful eviction and most acts of harassment will be a breach of this covenant.

(2) Breach of contract in general

Any other breach of a term of the tenancy or licence agreement will be actionable by the occupier. So if a landlord evicts a tenant before the end of the tenancy, for example, before giving notice to quit, he will be in breach of contract. Similarly, if the landlord agrees to provide gas and electricity to a house and then withdraws these facilities, he will again be in breach.

Actions in tort

(1) Trespass to land

A tenant has the right to exclusive possession of the premises which have been let to him. If the landlord (or anyone else) enters those premises without permission he is liable for trespass unless the landlord has entered for a lawful purpose, e.g. to inspect or do repairs under the tenancy agreement. Licensees who do not have the right to exclusive possession cannot sue in trespass.

(2) Trespass to the person

Harassment and unlawful eviction are frequently accompanied by violence or threats of violence. These may well amount to the torts of assault and battery (which can also be criminal offences). Battery is the infliction of physical violence on another without lawful excuse; assault is any act which puts a person in immediate and reasonable fear of battery. This cause of action will be available to both tenants and licensees.

(3) Trespass to goods

If, in the process of harassing or evicting an occupier, a landlord damages the occupier's furniture or other personal belongings, this would amount to trespass to goods, i.e. unlawfully damaging someone else's property. If the landlord detains or otherwise deprives the occupier of the use of the goods, this might amount to a special tort called 'conversion'. Both tenants and licensees can use this cause of action.

(4) Section 3 of the Protection from Eviction Act 1977

Section 3 of the Act provides that when a tenancy or licence which is not 'statutorily protected' comes to an end, but the former tenant continues to reside on the premises, he cannot be evicted without a court order. Any evictions of such a tenant will give rise to an action in tort for breach of statutory duty.

The definition of a statutorily protected tenancy excludes assured and assured shorthold tenancies under the Housing Act 1988 and protected tenancies under the Rent Act 1977. Tenancies and licences will also be excluded if:

- the occupier shares accommodation with the landlord or licensor who occupies the premises of which the shared accommodation forms part as his only or principal home
- the occupier shares accommodation with a member of the landlord's or licensor's family who occupies the premises of which the shared accommodation forms part as his only or principal home.
- they confer the right to occupy for the purpose of a holiday
- they were granted other than for money or money's worth (i.e. assets with a monetary value such as stocks and shares).

(5) Breach of Section 27 of the Housing Act 1988

Section 27 creates a statutory tort if a landlord:

- attempts unlawfully to deprive a residential occupier of his occupation and the occupier leaves as a result; or

- knowing or having reasonable cause to believe that his conduct is likely to cause a residential occupier to give up his occupancy, commits acts likely to interfere with the peace or comfort of the residential occupier or members of his household and the occupier leaves as a result.

Note that this tort is satisfied only if the residential occupier actually gives up occupancy; this cause of action cannot be used in cases of harassment which have forced the occupier to leave. Equally, there will be no liability under Section 27 if the occupier is reinstated in the property either by the landlord or by an order of the court.

The landlord has a defence to this action if he can prove that he had reasonable cause to believe that the occupier had ceased to live in the premises, or that he had reasonable grounds for his conduct. There is a special measure of damages for this tort (see below).

Remedies in civil proceedings

Damages

The basic remedy for breach of contract or tort will be damages, or compensation for loss. The measure of damages, i.e. the amount that can be recovered, will vary depending upon the cause of action alleged.

Measure for Section 27 actions

For actions under Section 27 of the Housing Act 1988 (see above) a special measure of damages is laid down (in Section 28). Normally, damages are assessed on the basis of the loss to the claimant; under Section 28 the damages are assessed on the basis of the gain to the landlord, in an attempt to prevent landlords from profiting from their wrongdoing.

The damages awarded will be the difference between the value of the premises with a sitting tenant and the value with vacant possession. This difference in value could be quite substantial (over £30,000 in one actual case) and both claimant and defendant must be prepared to provide valuation evidence where a claim under Section 27 is being brought. The amount of the damages payable may be reduced by the court if the prior conduct of the tenant was such that it would be reasonable to reduce the damages or the tenant has unreasonably refused an offer of reinstatement.

With regard to the above points, it is not unknown for tenants to harass and assault landlords and so a reasonable reduction of damages might be available to a landlord who had decided to take the law into his own hands by way of retaliation. If the tenant has suffered a series of unpleasant events, it would not be considered unreasonable for him to refuse reinstatement when, in his mind at least, he might be placing himself at further risk.

Measure in other actions

Under the normal laws of tort, damages are designed to put the claimant in the position he would have been in had the tort *not* been committed. In contract law, on the other hand, damages are designed to put the claimant into the position he would have been in *had* the contract been fulfilled.

Obviously, in bringing a claim, full details of all losses suffered because of the landlord's actions should be kept. These will include the cost of any alternative accommodation that was necessary, the cost of damage to furniture, clothes, and so on. Some losses, such as physical injury or mental stress suffered, are difficult to quantify and will be quantified by the court only if the case is successful.

Exemplary damages

Exemplary damages are available only for actions in tort, and will be awarded only where the defendant's conduct has been calculated to make a profit over and above any damages he would have otherwise had to pay to the claimant. They are available in unlawful eviction cases to teach wrongdoers that tort does not pay. It is not necessary to show that the landlord actually made a profit in order to claim exemplary damages, nor are they limited to the amount of profit actually made. They must, however, be specifically asked for in the particulars of claim. Although not available in contract actions, the special measure of damages under Section 27 of the Housing Act 1988 has a similar objective (see opposite).

Aggravated damages

Aggravated damages are also available only in relation to actions in tort, but unlike exemplary damages they need not be specifically claimed by the claimant. They are similar in many respects to exemplary damages, the difference being that there is no need to show an element of calculation on the defendant's part. They are awarded primarily in cases of particularly unpleasant conduct by the landlord.

Injunctions

Awarding damages in harassment and unlawful eviction cases will not necessarily provide the occupier with a full solution to his problem. An occupier who has been awarded damages but remains in occupation will want protection and reassurance that the harassment will not be repeated; an occupier who has been unlawfully evicted may want to be reinstated in the property; an occupier who has been deprived of his personal belongings will want them restored to him. The appropriate remedy in such cases will be an injunction. If an occupier fears that he may suffer unlawful eviction in the future he may also seek an injunction to restrain the landlord from such conduct. Unlike damages, however, an injunction is a discretionary remedy, which means that even if the tenant's case is proved the court does not have to grant an injunction; it will do so only if it thinks damages are an inadequate remedy. Furthermore, an applicant who delays bringing his case to court may fail to obtain an injunction, as may an applicant who has himself been guilty of violence against the landlord. However, neither of these circumstances would prevent a claim for damages.

An injunction may be made by the court as a final order or as an interim order. A final order is made on the final determination of the case, which may well be several months after the commencement of the proceedings. Obviously, in harassment cases such a delay will be unacceptable and so an interlocutory or interim injunction should be applied for. This will remain in force until a specified date, but will not necessarily reflect the final outcome of the case.

Interlocutory relief is not available as of right; various conditions must be satisfied. However, in harassment cases this should not cause any problem.

The requirements which must be satisfied are:

- that there is a serious case to be tried; and
- that damages would not be adequate compensation; and

- that it is more convenient to grant an injunction rather than to await the outcome of the full trial.

The applicant will usually be required to give an undertaking to compensate the landlord if it is later found that the order should not have been made. Even if the applicant has public funding (and therefore unable to give a financially worthwhile undertaking), this should not prevent the making of an interlocutory order in appropriate cases.

Normally an injunction is ordered by the court only after both sides to the action have been heard. However, in an emergency, an order without notice can be obtained, i.e. an order made on the hearing of evidence from the applicant only. This kind of injunction is sought in many harassment and unlawful eviction cases where the occupier requires a speedy remedy.

Obtaining emergency relief

It is possible to bring proceedings for harassment or unlawful eviction on a 'self-help' basis, but it should be borne in mind that speed and accuracy are of the utmost importance if effective relief is to be obtained. As far as possible, therefore, professional help should be sought.

If you are eligible for public funding, a solicitor can be instructed at little or no cost. If not, assistance may be obtained from law centres, housing advice centres and Citizens Advice Bureaux. The local office of the county court (at which the proceedings have to be commenced) will also be helpful in providing the correct forms and ensuring that they have been properly completed, but it must be appreciated that the county court staff are not able to conduct cases in person on behalf of litigants.

Information needed to bring a court action

Whether you are instructing a solicitor or bringing the proceedings yourself, you will need to equip yourself with a large amount of information in order to commence the court proceedings.

The information should include:

(1) the precise identity of the property, including the postal address
(2) the tenancy agreement and the rent book (if applicable). In a case of unlawful eviction it may well not be possible to obtain

these owing to the fact that they are kept in the property from which the tenant has been evicted

(3) the landlord's full name and address. It is important that some indication can be given to the process-server as to the landlord's likely whereabouts. The full names and addresses of anyone else involved in the harassment or eviction should also be obtained if at all possible

(4) full and precise details of the alleged harassment or the circumstances of the unlawful eviction. If there are any potential witnesses to the alleged acts, their names and addresses should be obtained. The clearer the details are of what has happened, the better the chance of obtaining effective relief.

Application on notice or without notice

Normally, notice of the proceedings should be served upon the landlord at least three days prior to the hearing of the application (an application 'on notice'), but in an emergency an application may be made without notice, i.e. an order made on the hearing of evidence from the applicant only. Most courts prefer the application to be made on notice if at all possible. If an application without notice is made, it will be valid only for a short time until a further hearing (on notice) can be held.

Contacting the landlord

Whether or not an application is to be made with or without notice, consideration should be given at the outset as to whether or not the tenant (or his solicitor) should contact the landlord. This course of action may well be ruled out due to the urgency of the situation. However, if at least telephone contact can be made, this may be helpful for a variety of reasons. It is usually preferable to settle the matter out of court if at all possible and it may be that the landlord does not realise he is doing anything unlawful. In any event, a full record should be kept of any contact with the landlord, because when an injunction application is made it is worth including details of the contact in a supporting witness statement as further evidence of the landlord's conduct.

Commencing the proceedings

Any tenant faced with unlawful eviction or serious harassment should seek professional advice from a solicitor, a CAB or the local authority's tenancy relations officer. Proceedings will take place in the county court (address in the telephone directory under 'Courts') – either the one for the area in which the premises are situated or the one for the area where the landlord lives.

The next step, for cases where an application without notice is to be made, is to warn the court (by telephone, fax or letter) about the application and to ascertain when and where a judge will be available to hear it. This can sometimes be a problem in rural areas where a judge is not in attendance every day, or even every week.

A claim form (available from the court) and a statement of case must be completed, listing the cause of action, the relief or remedy sought and the material facts on which the tenant is relying.

An application notice should also be completed, showing:

- the terms of the injunction applied for
- a statement of truth or affidavit (sworn statement) setting out the case supported by a statement of grounds for making the application
- any witness statements relied upon, plus copies for service.

These should set out all the events and facts upon which the tenant seeks to rely in order to seek the injunction against the landlord.

A court fee payable (check the amount when applying).

Serving the documents

If the application for the injunction is to proceed on notice the landlord should be served, at least two days before the hearing, with:

- the application notice
- the statement of case and any affidavit or witness statement in support
- any witness statements intended for use at the hearing.

The landlord must also be served with the appropriate documents, in due course, in the case of an urgent 'without notice' application.

The court hearing

Unless otherwise directed, every application (except those made without notice) shall be made in open court. The application will be made to a single judge sitting alone without a jury. Many judges, however, hear applications in chambers. The tenant(s) and any witnesses should attend and be prepared to give oral evidence, even though the court will have received their written statements.

The tenant will outline his case and bring evidence to support his allegations. The landlord will then present his defence. Often the judge will be prepared to accept an undertaking from the landlord as to his future conduct without making a formal order. However, the landlord would still be in contempt of court should he not comply with such an undertaking.

The court order

The form of the injunction will be decided by the judge, but a draft order should be supplied by the tenant or his solicitors. It should contain a warning that failure by the landlord to comply may result in imprisonment for contempt of court. The injunction should normally be served personally on the landlord.

Enforcement of the order

If the landlord breaches the injunction, the tenant should apply to the court for the landlord's committal to prison for contempt. The tenant should make the application to the court that made the injunction in the first place, specifying when and how the landlord has broken the injunction. The matter will be listed for a hearing and the application should be served personally on the landlord. If proven, the court has very wide powers to imprison or fine the landlord for breaching the injunction.

Abuse by residential landlords

The self-help voluntary organisation Campaign for the Abolition of Residential Leasehold (CARL)★ provides home counselling to victims of landlord bullying – which could take the form of physical harassment, entering the tenant's premises without permission or overcharging for management services. The main objective of CARL is to lobby Parliament to protect leaseholders and ultimately to see leasehold replaced by commonhold.

Q *My landlord came to see me yesterday and said that if I did not leave my flat by the end of the week he would come round with his mates and throw me out on the street. Can he do this?*

A No. He can legally obtain possession only by means of a court order. You should seek legal advice immediately and obtain an injunction against the landlord to prevent him taking any action such as he has threatened. You do not need to wait until he has actually carried out his threats before going to court.

Q *My landlord wants me to leave my flat, even though I am an assured tenant and have security of tenure. He has now offered me £1,000 to leave by the end of the month. Is this legal?*

A Provided that your landlord is not making any threats against you about what will happen if you do not leave, this is lawful. But you do not have to accept his offer; you have security of tenure and can stay on until he can prove a ground for possession against you. If you do choose to accept his offer, you will have to leave; it is up to you to decide whether losing your home is worth £1,000.

Q *My landlord has forced me to leave my flat. He made my life a misery for months, by banging on the door in the middle of the night, turning off the electricity for days at a time, threatening me with violence and so on. I eventually found somewhere else to live and have moved out. I don't want to go back there, but I don't want him to get away with it. What can I do? I am working so am not eligible for legal aid.*

A It certainly seems that you have the right to bring proceedings against the landlord under Section 27 of the Housing Act 1988 and possibly to obtain substantial damages. As you are aware, however, you would have to finance these proceedings yourself. Another possibility is to contact your local tenancy relations officer and see whether he would be willing to bring criminal proceedings against your landlord for harassment. The court could also award you compensation in criminal proceedings, although the amount would probably not be as large as under Section 27 proceedings.

Chapter 14

Possession proceedings

If a tenant at the end of a tenancy is not prepared to vacate the property voluntarily, the landlord will usually need to commence possession proceedings in the local county court. Similarly, if the tenant breaches the tenancy agreement (for example, by not paying the rent so that arrears have accumulated) the landlord cannot normally regain possession without a court order.

If a landlord resorts to obtaining possession without a court order this will normally amount to unlawful eviction, for which the landlord may be ordered to pay substantial damages, an injunction, a fine or even, in extreme cases, be sent to prison. It is therefore essential that the landlord obtains the appropriate court order and follows the correct procedure. This chapter explains the need for a court order and the procedures for obtaining it.

Why a court order might be needed

The two most common reasons for requiring possession are that the tenancy has expired and the landlord does not wish to renew it, or that the tenant has fallen into arrears with the rent or has committed other breaches of the letting agreement. In both cases a court order will usually be needed if the landlord is to regain possession. The court needs to know that the tenancy or licence has been properly terminated, the landlord has served valid and correct notices and (where the court has a discretion as to whether a possession order should be made) that it is reasonable to award possession to the landlord.

There are however cases where the landlord does not need a court order and is allowed to re-enter the property without one, but even in cases such as these, if violence is used the landlord will be guilty of a criminal offence and can be prosecuted. Hence, if the tenant or occupier is likely to resist the landlord's re-entry, a court order should be obtained to remove the possibility of a criminal offence being committed.

The exceptional cases in which a court order is not needed are called 'excluded licences or tenancies'.

Excluded licences or tenancies

These include resident landlords where the following conditions exist:

- before the tenancy/licence was granted, the landlord/licensor occupied the property as his only or main residence and, under the terms of the agreement, the occupier now shares accommodation with the landlord/licensor; or
- the occupier shares accommodation with a member or members of the landlord's family and the following conditions also apply:
  (a) the landlord/licensor's main home is in the same building (unless it is a purpose-built block of flats)
  (b) a member of the landlord/licensor's family shares accommodation with the tenant/licensee ('family' is widely defined to include spouses, children, parents, grandparents, grandchildren, brothers, sisters, uncles, aunts, nephews and nieces).

Other excluded tenancies/licences are:

- holiday lets – where the occupier fails to vacate property let for the purpose of a holiday
- gratuitous lettings – where the accommodation is made available rent-free to the tenant or licensee
- squatters and trespassers – where the tenancy/licence was given to a squatter or trespasser as a temporary measure
- hostels – where the accommodation is in a residential hostel.

In all other cases, including tenancies governed by the Rent Act 1977 (protected and statutory tenancies), the Housing Acts 1988 and 1996 (assured and assured shorthold tenancies) and public-sector tenancies governed by the Housing Act 1985 (secure tenancies), a court order is essential.

The procedure and formalities for obtaining a court order vary according to the type of tenancy or licence, but essentially they all require the landlord/licensor to:

- show that the tenancy has ended and that the appropriate termination notices have been given
- prove that the landlord has grounds for possession, and
- if the ground is a discretionary ground (as opposed to a mandatory ground), show that it is 'reasonable' for the court to grant possession.

These points are considered below in the context of:

- assured shorthold tenancies
- assured tenancies
- Rent Act 1977 tenancies
- public-sector tenancies
- other lettings.

Assured shorthold tenancies

If the landlord wants possession because the tenancy has expired and does not wish to renew it or if, in the case of a periodic assured shorthold tenancy, the landlord simply wishes to terminate it without wishing to grant a new tenancy to the same tenant, the procedures are as follows.

(1) **Ending of tenancy** The landlord must give at least two months' notice under Section 21 of the 1988 Act ('Section 21 notice') requiring possession when the notice expires. The Court cannot make a possession order in the first six months after the grant of the tenancy. If the tenancy was granted initially for more than six months, the tenancy cannot take effect before the fixed term expires. Therefore, if the tenancy was granted for 12 months, the notice cannot be effective until the end of the 12 months. If the landlord seeks possession before the agreed fixed term expires or during the first six months, this must be based on a ground for possession (see 'Assured tenancies', page 179).

   The Act does not specify a 'prescribed' form of notice but it must be in writing and it must require possession to be given after a specified date, which cannot be sooner than two months after the notice is served on the tenant. Most law stationers can supply printed forms, which may vary slightly. A specimen is given below.

Housing Act 1988
Section 21
Notice requiring possession

To: [name of tenant(s)]
of: [address of tenant(s)]
From: [name of landlord]
of: [address of landlord]

I/We hereby give you notice that I/we require possession of the dwelling-house known as [address of property]

after: [date of expiry of notice]
by virtue of Section 21 of the Housing Act 1988.

Dated: [date of signature]

Signed: [signature of landlord or landlord's agent]

Note that:

- if the tenancy was for a fixed term, the date specified cannot be any earlier than the expiry date of that fixed term
- if the tenancy was periodic or the fixed term has expired before the notice is given, the date specified must be the last day of a rental period. Therefore, if the tenancy is a monthly tenancy and the rent day is the 15th of the month, the date specified must be the 14th of a subsequent month at least two months after the date of service
- the two-month notice period is a minimum – it can be more than two months and still be valid. For example, if a six-month tenancy was granted there would be nothing legally wrong with the landlord serving the Section 21 notice on or soon after the grant of the tenancy, to take effect at the expiry of the tenancy.

(2) **Grounds for possession** In the case of an assured shorthold tenancy the landlord simply needs to show that the tenancy has ended and that the Section 21 notice has been served and has expired. He does not need a ground for possession, being

entitled to a possession order as of right. The usual procedure for obtaining such an order, called an 'accelerated possession action', is described below.

(3) **Reasonableness** The landlord does not have to show it is reasonable to grant possession. Once the correct Section 21 notice has been served and the court is satisfied that the tenancy is an assured shorthold, it must grant an order for possession.

Accelerated possession proceedings

These are commenced in the county court for the area where the property is situated. Your local county court will confirm which court has jurisdiction. Once you have established which is the right county court, ask for the forms for an accelerated possession action and the explanatory leaflet on filling them in. The most important form is the 'Claim form for possession of property (accelerated procedure) (assured shorthold, tenancy), reproduced in this chapter. You can download it from the Court Service website.*

The claimant is the landlord, and he should fill in his name and address. The defendant's (tenant's) name(s) and address (the tenanted property) should also be inserted. The amount of the court fee should be checked at the court office and paid by the landlord in order that the action can commence.

The application is supported by a witness statement, printed on the inside pages of the application form.

The landlord (claimant) will also need to supply:

- a copy of the tenancy agreement
- the notice stating that the tenancy would be an assured shorthold if the tenancy began before 28 February 1997 (not required if the tenancy began after that date)
- in all cases, the notice requiring possession served under Section 21 of the Housing Act 1988.

It is most important that the form and the witness statement are properly completed, otherwise the court is likely to reject the application.

The completed form and statement plus a copy for each defendant must be filed at court along with the court fee. The court will serve

Claim form for possession of property
(accelerated procedure)
(assured shorthold tenancy)

In the	
Claim No.	

Claimant
(name(s) and address(es))

SEAL

Defendant(s)
(name(s) and address(es))

The claimant is claiming possession of:

for the reasons given in the following pages.
[The claimant is also asking for an order that you pay the costs of the claim.]

IMPORTANT - TO THE DEFENDANT(S)

This claim means that the court will decide whether or not you have to leave the premises and, if so, when. There will not normally be a court hearing. You must act immediately.

Get help and advice from an advice agency or a solicitor.
Read all the pages of this form and the papers delivered with it.
Fill in the defence form and return it **within 14 days** of receiving this form.

The notes on the last page of this form tell you more about what you can do.

Defendant's name and address for service

Court fee	£
Solicitor's costs	£
Total amount	£

Issue date	

N5B Claim form for property (accelerated procedure)(assured shorthold tenancy) (10.01)   *Printed on behalf of The Court Service*

	Claim No.	

1. The claimant seeks an order that the defendant(s) give possession of

   ("the premises") which is a dwelling house [part of a dwellinghouse].

2. On   , the claimant entered into a written tenancy agreement with the defendant(s).
   A copy of it, marked "A" is attached to this claim form.
   [One or more subsequent written tenancy agreements have been entered into. A copy of the most recent
   one, made on   , marked "A1", is also attached to this claim form.]

3. Both the [first] tenancy and the agreement for it were made on or after 28th February 1997.

   a) No notice was served on the defendant stating that the tenancy would not be, or continue to
   be, an assured shorthold tenancy.

   b) There is no provision in the tenancy agreement which states that it is not an assured shorthold tenancy.

   c) The "agricultural worker condition" defined in Schedule 3 to the Housing Act 1988 is not fulfilled
   with respect to the property.

   (or)

4. Both the [first] tenancy and the agreement for it were made on or after 15 January 1989.

   a) The [first] tenancy agreement was for a fixed term of not less than six months.

   b) There was no power for the landlord to end the tenancy earlier than six months after it began.

   c) On the   19   (before the tenancy began) a notice in writing, stating that the tenancy
   was to be an assured shorthold tenancy, was served on the defendant(s). It was served by:

   d) Attached to this claim form is a copy of that notice marked "B" [and proof of service marked "B1"].

   e) There was not a tenancy of a dwelling (other than an assured shorthold tenancy), under which the
   claimant was the landlord and the defendant(s) (or at least one) was a tenant, in existence immediately
   before the [first] tenancy agreement [nor before any subsequent tenancy agreement].

5. Whenever a new tenancy agreement has replaced the first tenancy agreement or has replaced a replacement
   tenancy agreement,

   a) it has been of the same, or substantially the same, premises, and

   b) the landlord and tenant were the same people at the start of the replacement tenancy as the landlord
   and tenant at the end of the tenancy which it replaced.

6. On the   20 , a notice in writing, saying that possession of the premises was
   required, was served upon the defendant(s). It was served by:

   The notice expired on the   20 .

   Attached to this claim form is a copy of that notice marked "C" [and proof of service marked "C1"].

Claim No.	

7. *(any further information, continue on separate sheet if necessary)*

8. If the defendant(s) seek(s) postponement of possession on the grounds of exceptional hardship, the claimant is content that the request be considered without a hearing.

9. The claimant asks the court

to order that the defendant(s) deliver up possession of the property.

[to order the defendant(s) to pay the costs of this claim.]

Statement of Truth

*(I believe)(The claimant believes) that the facts stated in this claim form (and any attached sheets) are true.
* I am duly authorised by the claimant to sign this statement.

signed _____ date _____

(Claimant)(Litigation friend(where claimant is a child or a patient)*)(Claimant's solicitor)
delete as appropriate

Full name _____

Name of claimant's solicitor's firm _____

position or office held _____
(if signing on behalf of firm or company)

Claimant's or claimant's solicitor's address to which documents should be sent if different from that on the front page.

	if applicable
Ref. no.	
fax no.	
DX no.	
e-mail	
Tel. no.	

Postcode

Notes for the defendant

The claimant has used the accelerated procedure because it is said you have an assured shorthold tenancy. If so, the court is not allowed to consider whether it is reasonable or fair to make the order for possession. Therefore, if what is written in the claim form and in the defence form make it clear that the claimant is entitled to possession, the court will make the order without fixing a hearing.

If you think there are reasons why the court should not make a possession order, you should consider getting advice from a solicitor or an advice agency immediately. If you dispute the claim, fill in the defence form and return it to the court office within 14 days of receiving the claim form. If you cannot give exact dates in your defence form, give them as nearly as you can. Make it clear that the dates you give are approximate. The judge can only take account of legally valid reasons.

You may qualify for assistance from Community Legal Service Fund (CLSF) to meet some or all of your legal costs. Ask about the CLSF at any county court office or any information or help point which displays this logo.

Court staff can only help you complete the defence form and tell you about court procedures. **They cannot give legal advice.**

If the court makes a possession order without a hearing, you will be entitled to apply, within 14 days of receiving the order, for it to be reconsidered. The application would have to show some good legal reason for varying or revoking the order.

Normally, if the court makes a possession order, it will tell you to leave the premises within 14 days. The judge can allow up to 42 days but only if satisfied that leaving within 14 days would cause you hardship which is exceptional (that is, worse than would usually be suffered by someone having to leave within 14 days). If you believe there are exceptional circumstances in your case, fill in section 9 of the defence form and return it to the court office. Usually, an order for possession in 14 days will still be made but a hearing will be fixed within the 14 day period. The judge will decide at the hearing whether or not to extend the period.

If the court orders you to pay the claimant's costs, normally the order requires payment within 14 days. If you would be unable to pay in that time, fill in section 10 of the defence form and give details of your means.

If you use the defence form, you **must** sign the Statement of Truth. Proceedings for contempt of court may be brought against a person who signs a Statement of Truth without an honest belief in its truth.

CERTIFICATE OF SERVICE
(completed on court copy only)
I certify that the claim form of which this is a true copy was served by me on

by posting it to the defendant(s) on

at the address stated on the first page of the claim form.

OR

The claim form has not been served for the following reasons:

Officer of the Court

Send documents for the court to the court office at

Telephone:
Fax:

Please address all correspondence to "The Court Manager".

the papers on the tenant(s) by post and will notify the landlord that this has been done.

The papers served on the tenant include a form of reply to enable him to lodge an objection to the landlord's application, should he wish to do so, and the grounds of his objection. This must be done within 14 days of service.

The matter is then referred to a district judge, who looks at the papers and the reply (if any) and decides whether possession should be ordered at this stage or the matter should be referred for a hearing. The procedure is designed to avoid the need for a hearing, so the judge will normally call for one only if the landlord's paperwork is not in order or the tenant has raised an issue that ought to be heard.

The accelerated possession procedure can deal only with possession claims, not other claims such as rent arrears. If the landlord wants rent arrears as well he should start an ordinary possession action (see page 185).

If the court is satisfied that the possession claim is made out and that there is no defence, it will make an order for possession and both landlord and tenant will be notified.

Assured tenancies

This section deals with fully assured tenancies, under which the tenant has full security of tenure under the Housing Act 1988 (see Chapter 3) or assured shorthold tenancies where the landlord is seeking possession before the agreed fixed term has expired.

(1) **Ending the tenancy** The landlord must service a notice under Section 8 of the Housing Act. This is a prescribed form:

Form No. 3

Housing Act 1988 Section 8 as amended by Section 151 of the Housing Act 1996.

Notice seeking possession of a property let on an Assured Tenancy or an Assured Agricultural Occupancy

- Please write clearly in black ink.

- Please tick boxes where appropriate

- Do not use this form if possession is sought on the "shorthold" ground under Section 21 of the Housing Act 1988 from and cross out text marked with an asterisk (*) that does not apply.

- This form should be used where possession of accommodation let under an assured tenancy, an assured agricultural occupancy or an assured shorthold tenancy is sought on one of the grounds in Schedule 2 to the Housing Act 1988.

an assured shorthold tenant where the fixed term has come to an end or, for assured shorthold tenancies with no fixed term which started on or after 28th February 1997, after six months has elapsed. There is no prescribed form for these cases, but you must give notice in writing.

1. To: ....

Name(s) of tenant(s)/licensee(s)*

2. Your landlord/licensor* intends to apply to the court for an order requiring you to give up possession of:

....
....
....

Address of premises

3. Your landlord/licensor* intends to seek possession on ground(s) .... in Schedule 2 to the Housing Act 1988, as amended by the Housing Act 1996, which read(s):

....
....
....

Give the full text (as set out in the Housing Act 1988 as amended by the Housing Act 1996) of each ground which is being relied on. Continue on a separate sheet if necessary.

4. Give a full explanation of why each ground is being relied on:

....
....
....

Continue on a separate sheet if necessary.

Notes on the grounds for possession

- If the court is satisfied that any of grounds 1 to 8 is established, it must make an order (but see below in respect of fixed-term tenancies).
- Before the court will grant an order on any of grounds 9 to 17, it must be satisfied that it is reasonable to require you to leave. This means that, if one of these grounds is set out in section 3, you will be able to suggest to the court that it is not reasonable that you should have to leave, even if you accept that the ground applies.

- The court will not make an order under grounds 1, 3 to 7, 9 or 16, to take effect during the fixed term of the tenancy (if there is one) and it will only make an order during the fixed term on grounds 2, 8, 10 to 15 or 17 if the terms of the tenancy make provision for it to be brought to an end on any of these grounds.

- Where the court makes an order for possession solely on ground 6 or 9, the landlord must pay your reasonable removal expenses.

---

5. The court proceedings will not begin until after:

....

Give the earliest date on which court proceedings can be brought

- Where the landlord is seeking possession on grounds 1, 2, 5 to 7, 9 or 16, court proceedings cannot begin earlier than 2 months from the date this notice is served on you (even where one of grounds 3, 4, 8, 10 to 13, 14A, 15 or 17 is specified) and not before the date on which the tenancy (had it not been assured) could have been brought to an end by a notice to quit served at the same time as this notice.

- Where the landlord is seeking possession on grounds 3, 4, 8, 10 to 13, 14A, 15 or 17, court proceedings cannot begin earlier than 2 weeks from the date this notice is served (unless one of 1, 2, 5 to 7, 9 or 16 grounds is also specified in which case they cannot begin earlier than two months from the date this notice is served).

- Where the landlord is seeking possession on ground 14 (with or without other grounds), court proceedings cannot begin before the date this notice is served.

- Where the landlord is seeking possession on ground 14A, court proceedings cannot begin unless the landlord has served, or has taken all reasonable steps to serve, a copy of this notice on the partner who has left the property.

- After the date shown in section 5, court proceedings may be begun at once but not later than 12 months from the date on which this notice is served. After this time the notice will lapse and a new notice must be served before possession can be sought.

---

6. Name and address of landlord/licensor*

To be signed and dated by the landlord or licensor or his agent (someone acting for him). If there are joint landlords each landlord or the agent must sign unless one signs on behalf of the rest with their agreement.

Signed .... *Date* ....
....

Please specify whether: landlord ☐ licensor ☐ joint landlords ☐ landlord's agent ☐

Name(s) (Block Capitals) ....
....

Address

....

....

....

Telephone—Daytime .... Evening...

What to do if this notice is served on you

- This notice is the first step requiring you to give up possession of your home. You should read it very carefully.

- Your landlord cannot make you leave your home without an order for possession issued by a court. By issuing this notice your landlord is informing you that he intends to seek such an order. If you are willing to give up possession without a court order, you should tell the person who signed this notice as soon as possible and say when you are prepared to leave.

- Whichever grounds are set out in section 3 of this form, the court may allow any of the other grounds to be added at a later date. If this is done, you will be told about it so you can discuss the additional grounds at the court hearing as well as the grounds set out in section 3.

- If you need advice about this notice, and what you should do about it, take it immediately to a Citizens Advice Bureau, a Housing Advice Centre, a law centre or a solicitor.

The grounds for possession are set out in Chapter 3. The Section 8 notice must specify a date before which proceedings cannot be commenced. If grounds 3, 4, 8 or 10–15 are to be used, the date specified must be a minimum of two weeks away. But in the case of ground 14 no minimum notice period of notice is required: the date specified can simply be the date of service of the notice itself.

For grounds 1, 2, 5–7, 9 and 16 the date specified in the notice must be at least two months after the date of service.

The rationale behind these rules on notice is that if the tenant is in default only a short period of notice (two weeks) is required, whereas if the reason for requiring possession is not the fault of the tenant, a longer notice period (two months) is needed.

The landlord must then wait for the Section 8 notice to expire before starting proceedings, on grounds which must be as stated in the notice.

(2) **Grounds for possession** The landlord must prove the relevant ground and that the Section 8 notice has been validly served.

(3) **Reasonableness** Some of the grounds are mandatory and others discretionary (see Chapter 3). If a mandatory ground is used and proven, the court has no discretion and must grant a

possession order in the landlord's favour. If a discretionary ground is used, the court must be satisfied that it is reasonable to grant a possession order. For example, if there are rent arrears of less than two months, the ground for possession will be discretionary, but it is unlikely that the court would grant an outright possession order for such minor arrears; at the most a 'suspended' possession order may be granted giving the landlord possession but at the same time stipulating that if the tenant pays the current rent, plus a specified amount of the arrears by instalments, the order is 'suspended' and the tenant who complies with it can stay in possession on those terms.

Rent Act 1977: protected and statutory tenancies

(1) **Ending the tenancy** If the tenancy is periodic, the landlord must serve a notice to quit containing the information laid down by the Protection from Eviction Act 1977 and the regulations made under that Act. The prescribed information is set out below in paragraph 2, but forms can change and landlords are advised to purchase the latest form of notice from a law stationer and use this when serving notice to quit.

NOTICE TO QUIT premises let as a dwelling
PROTECTION FROM EVICTION ACT 1977

To: [tenant: insert details]
Property: [insert address]
From: [landlord: insert details]

1. The Landlord gives you, the Tenant, NOTICE TO QUIT the Property on [insert date: this must be the last day of a rental period or the first day of a new rental period and, in either case, must be at least one full rental period after the date of service and not less than four weeks in the future] or, if later, the next date (being at least four weeks from the service of this notice) on which a complete period of your tenancy expires.

2. You are given the following information:

2.1 If the tenant or licensee does not leave the dwelling, the landlord or licensor must get an order for possession from the court before the tenant or licensee can lawfully be evicted. The landlord or licensor cannot apply for such an order before the notice to quit or notice to determine has run out.

2.2 A tenant or licensee who does not know if he has any right to remain in possession after a notice to quit or a notice to determine runs out can obtain advice from a solicitor. Help with all or part of the cost of legal advice and assistance may be available under the Legal Aid Scheme. The tenant/licensee should also be able to obtain information from a Citizens Advice Bureau, a Housing Aid Centre or a rent officer.

This does not apply to premises which are let or occupied as specified in Section 5(1B) of the Protection from Eviction Act 1977.

Signed:
Landlord or landlord's agent

Name and address of landlord or landlord's agents:

The minimum notice period in such cases is four weeks, but the precise notice period will depend on the rental periods. If the tenancy is monthly, at least one calendar month's notice is required, expiring at the end of a rental period. For example, if the rent is payable on the 15th of the month, at least one month's notice expiring on the 14th of a subsequent month must be given. In practice, a notice specifying the 14th or the 15th of the month will be accepted by the courts. If a different date is specified this will invalidate the notice. However, the notice does contain a fallback provision stating that the tenancy will terminate at an appropriate end of a rental period, should the date specified be later than the date stated in the notice. This fallback provision should be relied upon only as a last resort if the tenant makes an issue about the validity of the notice in relation to the expiry date specified.

(2) **Grounds for possession** In Rent Act cases the landlord must prove a ground for possession. These do not have to be specified in the notice, but they will have to be pleaded in the court action. Some of the grounds are mandatory, others discretionary. Significantly, rent arrears, no matter how large the amount, are always discretionary grounds in Rent Act cases (unlike those under assured and assured shorthold tenancies, where serious arrears are mandatory grounds). All the grounds are set out in Chapter 7.

(3) **Reasonableness** If a discretionary ground is relied upon, the court must be satisfied that it is reasonable to grant an order for possession. In rent arrears cases it is normal for the order to be suspended, in that it will usually provide that if the tenant pays the current rent and also a specified amount of the arrears with each subsequent rental payment the order will not be implemented.

Possession actions for ordinary assured tenancies or shortholds before the tenancy has expired

Normally the landlord will have to commence an ordinary possession action as described below, but the quicker 'accelerated possession action' can be used as an alternative if grounds 1, 3, 4 or 5 are relied upon. In this event, a slightly different application form is needed (available from the local county court).

An ordinary possession action, on the other hand, takes time and usually involves a court hearing, even if the tenant has no defence. It is started by issuing a 'Claim form for possession of property' (see overleaf) supported by a 'Particulars of claim (rented residential premises)' form (both forms are available from the court or can be downloaded from the Court Service website*).

The forms must be filled in and filed at the local county court for the area where the property is situated. A copy for each tenant must also be filed, along with the court fee.

The court will then serve the Claim form and Particulars of claim and fix a date for a hearing, which will be notified to both parties. The tenant may file a defence or a reply if he disputes the landlord's claim for possession. Rent arrears may also be claimed in this type of action.

The matter will be listed before either a district judge or a circuit judge, who will hear both parties give evidence. The judge must be satisfied that the landlord has made his case, that the tenant has no defence and, if the landlord is relying upon a discretionary ground for possession, that it is reasonable to make a possession order.

The detailed procedural rules are contained in Part 55 of the Civil Procedure Rules.

Claim for possession: form N5

Claim form for possession of property

In the

Claim No.

Claimant
(name(s) and address(es))

SEAL

Defendant(s)
(name(s) and address(es))

The claimant is claiming possession of :

which (includes) (does not include) residential property. Full particulars of the claim are attached.
(The claimant is also making a claim for money).

This claim will be heard on: 20   at   am/pm

at

At the hearing
• The court will consider whether or not you must leave the property and, if so, when.
• It will take into account information the claimant provides and any you provide.

What you should do
• Get help and advice immediately from a solicitor or an advice agency.
• Help yourself and the court by **filling in the defence form** and **coming to the hearing** to make sure the court knows all the facts.

Defendant's name and address for service

Court fee	£
Solicitor's costs	£
Total amount	£

Issue date	

N5 Claim form for possession of property (10.01)

Printed on behalf of The Court Service

	Claim No.	

Grounds for possession

The claim for possession is made on the following ground(s):

☐ rent arrears

☐ other breach of tenancy

☐ forfeiture of the lease

☐ mortgage arrears

☐ other breach of the mortgage

☐ trespass

☐ other *(please specify)* _____

Anti-social behaviour

The claimant is alleging:

☐ actual or threatened assault

☐ actual or threatened serious damage to the property

See full details in the attached particulars of claim

Does, or will, the claim include any issues under the Human Rights Act 1998? ☐ Yes ☐ No

Statement of Truth

*(I believe)(The claimant believes) that the facts stated in this claim form are true.
* I am duly authorised by the claimant to sign this statement.

signed _____ date _____

*(Claimant)(Litigation friend *(where the claimant is a child or a patient)*)(Claimant's solicitor)
delete as appropriate

Full name _____

Name of claimant's solicitor's firm _____

position or office held _____
(if signing on behalf of firm or company)

Claimant's or claimant's solicitor's address to which documents or payments should be sent if different from overleaf.

Postcode

	if applicable
Ref. no.	
fax no.	
DX no.	
e-mail	
Tel. no.	

Particulars of claim for possession

(rented residential premises)

In the

Claim No.

Claimant

Defendant

1. The claimant has a right to possession of:

2. To the best of the claimant's knowledge the following persons are in possession of the property:

About the tenancy

3. (a) The premises are let to the defendant(s) under a(n) tenancy which began on

   (b) The current rent is £   and is payable each (week) (fortnight) (month). (*other*   )

   (c) Any unpaid rent or charge for use and occupation should be calculated at £   per day.

4. The reason the claimant is asking for possession is:

   (a) because the defendant has not paid the rent due under the terms of the tenancy agreement.
(Details are set out below) (Details are shown on the attached rent statement)

   (b) because the defendant has failed to comply with other terms of the tenancy.
Details are set out below.

   (c) because: (including any (other) statutory grounds)

N119 Particulars of claim for possession (rented residential premises) (10.01)   *Printed on behalf of The Court Service*

188

5. The following steps have already been taken to recover any arrears:

6. The appropriate (notice to quit) (notice of breach of lease) (notice seeking possession) (*other*   ) was served on the defendant on
                   20   .

About the defendant

7. The following information is known about the defendant's circumstances:

About the claimant

8. The claimant is asking the court to take the following financial or other information into account when making its decision whether or not to grant an order for possession:

Forfeiture

9. (a)   There is no underlessee or mortgagee entitled to claim relief against forfeiture.

or (b)   of

is entitled to claim relief against forfeiture as underlessee or mortgagee.

What the court is being asked to do:

10. The claimant asks the court to order that the defendant(s):

   (a) give the claimant possession of the premises;
   (b) pay the unpaid rent and any charge for use and occupation up to the date an order is made;
   (c) pay rent and any charge for use and occupation from the date of the order until the claimant recovers possession of the property;
   (d) pay the claimant's costs of making this claim.

Statement of Truth

★(I believe) (The claimant believes) that the facts stated in these particulars of claim are true.
★I am duly authorised by the claimant to sign this statement.

signed ——————————————— date ————————
★(Claimant) (Litigation friend *(where claimant is a child or a patient)* (Claimant's solicitor)
★delete as appropriate

Full name ————————————————————————

Name of claimant's solicitor's firm ————————————————

position or office held ————————————————————
                    (if signing on behalf of firm or company)

Public-sector tenancies

If the landlord is a local authority, the Housing Act 1985 will apply, but if the landlord is a housing association and the tenancy was granted on or after 15 January 1989 the rules relating to assured and assured shorthold tenancies will normally apply. Hence, the following is confined to council houses and flats.

(1) **Ending the tenancy** The local authority or other public-sector landlord must serve a notice seeking possession, in a prescribed form. At least four weeks' notice of intention to commence proceedings must be given. The actual notice period will depend on when the rent is payable: if it is payable monthly, at least one calendar month's notice is required. Once the notice has been given it remains valid for 12 months, so the landlord can start proceedings at any point within that time.

(2) **Grounds for possession** The landlord will need to prove a ground for possession (unless it is an 'introductory tenancy'). The grounds are set out in Chapter 10 and the appropriate one(s) will be specified in the termination notice.

(3) **Reasonableness** If a discretionary ground is relied upon, such as rent arrears, the court must be satisfied that it is reasonable to grant possession. Again, the court may, and frequently does, suspend the order for possession on condition that the tenant pays the current rent and part of the arrears with each subsequent rental payment.

Other tenancies

Some tenancies are not covered by the above rules and tenants enjoy no security of tenure. Examples include cases where the landlord is resident (see page 32). Even in these cases the landlord will need to show that the tenancy has come to an end or the licence to occupy has been terminated.

For a possession order to be made, an ordinary possession action in the local county court will need to be started, with a hearing before a judge.

(1) **Ending the tenancy** If the tenancy or licence was granted for a fixed term and this expires, no notice to quit is strictly required. Possession proceedings could be started immediately after the fixed term expires. If it is periodic, however, the landlord must give 'reasonable notice'. The agreement itself may specify the notice period, in which case the express terms of the agreement must be complied with. If no express terms apply, the landlord must give 'reasonable notice'. The period of four weeks which applies to most residential occupiers is a guideline as to what is

reasonable and the landlord should always regard this as the minimum period, to be on the safe side.

(2) **Grounds for possession** In these cases no ground for possession is required. The tenants have no security of tenure and the court has no discretion. Once the fixed term or, if the tenancy is periodic, reasonable notice to quit or terminate has expired, the landlord can start proceedings for possession.

(3) **Reasonableness** The landlord does not have to show that it is reasonable to grant possession, and the court has no discretion is such cases.

The hearing of a possession action

The landlord should attend the hearing, which will normally be before the district judge. The landlord will need to give evidence and produce the tenancy agreement and a copy of the notice to quit or other appropriate termination notice, together with proof of service if the papers were served otherwise than by the court itself. The tenant is entitled to attend and make representations. If it is a case where the landlord is relying upon a discretionary ground for possession, the judge must also be satisfied that it is reasonable to make an order for possession.

The possession order

If the judge is satisfied that the landlord is entitled to a possession order he will order that the tenant yields possession within a specified period, usually 28 days. If, however, the landlord is relying upon a discretionary ground for possession the court may suspend the order, which means that if the tenant complies with the obligations set out in the order (such as paying off rent arrears by instalments) the giving of possession is held in abeyance. Only if the tenant defaults can the landlord go back to the court to make the suspended order absolute and, even then, the court can review the matter and suspend it yet again if it feels this is appropriate.

If the landlord is relying upon a mandatory ground (such as serious rent arrears under an assured or assured shorthold tenancy) the court should order possession within 14 days and generally has no discretion about awarding possession.

The different types of order are outlined below.

Absolute order for possession

This means that the tenant must leave the property on the date specified in the order. An absolute order will be appropriate where the landlord proves a mandatory ground for possession. For example, if the tenancy is an assured shorthold and the landlord has served the appropriate notices, the court has no choice but to make an order for possession requiring the tenant to vacate 14 days after the date of the hearing. The only discretion the court has in this case is to postpone the date for giving of possession for up to 42 days, but only if the tenant will suffer exceptional hardship. The onus is on the tenant to prove this. At the end of the stated period the tenant must vacate. Twenty-eight days is the normal discretionary period allowed by the court in possession cases.

An absolute order for possession would also be appropriate in the case of an ordinary assured tenancy (not a shorthold) when the landlord has served the requisite notice – for example, basing possession on ground 1: owner-occupier (see pages 45–6). In cases where the tenant has no statutory protection under the Rent Acts or the Housing Acts (for example, where there is a resident landlord) the court again must make an absolute order for possession.

Suspended order for possession

If the landlord proves a discretionary ground, the court may make an order for possession but suspend the operation of the order if certain conditions are satisfied. Suspended orders are frequently used in rent arrears cases. Very often the court will make an order for possession which provides that if the tenant pays the current rent plus a certain amount of arrears each week or month, the order will be suspended and the tenant cannot be evicted. However, if he breaches the terms of the order the landlord may apply again to the court for the order to be made absolute or for an immediate warrant for possession to be issued, depending on the circumstances.

Adjournment

In cases where the landlord is relying upon discretionary, not mandatory, grounds for possession the court need not make an order for possession at all. It may simply adjourn the proceedings, either to a later date or indefinitely, subject to certain terms and conditions. An adjournment may be appropriate if the tenant's conduct does not constitute a serious breach of the tenancy agreement, such as in a case based on rent arrears. The court could, in the first instance, adjourn the case on condition that the tenant pays the current rent plus a certain amount of arrears each week or month. This is rather like a suspended order for possession, the difference being that no order for possession has in fact been made, which means that the landlord would have to re-apply to the court for a possession order if the tenant did not adhere to the terms. On the second occasion the court may make either a suspended order for possession or an absolute order for possession depending on the seriousness of the case and the tenant's circumstances.

Order against the landlord

If the landlord fails to make out a claim for possession (say, by failing to serve the appropriate notices or serving defective ones) the landlord's proceedings may be dismissed. If this happens, the tenant can apply for an order for costs against the landlord (see below). If the tenant has made a counterclaim against the landlord (perhaps for breach of the landlord's repairing obligations, see Chapter 12) and succeeds with his claim, an order for damages may be awarded against the landlord.

Legal costs incurred in possession proceedings

Responsibility for the legal costs incurred in possession proceedings is always a matter for the court's discretion. If a possession order is made against the tenant, the tenant may be ordered to pay some or all of the landlord's legal costs in bringing the proceedings. On the other hand, if the landlord fails and the tenant has incurred legal costs there may be an order for costs against the landlord. The successful party at the hearing will normally make an application for costs as appropriate.

Enforcement of possession orders

If the tenant fails to vacate in accordance with the court order, the landlord cannot simply walk back in. The order can be enforced only by the court bailiff. To achieve this, the landlord must apply for a 'warrant for possession'. The bailiff will then arrange to carry out the eviction.

Q *I let my flat to a tenant under an assured shorthold tenancy which has now expired. The tenant shows no sign of leaving voluntarily. How can I obtain possession?*

A If you have not already done so, you should serve a notice on the tenant under Section 21 of the Housing Act 1988, allowing at least two months' notice before the date specified for possession, which must be the last day of a rental period. If you served the notice before the expiry of the tenancy, you must make sure that the notice period has expired before you start court proceedings.

Assuming that the tenant does not leave by the due date, you may start either an ordinary possession action (in which case there will be a court hearing which you must attend to prove your case), or an accelerated possession action which will not require a hearing. You may not use the accelerated procedure if you are also claiming rent arrears.

Q *I let my house under an assured tenancy on a monthly basis. The tenant has not paid any rent for two months. How can I get possession?*

A You must first serve a notice on the tenant in the prescribed form under Section 8 of the Housing Act 1988, specifying the grounds upon which you are claiming possession. In your case, these will be grounds 8, 10 and 11. You must attach to the notice full details of the grounds and the rent arrears and then allow two weeks before you start court proceedings.

When the notice expires you must file a county court claim and particulars of claim form (both available from the county court).

If the tenant does not leave voluntarily you must attend court on the hearing date given and prove your case. You will have to provide details of the rent arrears and produce the tenancy agreement. If you prove only grounds 10 or 11 (which are discretionary), you will have to satisfy the court that your request for possession is reasonable. Much will depend on whether or not the tenant opposes your application.

Q *I am a resident landlord letting a bedsitter in my home to a student. I am not happy with the tenant and want him to leave. Do I need a court order?*

A Strictly speaking, you do not need a court order as this is an excluded tenancy. However, the safest option is to start possession proceedings in the county court. You must first give your tenant 'reasonable notice' of the termination of the arrangement (four weeks, say, although the period is not laid down in law), and if he remains after that time you should start court proceedings immediately. As long as you can prove that you have been a resident landlord throughout the tenancy and that you followed the correct procedure to terminate the agreement, you have a right to possession. The court cannot exercise discretion in this matter.

Chapter 15

Defending possession proceedings

If you are a tenant facing possession proceedings, eviction is not inevitable. You should seek legal advice as soon as possible. The landlord will normally require a court order to evict – he cannot just change the locks and walk back in. Moreover, if you are threatened with unlawful eviction or the landlord tries to harass you into leaving, there are many ways in which you can prevent this happening (see Chapter 13). Most local authorities have a department to help tenants faced with situations of this sort. Help is also available from Citizens Advice Bureaux, Housing Advice Centres, law centres or from local lawyers who hold free law clinics or free initial interviews to deal with cases of this sort. You may also qualify for legal aid (public funding). If the case has already progressed to court, a duty solicitor may be available to advise you, or represent you at the hearing.

The following factors should also be taken into account:

- **court order** The landlord cannot normally evict a tenant without one. If he does, or tries to do so, he will probably be committing a criminal offence, in which case the tenant can seek a court injunction to prevent him from breaking the law. In certain cases (for example, where the landlord is resident: see pages 32–4), the landlord may not strictly need a court order for eviction, but even in this situation he must not use any violence to evict the occupier: if he does, he commits a criminal offence. Therefore, if you make it clear that you cannot or will not be able to leave when the landlord gives you notice to quit, he must get a court order
- **technicalities and evidence** The landlord cannot get a possession order without showing to the court that he is entitled to it.

Where appropriate, the landlord must show that he has given the correct notices and followed the correct procedure. Very often landlords make procedural or technical mistakes. If the tenant or his adviser spots any such mistakes, they may well lead to the case being dismissed or adjourned

- **security of tenure** If you have a fully assured tenancy (see page 40), a protected tenancy (see page 91) or a secure tenancy (see page 120) you will normally have security of tenure, which means that the landlord has to show that he has grounds for possession laid down by law. If the landlord cannot prove such a ground, or if the ground is proven but is discretionary, the tenant can argue that the landlord is not entitled to possession or that it is unreasonable for a possession order to be made

- **counter-claim** If the landlord has not fully complied with his side of the tenancy agreement – for example, by not repairing the property when the law says he must – this can form the basis of a counter-claim by the tenant for compensation

- **the right to be heard or to make representations** The tenant has the right to reply to a possession summons by returning the court form completed within 14 days of receipt of the claim form – even if the tenancy is an assured shorthold and the landlord has opted for the accelerated possession procedure (see page 174). At any hearing the tenant has the right to be present in person with or without a lawyer to argue his case.

Checking the termination notice

The landlord must normally serve an appropriate notice, requiring the tenant to quit the premises, informing the tenant that the landlord requires possession on or after a certain date, or warning the tenant that possession proceedings are about to commence. The precise notice will depend on the type of tenancy.

- **assured shorthold tenants** Such tenants should be served with a notice requiring possession under Section 21 of the Housing Act 1988. This must be of at least two months' duration and the court cannot order possession until the tenancy has lasted for at least six months or, if the tenancy is for longer than six months, until the date when the fixed term expires. Hence, if the landlord has not given the correct notice or the date for termination is too early, the notice is invalid. Further, if the tenancy is periodic, the date specified must be the last day of a rental period; if it is not, again the notice is invalid – so check both the form of notice and the termination date specified.

- **assured tenancies or shortholds not yet expired or of less than six months' duration** Where these apply, the landlord must serve a notice under Section 8 of the Housing Act 1988. It must be in the prescribed form, stating the ground or grounds upon which the landlord relies and, if based on rent arrears, must give details of the arrears. Any inaccuracies may form the basis of a defence.
- **Rent Act tenancies** The landlord must serve a notice to quit/determine.

Filing a defence or counter-claim

The tenant has 14 days in which to respond to a termination notice; the forms to fill in and return will be sent with the summons. Always complete these, even if you feel you have no defence. It may help you gain time, either by extension of the possession date and/or extra time to pay rent arrears if these are being claimed.

It is always worth considering taking legal advice. Often, landlords have not complied with formalities. For example, the notices that the landlord is required to give may have incorrect dates in them or may have not been served properly. Having these points checked out before conceding the landlord's case could help a good deal. In any event, the court may well have some discretion as to whether or not to grant possession, particularly in cases that are not assured shorthold tenancies.

Chapter 16

Finance and tax

Buying a house or a flat to rent out as an investment for the future requires careful consideration. The choice of property, its suitability for letting and the likely amount of income and expenditure need checking out, preferably with a surveyor, valuer or reputable letting agent, and meanwhile arrangements for paying for the property will need to be put in hand. This chapter looks at ways of managing the capital cost of acquisition and the tax consequences of letting.

'Buy-to-let' mortgages

For prospective landlords seeking mortgage finance to buy a property to let there are now many 'buy-to-let' mortgage schemes on the market and it is well worth shopping around for the best deal.

Many mortgage lenders will want to ensure that the rental income will be at least be 125 per cent of the mortgage repayments so that the projected rental income will cover not only the monthly repayments but also provide enough extra to cover running costs and void periods between the end of one tenancy and the grant of another. Some insist that the property is professionally managed.

The maximum amount that can be borrowed per property also varies from lender to lender. Some will not lend more than 75 per cent of the value of the property, but others may be prepared to lend up to 85 per cent of the valuation.

Interest rates vary too, but most lenders in this type of scheme charge lower interest rates than would be levied for commercial purposes and most charge only a little more than they would if the money were being borrowed to purchase the property as a main residence. The repayment period can, in many cases, be up to 25 years or even longer depending on the choice of repayment and plan.

Typical deals usually have the following sorts of conditions attached:

- rental income must cover at least 125 per cent of monthly mortgage repayments based on the lender's standard rates of interest
- the basis of the letting must be an assured shorthold tenancy *or* to a company *or* a holiday let
- the letting agent must provide written confirmation of the anticipated rental income
- the borrower's earned income must be at a specified minimum level in relation to the amount borrowed
- a minimum valuation will apply: for example, some lenders will not lend on properties below the value of £40,000; there is usually also a ceiling on the amount that can be borrowed.
- a choice of repayment methods is likely to be available: for example, capital and interest repayment, interest-only linked to an ISA or pension fund, and so on
- a first legal charge (mortgage) will be made on the property as security for the loan.

These conditions are just examples. It makes sense to seek advice from an independent financial adviser before signing up for a loan to ensure that you are opting for the most appropriate deal.

Rentals and tax

All forms of income are liable to income tax, and the profit a landlord makes is no exception. In addition, if the rental property is sold, a capital profit may be subject to capital gains tax. These basic principles may be modified if the property is the landlord's own home (or a room within it) or is a furnished holiday let.

Income tax on rents

The profit a landlord makes in each tax year (running from 6 April to the following 5 April) from his rental business is assessed under the provisions of Schedule A of the Income and Corporation Taxes Act 1988. Note that:

- it is only the *profit* after deducting allowable expenses (see opposite) which is taxed
- as the Inland Revenue requires the landlord to calculate his profit for each tax year, it makes sense to keep records for tax years rather than calendar years, and thus avoid having to apportion figures
- all rental activities are aggregated (for example, the income and costs from letting Bleak House furnished, and 17 Jarndyce Terrace and 6 Dickens Street unfurnished) and treated as if they constituted a single business. The analogy with a trading business assessable under Schedule D is not taken any further: hence, for example, pension contributions cannot be set against rental profits; neither are the rental properties eligible for inheritance tax business property relief. Schedule A income, though unearned, is subject to the normal rates of income tax and not those applying to investments.

Calculating profit

Strictly, the legislation demands that 'rental profit' be calculated on an *earnings* basis. In accountancy terms this means recognising both receipts and payments when they fall due, rather than when they are actually made.

Therefore, a rent payable in advance on the normal quarter days should be recorded as received on 25 March regardless of when (or even whether) the tenant actually paid it. Twelve days' worth (25 March to 5 April) would fall into the first tax year, and the balance (from 6 April) would fall into the second. Similarly, a builder's invoice dated 20 April 2001 for repairs done in March 2001 and paid on 30 May 2001 should be recorded as an expense for the tax year to 5 April 2001, the year to which the work related. The expense of an annual insurance premium of £1,200 paid on 30 December 2001 for the year from 1 January 2002 would also be apportioned between the relevant tax years, on a daily basis.

To simplify matters, the Inland Revenue will, by concession, accept a straightforward 'cash' basis of accounting. If this is adopted, income is recognised only when it is received. The whole insurance premium for the calendar year 2002 would be deducted as an expense of the tax year 2001–2, and record-keeping simplified by recording the builder's invoice as an expense for tax year 2001–2 when it is paid on 30 May 2001. The Revenue insists that all the following conditions are fulfilled before the cash basis can be used:

- total gross receipts of the rental business do not exceed £15,000
- rents are received weekly or monthly
- expenses are paid promptly
- the cash basis is used consistently, and
- the result is not substantially different from the earnings basis.

Income

Income tax, as a judge once famously declared, 'is a tax on income'. This aphorism reflects the fact that it is only income (as against capital) profit which is dealt with under Schedule A; similarly, expenditure of a capital nature is not deductible. All forms of rent are Schedule A income, whether from furnished or unfurnished lettings. So too are any separate charges made to tenants for the hiring of furniture, or service charges to meet the landlord's responsibility for the upkeep of common parts of the building.

Receipts under an insurance policy covering non-payment of rent are assessable as part of the Schedule A business. 'Key money' might also be caught by these rules, but a straight deposit which is refundable if the property is vacated in good order is not. At the end of the lease the amount of any deposit which the landlord retains is treated as a normal income receipt, to offset the cost of repairs claimed as expenses.

There are special rules designed to bring a premium, a capital sum charged for the grant of a lease, into the scope of Schedule A.

On the other hand, charges a landlord makes for additional services such as meals or laundry, beyond those normally provided by a landlord, may be treated as a separate trading enterprise and taxable under Schedule D Case I. If the landlord charges interest on rent paid late, the interest received is assessed separately from the Schedule A receipts, under Schedule D Case III.

Deductible expenses: general principles

Whether an expense is an allowable deduction from income, thus reducing taxable profit, is determined by answering two questions. First, is the expense of income? Second, was it incurred (in the words of statute) 'wholly and exclusively' for the purposes of the rental business?

The first question rules out capital expenditure. The initial cost of buying the investment property is clearly a capital outlay, but what about renovations? When do running repairs become capital improvements? Although each case depends on its own facts the position is broadly as follows. If the property is in a lettable state when acquired (even at a reduced rent) then redecoration costs are allowed against rents received. If however, a dilapidated property is bought cheaply and needs substantial work done before it can be let, the cost of improvement is a capital matter, and not allowed against rents.

Sometimes the improvement is so incidental to the repair, particularly where modern materials are used to replace traditional ones, that the whole cost is allowed as a current expense – for example, replacing cast-iron guttering with plastic, or wooden window frames with single-glazed PVC windows. Even where there is an element of improvement, such as wooden window frames being replaced by double-glazed PVC units, by concession the Revenue allows a part deduction equivalent to the estimated cost of the notional repair; here the figure would be the cost of installing single-glazed PVC window frames.

The second requirement, that the expenditure be incurred 'wholly and exclusively' for the purposes of the rental business, rules out any element of personal use or benefit. A landlord cannot charge against his Schedule A income wallpaper and paint used to decorate his own home. Less obviously, the landlord is not permitted to make a charge for the time he spends collecting rents or managing properties: his recompense is the profit from his Schedule A rental business. Reasonable wages paid to members of his family for work actually performed (and recorded) will be allowable.

Travelling expenses

Travelling expenses incurred when checking the current state of properties or collecting rents are allowable deductions. If a car is used partly for business and partly for private use, it is possible to work out the proportion of the running costs attributable to the business use. (The initial cost of the car purchase is not allowable.)

As an alterative to the meticulous record-keeping needed to keep track of such travelling expenses, a simpler method that may be used if the rental income is less than the VAT threshold, currently £54,000, is to use the Inland Revenue Authorised Mileage Rate (AMR) and apply it to the recorded mileage. For the tax year 2001–2 the rates depend upon the car's capacity, and whether the mileage is for the first 4,000 miles or the excess, which attracts a lower rate:

up to 1,500 cc	40p	(25p)
1,501–2,000 cc	45p	(25p)
over 2,000 cc	63p	(36p)

For the tax year 2002–3 and subsequently, a single rate (regardless of engine capacity) will apply:

for the first 10,000 miles	40p per mile
for each additional mile	25p per mile

The AMR rates do not include interest payable on a loan to buy the vehicle; the proportion of such interest attributable to business usage may be claimed as a separate Schedule A expense. As the rates include an allowance for capital depreciation, adopting them saves the necessity of calculating the part of the capital cost of the vehicle attributable to the business which might otherwise be eligible for a capital allowance.

Interest payments

Interest paid on any loan taken out to buy an investment property (or to improve or repair it or buy furniture) is allowed as an expense against rental profits under normal principles. Interest on an overdraft taken out to fund the rental business is equally allowable; however, care should be taken to ensure that the overdraft does not finance any private expenditure, including personal withdrawals.

Usual expenses

Subject to the general principles outlined above the following revenue expenses will normally be deductible in computing the profits of the rental business: council tax, water rates, insurance premiums (property and non-payment of rent), repairs, advertising for tenants, legal costs (unless for a first letting of more than one year), finance costs, interest payments and travelling expenses.

If profits are computed on the earnings basis so that rent is counted as income when due, if it turns out to be irrecoverable the bad debt can then be treated as an expense. On the other hand, if the cash basis is adopted, non-payment by a tenant simply means that there is no income to be recorded.

Capital allowances

Only current (or income) expenditure can be claimed as a Schedule A expense (see page 203). However, a capital allowance may allow some of the capital cost of machinery and plant used in the letting business to be set against income profit. Assets used in residential accommodation (central heating boilers, cookers, refrigerators, and so on) are ineligible. But the cost of tools to effect repairs (including ladders), computers and other equipment used in the business is eligible. Vehicles are too, but are subject to detailed rules and conditions.

For 'small' businesses with a turnover below £11.2m and assets below £5.6m, 40 per cent of the cost of machinery and plant acquired after 2 July 1998 can be deducted from income in the year of acquisition. In later years, the reducing balance of expenditure attracts a 25 per cent writing-down allowance.

EXAMPLE

In June 2001 Andy buys for £2,000 an industrial cleaning machine for use in his rental business.

He can deduct £2,000 × 40% = £800 from his rental profits for 2001–2; in 2002–3 his writing-down allowance will be £1,200 × 25% = £300. By 2003–4 the £2,000 cost of the asset has been written down by £800 + £300 to £900; the writing-down allowance will be £900 × 25% = £225.

Furnished lettings

A furnished let entails the added cost of providing furniture and furnishings. In principle, such outlay should be regarded as capital expenditure, and is therefore not subject to relief as an expense against the rental income. Neither are capital allowances available for the furnishings used in residential accommodation. However, the Inland Revenue allows the landlord a choice. He may deduct from income a wear-and-tear allowance of 10 per cent of the rent net of council tax and any similar charges which would normally be borne by the tenant. This flat-rate allowance has the attraction of simplicity. Alternatively, the landlord may deduct the full cost of renewing individual items such as beds and carpets, as and when the expenditure is incurred.

Note that the original outlay is not allowable – only the subsequent cost of replacing damaged or worn out furniture and furnishings. Whichever method is adopted it must be used consistently; a landlord is not permitted to change to a more favourable basis from year to year.

Rent-a-room relief

This scheme provides a simplified method for taxing the profit obtained from letting a furnished room (or rooms) in the landlord's own home to a lodger. If the annual gross receipts are not more than £4,250 (a figure which may gradually increase in future years), the income is wholly exempt. If it is greater, the taxpayer has the option to have the excess income (ignoring any expenses) taxed as Schedule A rental profit; if he does not exercise the option he will be taxed in the normal way on the profit from his gross receipts less deductible expenses.

Providing services such as meals or laundry may be regarded as a separate trading activity (see page 203).

Furnished holiday lettings

Although the profits from furnished holiday lets are assessed under normal Schedule A principles, any losses are classed as true trading losses attracting more generous reliefs; in addition, for capital gains tax purposes, business reliefs apply.

Broadly, to attract this treatment the property must be:

- available for holiday lets for at least 140 days a year
- actually let for at least 70 days, and
- not occupied by the same person for over 31 days in any seven months.

The final condition prevents student lets from qualifying.

Losses

If the expenses and capital allowances for any year exceed the income, the landlord has sustained a Schedule A loss. This cannot be set against other forms of income to obtain immediate relief; the only option is to carry the loss forward and set it against Schedule A profits of future years, as and when they arise.

Capital gains tax

Whilst the rental profit is subject to income tax, the ultimate capital profit generated when the investment property is sold for more than it cost will normally attract capital gains tax (CGT). Such property would be unlikely to attract the exemption attributable to a taxpayer's principal private residence. Any expenditure on capital improvements (which would not have attracted relief as an income expense – for example, the additional cost of double-glazing) is deductible, as are any professional charges incurred on the purchase and sale.

The taxable gain is subject to two further reductions:

(1) by increasing the cost of acquisition and subsequent improvements in line with the Retail Prices Index up to April 1998, an indexation allowance strips out the inflationary element of the gain

(2) for each complete year of ownership after 6 April 1998 (and with a 'bonus' year added for property owned on 17 March 1998), the indexed gain is tapered, so that less is ultimately taxed. There is no taper for the first two years, but for the third and each subsequent complete year of ownership to a maximum of ten years, the taxable gain is discounted by 5 per cent. This, the less favourable rate of taper for non-business assets, applies to let residential property. Having applied the deductions for indexation and taper, each tax year a taxpayer is entitled to an annual exemption against any outstanding gains, £7,500 for 2001–2.

EXAMPLE

Jayne bought 49 Sebastopol Terrace in October 1995 for £80,000 and incurred survey and legal charges of £3,440. She spent £12,000 on upgrading the property in January 1996 and then let it. In June 2001 Jayne sells the property for £120,000 and pays estate agent and legal costs of £3,000. The RPI rose by 8 per cent between October 1995 and April 1998, and by 7 per cent between January 1996 and April 1998.

			£
Sale price			121,000
less:	professional charges		3,440
Net proceeds of sale			117,560
less:	acquisition cost	80,000	
	acquisition expenses	4,000	
	improvements	12,000	96,000
Unindexed gain			21,560
less:	indexation allowance		
	£84,000 × 8% =	6,720	
	£12,000 × 7% =	840	6,560
Indexed gain			15,000

Tapered (and taxable) gain [3 complete years, 6 April 1998–5 April 2001 + 1 'bonus' year = 4 'relevant' years; ignoring first 2, indexed gain can be discounted by 10%]

			£
£15,000 × 90% =			13,500
less:	annual exemption*		7,500
	Chargeable gain		6,000

*assuming no other gains in year

The final chargeable gain is added to the top slice of the taxpayer's taxable income. To the extent that it falls within the taxpayer's starting or basic rate bands it is subject to a 10 per cent or 20 per cent CGT charge, and to the extent it exceeds them it attracts CGT at 40 per cent.

Letting landlord's own home

The income tax and CGT principles discussed above are modified slightly when a landlord lets his own home, possibly while he is working in another part of the country or abroad.

Income tax

What constitutes income or expenditure is unchanged; the exception lies in the tax treatment of interest payments on the mortgage. The full amount of interest paid can now be set against the Schedule A rental income.

If the landlord lets out part of the house and occupies the rest the Inland Revenue, by concession, allows the interest to be apportioned (usually on the basis of the number of rooms occupied by landlord and tenant respectively) and the interest attributable to the let part will be deductible from rents received. Further apportionments may be necessary if the arrangements alter during the course of the year.

Capital gains tax

The gain realised on the sale of one's own home is normally exempt. The gain realised on the sale of an investment property is taxable. Those distinctions become blurred when, for example, the property is let while the owner works away from home for a few years.

Certain periods of absence do not jeopardise the exemption, provided the taxpayer occupied the house as his main residence both before and after the absence; these allowable periods are cumulative and include:

- any time working abroad
- up to four years in total working elsewhere in the UK
- absences for any reason totalling three years.

In addition, the final three years of ownership are ignored when calculating the extent of non-occupation.

Even if absences exceed the permitted periods, provided the property has been let any outstanding chargeable gain will be exempt up to the lesser of £40,000 or the amount exempt by virtue of the owner's occupation. Given all these generous relaxations, forced absences are unlikely to jeopardise the owner-occupier's exemption.

EXAMPLE

Lavengro has owned his home for 18 years. The gain, after indexation and taper relief, amounts to £180,000; he has had various periods of occupation and absence:

1 year	at home	exempt –	occupation
2 years	working in UK	exempt –	2 years, any reason
3 years	at home	exempt –	occupation
3 years	working in UK	exempt –	1 year, any reason
			2 years, UK work
2 years	at home	exempt –	occupation

6 years	working in UK	exempt –	2 years, UK work
			2 years chargeable
		exempt –	2 years, part of last
			3 years
1 year	at home	exempt	1 year, part of last
			3 years

Although Lavengro has been out of occupation for 11 years during his 18 years' ownership, provided he did not have another main residence elsewhere, only two of those years of absence are chargeable:

$$£180,000 \times {}^{2}/_{18} = £20,000 \text{ chargeable gain (the rest is exempt).}$$

The chargeable gain is within the £40,000 limit attributable to letting, and is exempt.

Lavengro's entire gain is therefore exempt.

Practicalities

The responsibility of recognising and declaring taxable income lies squarely with the individual, with substantial penalties and ultimately imprisonment facing those who default on their obligations. When starting a rental business, the landlord must inform the Inland Revenue office which handles his affairs no later than 6 October after the end of the relevant tax year.

The Inland Revenue will then issue a self-assessment return (and explanatory notes) requiring the landlord to give details of that Schedule A income. Provided gross receipts are less than £15,000, a simple three-line statement (income less expenses equals profit) is acceptable. If the return is submitted by 30 September (or within two months if issued after 31 July) the Inland Revenue will calculate the amount of tax payable. Otherwise, the taxpayer must both submit his return and calculate (correctly) his own tax by the following 31 January. Once the landlord is 'in' the tax system, each April the Inland Revenue will automatically issue a return for the previous tax year. Instead of all the tax being paid in arrears by a single lump sum on 31 January after the tax year, if over £500 was payable the previous year, for the current year payments on account based on last year's profits will be due on 31 January within and on 31 July after the tax year; the payment on 31 January after the tax year will be for any outstanding balance due or refundable. Failure to pay any tax when due renders the defaulter liable to interest on the outstanding sum, and the possibility of further penalties.

As the Inland Revenue can make random enquiries of any tax-payer, as well as specific investigations where they have suspicions (perhaps through a tip-off from a disgruntled tenant), it is essential for a landlord to protect himself by maintaining accurate records and keeping all receipts, bank statements and invoices for at least six years.

For further information on the tax aspects of letting, the free Inland Revenue booklet IR150, *Taxation of Income from Land*, is available from any Inland Revenue Enquiry Office or from the Inland Revenue website.* It is invaluable.

EXAMPLE

Hector, whose other earnings make him a higher-rate taxpayer, starts renting properties in August 2001 and makes a taxable profit of £10,000 during tax year 2001–2. He should inform his tax office by 6 October 2002 at the latest. He must file his return and pay the 40 per cent tax due by 31 January 2003 Payments on account for 2002–3 of £2,000 are due on 31 January 2003 and 31 July 2003 respectively. His profits for tax year 2002–3 are £15,000, giving an income tax liability at 40 per cent of £6,000. The sum of £4,000 has already been paid on account. The outstanding balance of £2,000 is payable by 31 January 2004.

Chapter 17

Long leases of houses: the right to buy or extend the lease

In certain areas of England and Wales houses were commonly sold on long leases, granting the right to occupy for a fixed period, rather than as freeholds, which grant the right to occupy forever. For houses, leases were often for 99 or even 999 years. Throughout the term of the lease, bought for a lump sum, a comparatively low rent, known as 'ground rent', would be paid. It bears this name because it is paid for the land on which the house stands. Ground rents for older properties might be only a few pounds a year, or a few hundred pounds in the case of more recently granted leases

Leasehold houses are often considered inferior to freehold houses, not only because of the limited term of ownership but also because owners of leasehold houses are more likely to have restrictions placed on them as to what they can and cannot do with their property. For example, building an extension or conservatory would usually require the landlord's permission. And although a 999-year lease might be seen to offer an ample length of occupation, a 99-year lease has a fast-diminishing value, becoming increasingly hard to sell as it approaches its expiry date: the classic case of a depreciating asset.

Commonhold & Leasehold Reform Bill 2001

At the time of writing, the Commonhold & Leasehold Reform Bill was proceeding through Parliament. This Bill will change the rights dealt with in this chapter. The proposed changes are set out in the relevant part of the chapter together with the existing law; before relying on the contents of this chapter, therefore, you should check to see whether the provisions of the Bill have been brought into force.

At the end of a long lease

On the expiry of a long lease, the tenant does not immediately have to leave; he is allowed to remain in occupation as an assured tenant under the Housing Act 1988. Hence, he has security of tenure and the landlord cannot obtain possession unless he can prove one of the usual assured tenancy grounds (see Chapter 3). But there is an extra ground for possession available to the landlord, which is the need for possession in order to redevelop the site, and this is obviously a potential worry for the houseowner.

However, the most immediate repercussion for the houseowner on the ending of the leasehold term will be the issue of rent. In place of the ground rent the tenant has been paying throughout the lease – a rent that was fixed perhaps a century ago at a few pounds a year – the rent would become a normal assured tenancy rent: a full market rent for both the land and the house. This could well amount to several hundred pounds a month.

Buy the freehold or extend the lease?

The Leasehold Reform Act 1967 confers on certain tenants of houses on long leasehold the right to acquire the freehold on their properties, often at a comparatively low cost. This right to buy is sometimes called enfranchisement. Alternatively, tenants can acquire an extended lease at a ground rent.

For these rights to apply various conditions must be fulfilled:

- there must be a house
- the house must be let on a long lease
- the house must be let at a low rent (but see page 216)
- the house must be tenanted by a qualifying tenant.

These criteria require consideration.

House

The Act applies only to houses, not to flats. (Similar rights are available to flat-owners, however: see Chapter 18.) 'House' is defined as any building designed or adapted for living in and reasonably so called, notwithstanding that the building is not structurally detached, or was not or is not solely designed or adapted for living in, or is divided horizontally into flats or maisonettes. In addition to ordinary purpose-built houses, whether detached, semi-detached or terraced, which are obviously designed for living in, the definition can include buildings which were not originally designed for this purpose (for example, barns, warehouses, windmills, stables) but were later converted or adapted for it.

The main problem is deciding whether a house can be 'reasonably so called'. If a windmill has been converted into a dwelling, is this a house 'reasonably so called' within the meaning of the Act? Almost certainly, it is. The definition can, however, cause problems in relation to shops with living accommodation attached and also with properties which have been converted into flats.

For shops with living accommodation attached, the leading authority is a House of Lords case concerning a purpose-built shop with a flat above. Both were included in the lease to the tenant. Although approximately 75 per cent of the property's area comprised the shop and 25 per cent the living accommodation, the House of Lords held that it was reasonable to call the accommodation a house within the 1967 Act, even though it was also reasonable to call it something else as well (in other words, a shop). Hence, it is only in exceptional circumstances that it will not be reasonable to call accommodation converted or adapted for living in a house.

Buildings converted into flats could potentially pose a problem. Many properties which were originally houses, especially large Victorian homes in cities, have been converted into flats. The legislation makes it clear that an individual flat cannot be a house, but the whole building of which the flat is part may nevertheless retain its characteristics as a house. For example, if a house is converted into four self-contained flats by the owner of a long lease of the whole house, who continues to occupy one of the flats while subletting the others, the long leaseholder could be in a position to enfranchise. The building looked at as a whole can still reasonably be called a house, notwithstanding the internal sub-division.

However, if a purpose-built block of flats is let to a tenant who occupies one flat and sublets the rest, the block of flats could not reasonably be called a house: it is a block of flats.

Long lease

The 1967 Act defines a long lease as one granted for a specific term exceeding 21 years. Periodic tenancies, such as one that runs from month to month, are excluded, no matter how long they may have been in existence. Note also that it is the length of the original term that matters. The fact that less than 21 years might remain unexpired when the rights are exercised is not relevant to this issue. Also, it need not be the original tenant who is claiming under the Act; over the years the lease could have been assigned many times.

Further, the fact that the lease may be terminated before it runs 21 years (for example, by forfeiture or break clause) can be ignored. If the long lease has expired but the tenant now has another tenancy of the property, the new tenancy is also usually deemed to be a long lease, although there are exceptions.

Low rent

The general rule is that the rent must not exceed two-thirds of the rateable value on the 'appropriate day'. The detailed rules, within the Act, are complex and depend (*inter alia*) on the date when the tenancy was granted. However, if the tenancy was granted on or after 1 April 1990 'low rent' means £1,000 p.a. or less if the property is in Greater London, £250 p.a. if the property is elsewhere.

In most cases the question of what constitutes a low rent can be safely ignored. The 1967 Act was amended in 1996 so that even if the low-rent test is not satisfied tenants have the right to enfranchise if the lease was originally granted for a 'particularly long term' – that is, for more than 35 years. Hence, if a lease was originally for longer than 35 years, as most will be, the low-rent test will be irrelevant as the tenant already has the right to enfranchise, subject to complying with the other conditions. Again, it is the length of the lease when granted, and not how long remains unexpired, which is relevant.

Note, however, that tenants will not have a right to an extended lease unless they can satisfy the low-rent test. The 'more than 35 years' rule applies only to enfranchisement.

The Commonhold & Leasehold Reform Bill will remove the requirement for a low rent in all cases.

Rateable value limits

Originally, high-value houses with high rateable values were excluded from the Act. These limits have now been removed in respect of enfranchisement, so the value, or rateable value, of the house has no bearing on the right to buy. However, the method of calculating the price to be paid for the freehold differs according to the rateable value of the property (see page 220).

Note also that the rateable value limits were not removed in relation to the right to take an extended lease. The limits are complex, partly because of the replacement of domestic rates with council tax, and depend upon where the house is located and the date upon which the lease was granted. If you wish to take an extended lease and you have a larger-than-average house, you should seek professional advice.

Qualifying tenant

Three years' residence is required for a tenant to qualify for enfranchisement. The Act itself does not use the expression 'qualifying tenant', but it does impose certain requirements which must be satisfied before the tenant qualifies for enfranchisement or an extended lease. The tenant must, at the date when he serves the notice exercising his rights, be occupying the house (or part of it) as his only or main residence and have done so for the last three years or for an aggregate of three years out of the last 10 years. It is the tenant who is seeking to exercise rights under the Act who must satisfy this residence rule; whether previous tenants resided at the property is immaterial.

The occupation need not be exclusively for residential purposes. For example, if the house has been used partly for business purposes, the business use may not disqualify the tenant. Moreover, subletting of part of the property does not disqualify the tenant provided he retains occupation of some other part as his only or main residence for the relevant period.

The Commonhold & Leasehold Reform Bill will remove this residence requirement. However, it will be replaced by a requirement that the tenant should have been the owner of the lease for at least two years prior to exercising the rights under the Act.

Houses held on trust

A beneficiary's occupation of the house under a trust or strict settlement counts as occupation for this purpose even though the legal estate is held by trustees. If the beneficiary is entitled absolutely to the house, he can, after the relevant period, exercise the rights himself.

If he is not absolutely entitled, the trustees/tenant for life can exercise the rights on his behalf.

Death of the occupier

If the tenant dies before exercising rights under the Act and the tenancy passes to a member of his family, the successor can in certain circumstances add his own qualifying period of residence (after the previous tenant's death) to the deceased's qualifying period of residence to make up the three-year minimum. However, this applies only in cases where the tenant dies while occupying the house as his only or main residence and the successor also resided in the house as his only or main residence and is still so resident at the date of the death of the tenant. 'Member of the family' is defined to include spouse, stepchildren, parents or parents-in-law.

The Commonhold & Leasehold Reform Bill will allow the personal representatives of a deceased tenant to enfranchise within six months of obtaining the grant of representation.

Enfranchisement or extended lease?

The tenant who satisfies the above conditions will normally wish to enfranchise. This means that the landlord must convey the freehold to the tenant at a price, and on the terms, referred to in the Act. Alternatively, the tenant may elect to take an extended lease. In this case, the landlord must grant the tenant a new lease for the unexpired residue of the term of the existing lease plus a further 50 years. The new lease will be, broadly, on the same terms as the existing lease and the rent will be the same until the expiry date of the existing lease, but thereafter the rent will be replaced by a ground rent fixed to reflect modern values; this will be reviewed after 25 years of the extra 50 years.

As explained below, the price the tenant pays for the freehold will, for most properties, be very low. It is therefore advisable for the tenant to acquire the freehold if this is at all financially possible; it will be cheaper in the long run than taking an extended lease and having to pay an increased ground rent for the period of the extension. As this is a rent fixed to reflect modern values, it could be several hundred pounds per year.

Although it is possible for a tenant to take an extended lease and then subsequently buy the freehold, at present this is possible only during the unexpired term of the original lease; once the lease has entered the period of the 50-year extension, it is no longer possible to buy the freehold. However, under the Commonhold & Leasehold Reform Bill, it will be possible to buy the freehold even after the commencement of the extension period.

The desire notice

The tenant must serve the landlord written notice (the 'desire notice'), in the prescribed form, of his wish to have either the freehold or an extended lease. This notice, normally the first step in the procedure to obtain the rights granted by the Act, is deemed to be a contract to buy the land. The landlord must within two months serve a 'notice in reply' admitting or objecting to the tenant's claim. (See the Act and the regulations made under it for details of the procedure.) Most landlords will accept as inevitable the fact that they are going to have to sell, and will agree to a sale without the need to follow the procedure laid down by the Act. The main argument will be over the price to be paid (see below).

Transfer of right

Although the desire notice is deemed to create a contract, it is generally personal to the tenant and is not assignable to third parties. However, if the tenant assigns the lease – to a purchaser, for example – he can assign the benefit of the desire notice at the same time to the assignee of the lease. The assignee could then proceed with the acquisition of the freehold or an extended lease even though the assignee does not himself qualify under the Act. This can be very important to a tenant who, perhaps, cannot afford to buy the freehold but finds difficulty in selling his lease due to the short term remaining. The seller can serve the desire notice, assuming he has lived in the house for the necessary three years, and then transfer the benefit of it to the buyer at the same time as he sells the lease to him. The buyer can therefore buy the short residue of the lease and then buy the freehold without having to wait for a further three years.

The price of the freehold

The Act lays down the principles and formulae for ascertaining the price and the appeals machinery if it cannot be agreed between the parties.

There are two methods of ascertaining the price, depending on the rateable value of the house and premises.

The valuation for most properties is very favourable to the tenant. It must be assumed for valuation purposes that the landlord is selling the freehold subject to the lease and on the assumption that this had been extended for a further 50 years under the Act and assuming the tenant is not the purchaser. It is therefore looked at as if the freehold is being bought largely for its investment income. Anyone, other than the tenant, buying the freehold would simply be buying the right to receive the rent until the lease (assumed to be extended by 50 years) comes to an end. That rent is likely to be fairly small – as will be the purchase price. The fact that the tenant can, on acquisition, merge the freehold and leasehold interests, thus acquiring the right to occupy the property forever, is ignored. This 'marriage value', as it is sometimes called, is not taken into account for lower-value properties.

Often, therefore, the tenant will pay a very low price for the freehold, in some cases only about 10 times the amount of the ground rent.

For high-value properties, the basis of valuation is less favourable to the tenant. The increase in value caused by the tenant owning both freehold and leasehold interests has to be taken into account. Also, an assumption has to be made that the tenant has no right to extend the lease. This would again tend to increase the price which the tenant has to pay.

In all cases of intention to enfranchise, it is wise to obtain the advice of a valuer at an early stage; this is particularly important in the case of larger properties likely to be sold for a substantial sum.

In addition to the purchase price the tenant must pay the landlord's reasonable legal and surveyors/valuation fees. In lower-value properties, these often exceed the amount of the purchase price. Disputes over price are dealt with by the Leasehold Valuation Tribunal.

Chapter 18

Long leases of flats: acquiring the freehold or an extension of the lease

When you buy a flat, you normally do not buy the freehold, which gives you the right to occupy the property forever, but instead acquire a long lease which gives the right to occupy for a fixed number of years. There are more than 1 million leasehold flats in England and Wales. But many 'long' leases are for only 99 years, or even less, and when there are fewer than 50 years left to run it can prove difficult to find a buyer. This is because banks and building societies are often reluctant to lend money on such a comparatively short length of lease.

Another common problem with blocks of flats is that disagreements often arise with regard to the maintenance and repair of the block. This is normally in the hands of the landlord or a management company, to which the tenants pay a service charge for repairs and day-to-day maintenance. Tenants often complain that landlords/management companies do not undertake work that needs doing, or that they overcharge for the services, or both.

The Leasehold Reform, Housing and Urban Development Act of 1993 gives flat-owners the right to join together and collectively buy the freehold in their block, which enables them to take over its management. As they collectively own the freehold, they are also able to grant themselves new long leases when their existing leases become unsaleable.

To acquire the freehold in their block, flat-owners must join together: no individual tenant can exercise the right independently of the other occupants of the block. Each tenant will therefore not be acquiring the freehold in his own flat; he will still have only a lease.

If, as a group, you cannot afford to buy the freehold in the block (which could be very expensive), flat-owners have the right to buy a new lease of their individual flats which will add a further period of 90 years to the length of their existing leases. For many people, and particularly where the existing system of management of the block is working satisfactorily, this will be a better option than buying the freehold. It will solve the problem of the lease becoming less attractive to prospective purchasers and, importantly, you can exercise this right on your own regardless of the other flat-owners.

Both the right to buy the freehold ('enfranchisement') and the right to buy a new long lease can be exercised without the landlord's consent, although there are limited grounds on which the landlord can resist a claim to enfranchise (see page 229).

For the right to buy the freehold, the building in which your flat is situated need not be let exclusively to tenants on long leases; some of the flats might, for example, be let on short-term tenancies.

Further, not all of the building need be let exclusively for residential purposes: some parts of the building could be used for business purposes, for example. However, as explained below, if a substantial part of the building is let for non-residential purposes, there will be no right to buy the freehold (although there will still be a right to obtain an extended lease).

The Act did not receive a universal welcome from landlords (the Duke of Westminster famously resigned from the Conservative Party over it). Some landlords may well prove hostile to any claims under the Act and insist that the provisions of the Act are complied with to the letter. Faced with such a landlord, it takes a determined (and patient) group of tenants to succeed in an enfranchisement claim. But remember that the law is on your side: although the landlord can make you jump through all the hoops laid down by the Act, he cannot stop you succeeding, as long as you persevere. Other landlords will adopt a more fatalistic approach and be prepared to agree a sale without strict compliance with all of the Act's conditions.

The conditions which must be met under the Act are somewhat complicated. When it is in force the Commonhold & Leasehold Reform Bill will make it easier for flat-owners to buy the freehold. It may also in some circumstances mean a reduction in the price payable.

Qualifying conditions

Basically, to claim the rights granted under the Act, the tenants and the block of flats itself must 'qualify' and, in the case of enfranchisement, a minimum number of the qualifying tenants must join in the purchase.

It is not necessary, however, for all of the qualifying tenants in a block to join in the purchase of the freehold. The right to enfranchise is exercised by the service of a notice on the landlord by the 'participating qualifying tenants'. To be valid this must be given by at least two-thirds of the qualifying tenants in the block. Furthermore, at least one-half of the participating qualifying tenants must satisfy the 'residence qualification' outlined below.

The Commonhold & Leasehold Reform Bill will abolish the residence requirement in its entirety. It will also abolish the rule that two-thirds of the qualifying tenants must join in the enfranchisement and replace it with a requirement that those seeking to enfranchise must occupy at least half the flats in the block.

Qualifying tenant

This is a tenant of a flat under a long lease at a low rent, all as defined by the Act. If the lease was granted for a 'particularly long term' (see below), it does not matter whether it is at a low rent.

- The tenant, as defined, can be a subtenant: hence, you would still have rights under the Act even if your immediate landlord did not himself own the freehold. This might be the case, for example, where you have a lease from a management company which itself took a lease of the whole block from the owner of the freehold.

  You will not be a qualifying tenant, however, if you occupy the property for the purposes of a business or if your immediate landlord is a charitable housing trust and the flat forms part of the accommodation provided by it for charitable purposes. Also, you will not qualify if you own qualifying leases of more than two flats in the same building.

- You have to be a tenant of a 'flat' – which, as defined by the Act, is a separate set of premises, whether or not on the same floor, constructed or adapted for living in, and either the whole or some material part of it lying above or below some other part of the building of which it forms part. The emphasis in the definition is that at least part of the flat should be above or below another part of the building. Therefore flats above shops are included, as are 'maisonettes': that is, two-storey dwellings, often above shops. Not included are some 'granny flats', i.e. those which are an extension to an existing building but not above or below part of it.

- 'Long lease' in this context means a lease that was originally granted for a term exceeding 21 years. It does not matter if you were not the original tenant, or if there are now fewer than 21 years left to run: you will still qualify.

- The interpretation of 'low rent' under the Act will depend on when it was first granted and will exclude any payments in respect of services, repairs, maintenance or insurance, even if these are stated to be payable as rent. Whether the rent is a low rent is assessed by considering the rent when the lease was first granted: the amount of rent currently being paid is irrelevant in this context.

  (a) *Lease granted before 1 April 1963* The rent must not have exceeded two-thirds of the letting value of the flat on the date of commencement of the lease. The letting value is the rent that a landlord could reasonably have charged had he let the flat on a short-term tenancy without a lump sum being paid, rather than selling it on a long lease.

  (b) *Lease granted on or after 1 April 1963 but before 1 April 1990* or *on or after 1 April 1990 in pursuance of a contract made before that date* The rent must not have exceeded two-thirds of the rateable value of the flat on the commencement of the lease.

  (c) *All other leases, i.e. those granted on or after 1 April 1990* The rent in the initial year must not have exceeded £1,000 if the flat is in Greater London, or £250 if elsewhere.

  These complicated provisions have caused many tenants great difficulties. Take a flat lease granted in the 1930s: it is far from easy for a tenant to establish, some 60 years later, what the letting value of a flat was in, say, 1936.

- 'A particularly long term' in this context means more than 35 years. This qualifying condition was introduced when, in 1996, Parliament realised the error of its ways. Tenants with leases originally granted for such a term have the right to enfranchise whether or not they were initially paying a low rent. The term in question is the length of the lease as originally granted, not how long remains unexpired. This change in the law will have made life much easier for most flat-owners wishing to enfranchise, as outside London, at least, most flat leases will have been originally granted for longer than 35 years.

The Commonhold & Leasehold Reform Bill will abolish the low-rent requirement for all leases.

Residence qualification

The residence qualification differs depending upon whether you are seeking to buy the freehold or to buy a new lease. However, if you own the flat jointly with someone else, only one of you need satisfy the residence rule.

• When you are seeking to buy the freehold, the qualification is that you must have occupied the flat as your only or principal home *either* for the last 12 months *or* for periods amounting to three years in the last 10 years.

  However, even if you do not satisfy this residence qualification, you may still be able to join in a purchase of the freehold. This is because only one-half of the tenants seeking to enfranchise need to have satisfied this residence rule. If you personally have not been resident for long enough, whether you can participate will obviously depend upon how many of the other tenants seeking to buy have satisfied the rule.

• When you wish to buy a new lease you must have occupied the flat as your only or principal home *either* for the last three years *or* for periods amounting to three years in the last 10 years.

This residence requirement means that flats belonging to limited companies will never be able to take advantage of the extension provisions. A company cannot occupy premises as its home, even if one of the directors is occupying the flat as his home. The requirement also excludes 'holiday' or second homes: the flat has to be the only or principal home. Foreign residents, whose principal home is abroad but who have a home in London, for example, will also be excluded. As mentioned above, in the case of an enfranchisement such tenants might still be able to join in if there are enough other tenants who satisfy the resident rule: for enfranchisement, only half of those joining in need to satisfy it.

The Commonhold & Leasehold Reform Bill will abolish the residence requirement for tenants wishing to buy the freehold and those wishing to take an extension. However, in the case of the latter, the requirement will be replaced by a rule that the tenant must have been the owner of the lease for at least two years.

Qualification of building in which flat is situated

Once you are a qualifying tenant and have satisfied the residence test, you will have the right to a new lease. The nature or type of building in which your flat is situated is irrelevant. It might be in a purpose-built block with lots of others, or it might be the only flat in a building otherwise used for non-residential purposes – for example, a flat over a shop. However, in order to be able to acquire the freehold, your flat must be situated in 'premises', as defined by the Act. They must:

- consist either of a self-contained building or a self-contained part of a building *and*
- contain two or more flats held by qualifying tenants *and*
- the number of flats held by qualifying tenants must not be less than two-thirds of the total number of flats in the premises.

Hence, even very small blocks of flats come within the legislation and the requirement that not less than two-thirds of the flats in the block must be held by qualifying tenants means that not all the flats in the block need be so held. In many blocks of flats, particularly in the London area, there will be a mixture of long leases and short leases. These blocks can still be enfranchised, subject to the two-thirds rule. Remember, though, that even if your flat is not within premises as defined for the purposes of enfranchisement, you will still be able to acquire a new lease for a further 90 years.

A building is a self-contained building if it is structurally detached.

Part of a building is a self-contained part if it consists of a vertical division of the building and its structure is such that that part could be redeveloped independently of the remainder. In addition, the services provided for the occupiers (by pipes, cables and so on) are or could be provided independently of the services provided for the rest of the building. Complicated though this sounds, it is intended to deal with the common situation of a long, low block of flats. These often have several separate entrances, one entrance leading to (say) flats 1–10, the next to flats 11–20, and so on. Assuming that the services could be provided independently to each segment of the building, then the tenants in flats 1–10 will be able to enfranchise independently of those in the rest of the block, and *vice versa*. This should simplify matters from the tenants' point of view, as it will certainly be easier for a small group of tenants to agree to enfranchise than for a much larger number to be involved.

'Premises' that do not qualify

Certain buildings are excluded from the right to buy the freehold or the right to buy a new lease, even though at first sight they might look as though they satisfy the conditions. These include buildings within the precincts of a cathedral, National Trust property and property owned by the Crown.

Also excluded, but only from the right to buy, are buildings where any parts occupied or intended to be occupied for non-residential purposes (for example, as a shop or office), exceed 10 per cent of the internal floor area of the premises as a whole. (For the purposes of this calculation, any common parts of the building are ignored.) This will exclude from the right to buy most buildings with shops on the ground floor and flats above. Remember, however, that qualifying tenants of such flats will still have the right to an extended lease.

The Commonhold & Leasehold Reform Bill will change this 10 per cent rule. In future, only if the floor area occupied for non-residential purposes exceeds 25 per cent will the building be excluded from the enfranchisement provisions. This will mean that many more buildings with shops on the ground floor and flats above will be brought within the enfranchisement provisions.

In addition, tenants may not be able to buy the freehold (but can still buy a new lease) if the building is a converted property containing four or fewer flats and the owner of the freehold (or an adult member of his family) has lived in one of the flats as his only or principal home for the last 12 months. Note that if the building was originally constructed as flats, or contains more than four flats, tenants will still have the right to enfranchise even if the freeholder lives in one of the flats.

Under the Commonhold & Leasehold Reform Bill, such converted properties will be excluded from the right to buy the freehold only if the present landlord effected the conversion himself.

Acquiring the freehold

What the purchase will comprise

If the qualifying tenants are collectively buying the freehold, the purchase will include not only the freehold of the premises in which the flats are situated but also certain other freehold property owned by the landlord, such as any garage, outhouse, garden or yard belonging to or usually enjoyed by the tenants of any of the flats. This will therefore cover situations where the lease includes, or gives the tenant a right to use, a separate garage or parking space. It will also include the grounds in which the block of flats is situated: the tenants will acquire the freehold to these as well.

The qualifying tenants are also required to acquire all superior leases. So if you are a subtenant – that is, the person who granted you your lease did not himself own the freehold but owned only a lease – you will have to acquire all superior leases as well as the freehold.

However, certain parts of the building may have to be leased back to the freeholder (see below).

Lease-backs

Although the tenants are buying the freehold, they will have to grant a lease of some parts of the building back to the freeholder from whom they have just bought it. This will be a lease for 999 years at a peppercorn rent. In effect this means that no rent is payable for the leased-back property.

The following must be leased back:

- flats let by the freeholder on secure tenancies: these are lettings by local authorities, so the requirement will apply only where the local council is the freeholder

- flats let by housing associations on tenancies other than secure tenancies: this will apply only where tenants are buying the freehold from a housing association.

The following are to be leased back if the freeholder so requires:

- units which are not flats let to qualifying tenants: this could include any parts of the premises which are let on a business tenancy, or on tenancies which are not long leases at a low rent; it will also include un-let flats. The landlord may therefore wish to have these units leased back so that he can continue to receive the rent or, in the case of un-let flats, make a profit by selling them on long leases.

  However, taking a lease-back in this way will inevitably reduce the price the landlord will receive for the freehold: the fact that the tenants buying the freehold will not enjoy the benefit of these rents or sales will reduce its value. A landlord will therefore have to obtain the advice of a skilled valuer as to whether it is better to sell the entire property and obtain a higher price or take the lease-backs, and the future profits attaching to them, in exchange for a lower price for the freehold he is currently selling. From the tenants' point of view, this reduction in price may be most welcome; the inclusion of commercial units and un-let flats in the purchase would undoubtedly increase to a considerable degree the price they are paying.

- a flat occupied by a resident landlord: a landlord occupying one flat in, say, a large converted house would, apart from taking the lease-back, have to vacate his flat when he sells the freehold to the tenants. Before the sale he will not have a lease of that flat, because you cannot grant a lease to yourself. He occupies it by virtue of his ownership of the freehold, which he is now selling and so unless he takes the lease-back he will have to leave. He may, of course, wish to do this anyway, given that the roles of landlord and tenant are to be reversed.

Opposition to the sale by the landlord

A landlord can dispute the right to enfranchise or to buy a new lease if he can establish that one or more of the qualifying conditions have not been complied with by the applicants.

However, a landlord can also oppose an enfranchisement claim if he can show that he intends to redevelop the whole or a substantial part of the premises. This ground for opposition will be possible only where not less than two-thirds of the long leases in the block are due to terminate within five years and the landlord cannot reasonably carry out his redevelopment without obtaining possession. In practice, it is unlikely that this ground of opposition will apply very often, but it would make sense for tenants seeking to enfranchise not to leave it until their leases have only – say – five years to run before they take action, to avoid the likelihood of this ground for opposition being used.

Cost of enfranchisement or buying an extended lease

This, of course, will in many cases be the crucial deciding factor as to whether the tenants wish to enfranchise or buy an extension.

Whether you are buying a new lease or the freehold in the whole block, you will be paying at least the full open-market price. It is therefore essential to seek the advice of a qualified valuer or surveyor at an early stage so that some idea of the price to be paid can be ascertained. There is no point in starting down the road to enfranchisement until you are sure you can afford the cost.

In the case of a purchase of the freehold you will pay the open-market price for the freehold and for any intervening leases that you have to include in the acquisition. Each will be valued separately.

In addition to the market value of the freehold you will also have to pay compensation to the landlord if your buying the freehold reduces the value of other property in the locality belonging to him. A landlord may, for example, own two blocks of flats in the same grounds. The acquisition of one block and the grounds by tenants might reduce the value of the other block; if that is so, you will have to compensate the landlord for that reduced value.

You will also have to pay the landlord's reasonable costs (as well as your own) in addition to the landlord's share of the 'marriage value'.

Under this principle, the value of the block of flats increases when both the leasehold and freehold interests belong to the same person – just as strawberries might be said to be enhanced by the addition of cream, or gin by the addition of tonic. If you own the freehold subject to the leases, all you are really entitled to is to receive the rent. If you own the lease, you have the right to occupy, but only for a limited amount of time, and the value of your lease will decrease as it gets shorter. Separately, the value of the lease and the value of the freehold might not be worth very much. When one person owns them both, that person has the right to occupy forever, rent-free; the value may then be much more than the combined total values of the freehold and leasehold interests valued separately. This is one of the few instances where two and two can really make five.

The landlord is entitled to at least 50 per cent of this increase in value, which, for some blocks of flats, could be a very substantial amount.

Precisely how much of the marriage value the landlord is entitled to is at present open to negotiation, subject to the 50 per cent minimum. The Commonhold & Leasehold Reform Bill provides that the landlord is entitled to a fixed 50 per cent of the marriage value: i.e., it will remove the present delays caused by the landlord arguing that he ought to be entitled to more than 50 per cent. The bill further provides that it is to be assumed that there is no marriage value where all the leases of the participating tenants have more than 80 years left to run.

The new owner of the freehold

Who this will be is entirely a decision for the participating qualifying tenants. As the maximum number of people who can legally own a piece of land is four, it will not usually be possible for all the flat-owners to become the new owners of the freehold. Someone will have to buy the freehold on their behalf. All those interested in buying the freehold should discuss this at an early stage and decide who will do this.

In the case of a small block, it may be advisable for the flat-owners themselves to buy the freehold jointly and then hold it in trust for themselves. This might be possible where only four flat-owners are joining in the enfranchisement. Where there are more than four flat-owners, it would be possible for them to nominate four people to buy the land on their behalf, but this could well lead to arguments as to which four should be nominated.

In most cases, however, to buy the freehold it will be necessary to set up a limited company of which the flat-owners are the shareholders. Usually each will own one share, the total number of shares in the company being the same as the number of flats. When a flat-owner sells his flat, he will also transfer his share in the company to the new owner.

The Commonhold & Leasehold Reform Bill will introduce a requirement that the freehold has to be purchased by a 'Right to Enfranchise' (RTE) company. This will be a private limited company, owned by the tenants. The company will have to comply with formal requirements laid down by the government and it will be the company (and not the tenants as at present) which will initiate the procedure to buy the freehold.

Initiating the procedure for buying the freehold

The purchase is initiated by serving the appropriate notice on the freeholder. However, this is not something you can do without professional assistance. A valuation prepared by a qualified valuer is essential. Legal advice will also be needed regarding the terms of the acquisition. First of all, in the case of acquisition of the freehold, the matter should be fully discussed with the other flat-owners to ensure that a sufficient number of them is interested. At present, two-thirds of the qualifying tenants in the block must join in the purchase of the freehold; under the Commonhold & Leasehold Reform Bill this will change to a requirement that the qualifying tenants wishing to enfranchise must occupy at least half the flats in the block. If sufficient are interested, the next step is to seek the advice of a valuer on the price.

Consideration will then have to be given as to how the purchase is going to be financed. Each individual tenant will have to pay a proportion of the price. If only one tenant cannot raise his share of the price, this may well prevent the enfranchisement going ahead. If all can be resolved, it will be appropriate to seek legal advice at that stage regarding the service of the relevant notice which initiates the purchase.

Note that once this initial notice has been served, although you can still change your mind and withdraw from the purchase, you will have to pay any costs incurred by the landlord up to that point (as well as your own). It is obviously desirable, therefore, to ensure the financing of the purchase before serving the notice.

Acquisition of a new lease by an individual tenant

While the right to buy the freehold must be exercised collectively, by a majority of the tenants joining together for the purchase, and getting agreement from enough tenants to do this might not always be possible, the right to buying a new lease can be exercised individually: you can act alone, independently of your neighbours.

When granted, the new lease will expire 90 years after the expiry date of the tenant's existing lease. It will be at a peppercorn rent (that is, a rent of no monetary value), but the tenant must pay a premium (to buy the lease) calculated in accordance with a formula laid down by the Act. Although the lease is to expire 90 years after the end of the existing lease, it will take effect immediately, replacing the existing lease.

Entitlement to a new lease

The qualifying conditions are slightly different from those for enfranchisement. The tenant must be a qualifying tenant (as defined on page 223) and must have occupied the flat as his only or main residence for the past three years or three years out of the last ten. In the case of joint tenants, only one need satisfy the residence requirement. The Commonhold & Leasehold Reform Bill will replace this residence requirement with a rule that the tenant must have owned the flat for at least the last two years. The other difference from the enfranchisement conditions is that the flat need not be in premises as defined by the Act, nor need there be a minimum number of flats in the building. So as long as you are tenant of a flat under a long lease and satisfy the residence requirement, you will have the right to have a new lease, even if there are no other flats in the building (for example, if your flat is a single flat over a shop) and even if the major part of the building is used for non-residential purposes.

Opposition by the landlord to the granting of a new lease

Assuming that the qualifying conditions are satisfied, the landlord can oppose the grant only if the tenant's existing lease is due to end within five years from the date of the tenant's request and at the end of that lease the landlord intends to demolish or reconstruct the building and cannot do so without obtaining possession of the flat. For this reason, it is advisable not to leave the application until the last five years of the current lease.

The price of the premium

The Act contains complicated rules for the calculation of the price to be paid for the new lease. This will be the sum of three elements:

- the reduction in the market value of the landlord's interest in the flat, comparing the value before and after the grant of the new lease, plus
- at least 50 per cent (an automatic 50 per cent when the Commonhold & Leasehold Reform Bill is in force) of the marriage value – the difference between the aggregate value of the freehold (and any superior leases) and the existing lease, compared with the aggregate value of the freehold etc. and the new lease, plus
- reasonable compensation for the reduction in the value of any adjoining property.

Professional valuation advice will be necessary at an early stage.

Effect of the grant of a new lease

Being granted a new lease will not prevent the tenant from joining in any future enfranchisement application. Indeed, the price to be paid for the freehold may well be reduced because of the existence of the new, longer lease. Note, however, that the landlord is entitled to insist on the inclusion in the new lease of a right to apply to court for possession for redevelopment purposes during the last 12 months of the term of the original lease or during the last five years of the new lease. In such a case, however, the landlord would have to pay full compensation to the tenant.

Once the new lease has been granted, you (or perhaps your children) can make another application for a further 90-year extension should the need arise.

Enfranchisement or new lease?

Which right should you exercise: buying the freehold or taking an extended lease?

To some extent this will depend upon your reasons for wishing to exercise either right. If you are concerned about poor maintenance or excessive service charges, these can be solved only by enfranchisement. However, under the Commonhold & Leasehold Reform Bill, flat-owners are to be given a new 'Right to Manage' their block – see page 262. This will enable them to take over the management of the block without the need to buy the freehold. In most cases, therefore, where you are concerned about poor management, it would make more sense to exercise this right and thus save yourself the expense of buying the freehold. But if you are happy with the maintenance arrangements, why bother buying the freehold? You and your fellow tenants will then be directly responsible for maintenance and repairs: are you sure you can do as good a job as the landlord is doing now? Do you want the hassle of being involved in this?

If you are happy with the maintenance arrangements and all you are concerned about is the comparatively short length of time left before your lease will expire, you would probably do better to go for the new lease. Doing this circumvents all the problems of getting a sufficient number of tenants to agree to enfranchise, which can be a problem, particularly if money is tight. And should the other tenants wish to enfranchise later, you can still join in if you wish.

When a lease runs out

Ideally, you should never get to the point when your lease runs out without having done something about it: either exercising your right to a new lease or joining with the other flat-owners to buy the freehold (and granting yourself a new lease). But it may well be that neither of these options is possible, for financial or other reasons, and the lease expires. Fortunately, not quite all is lost.

You will not have to give up possession at the end of your lease; you will be allowed to remain in possession as an ordinary assured tenant. So you will have full security of tenure. But you will have lost your capital asset, the value of the flat that you bought. You are now just a tenant renting property, and as an assured tenant you will be paying the full market rent for the house, not just the ground rent you were paying before. So the rent could well rise from a few pounds a year to hundreds of pounds per month. And although you have security of tenure, the landlord will be able to obtain possession on one of the usual assured tenancy grounds. One of these grounds (ground 6) allows a landlord to seek possession if he intends to demolish or reconstruct the property or the building of which it forms part. Hence, your best course of action will always be to exercise your rights under the Act if at all possible.

If you take an extended lease and allow that to expire (that is, you do not take a further extension), at the end of that new lease you will have no protection from the law and the landlord will be able to insist on your leaving.

An alternative to the 1993 Act

Tenants' right of first refusal

As well as the right given by the 1993 Act to force the landlord to sell the freehold, flat tenants are also given a right of first refusal in certain circumstances. This right is given by Part I of the Landlord and Tenant Act 1987 and requires a landlord who is intending to make various dispositions of the block containing the flats first to offer to dispose of the block on the same terms to the tenants. The tenants can then collectively accept or reject this offer. The Act therefore applies only where a landlord is himself planning to dispose of his interest, unlike the 1993 Act under which the tenants can insist on a sale at any time as long as the qualifying conditions are met.

The 1987 Act was originally rushed through Parliament in the days before the 1987 General Election. It was not well thought-out and was often ignored by landlords; but in 1996 it was revamped and made more effective. The advantage of taking the opportunity to buy under these provisions is that the method of calculating the price is different from that under the 1993 Act and hence may well result in a lower price being payable. Note also that the qualifying conditions are different from those under the 1993 Act, which means that some tenants will find that they have rights under this Act but not under the 1996 Act – and *vice versa*. In particular there is no residence requirement under this Act.

Qualifying conditions

The following conditions must be satisfied before tenants can claim rights under the Act:

- the premises in which the flats are situated must come within the Act
- the landlord must not be an exempt landlord
- the tenants must be qualifying tenants, and
- the landlord must be proposing to make a relevant disposal.

Each of these conditions requires consideration.

The premises

These must consist of a building:

- divided into at least two flats occupied by qualifying tenants
- in which not more than 50 per cent of the floor area is used for non-residential purposes, and
- where the number of flats held by qualifying tenants exceeds 50 per cent of the total number of flats in the building.

Note how these provisions differ from the 1993 Act; in particular the '50 per cent non-residential' rule, as opposed to the figure of 10 per cent under the 1993 Act, will mean that many flats over shops or other commercial premises will have rights under this Act but not under the 1993 Act.

The landlord

The landlord must not be an 'exempt landlord'. Although the Act applies to most landlords, some are excluded by the Act. These include various public-sector landlords, such as local authorities, the Housing Corporation (Housing for Wales in Wales) and some housing associations. In the private sector, resident landlords are excluded. For the purposes of this Act, a resident landlord is one who lives in another part of the same building as his only or main home and has done so for the past 12 months and the premises are not a purpose-built block of flats.

Qualifying tenants

These are defined by exclusion of certain types of tenants. All residential tenants qualify *unless* the tenancy falls into one of the following categories:

- a protected shorthold tenancy
- a business tenancy under the Landlord and Tenant Act 1954

- a tenancy terminable on the ending of employment
- an assured tenancy (including a shorthold).

All tenancies other than these qualify. Therefore, not only tenants with long leases at low rents but also those with protected tenancies within the Rent Act 1977 will qualify.

Relevant disposal

For the right of first refusal to apply, the landlord must be intending to make a relevant disposal – which means *any* disposal by the landlord of *any* interest in the block, other than those specifically excluded by the Act. A contract to make a relevant disposal is itself a relevant disposal.

The disposals specifically excluded include:

- the grant of a tenancy of a single flat
- the grant of a mortgage
- a disposal to a trustee in bankruptcy or a liquidator
- a disposal pursuant to a compulsory purchase order
- transfers ordered by the court in matrimonial and succession proceedings
- a gift to a member of the landlord's family
- a gift to charity
- the surrender of a lease pursuant to a provision in the lease
- a disposal to the Crown
- a disposal within an associated group of companies, but only if the companies have been associated for at least two years.

The last exception allows companies to transfer the ownership of the flats to, for example, a subsidiary company without falling foul of the Act. The requirement that the companies have been associated for at least two years is an anti-avoidance provision. Previously, some landlords would set up a wholly owned subsidiary and transfer the flats to that new company. To avoid the need to serve a Section 5 notice on the tenants (and the delay that that would cause to the transaction), the landlord, instead of selling the flats, would sell the new company which owned the flats. This neat way of circumventing the Act has now been removed by the two-year requirement.

Procedure for disposal by landlord and acquisition by tenants

If a landlord proposes to make a relevant disposal, he must first serve a 'Section 5' notice on at least 90 per cent of the qualifying tenants. The notice must detail the terms of the proposed disposition, including the price, and state that the notice constitutes an offer to dispose of the property on the same terms to the tenants. For the offer to be accepted, at least 50 per cent of the qualifying tenants must agree (as opposed to two-thirds of them under the 1993 Act). They must accept the offer within the period stated in the notice, which must be not less than two months after service. The purchasing tenants then have another two months within which to nominate a person or other entity (for example, a company controlled by them) who will purchase the landlord's interest on the tenant's behalf.

If such a nomination is made, the landlord can then serve a notice within one month of the nomination stating that he no longer intends to proceed with the disposal. If he does not withdraw, he must then send a contract for the disposal to the nominated person/company. The nominee then has a further two months in which either to withdraw or offer to exchange contracts.

As can be seen, this procedure is somewhat long-winded. If the landlord decides to sell at an auction sale, then a slightly different procedure applies. The Section 5 notice must then be served not less than four months and not more than six months before the auction.

Criminal sanctions

The Act makes it a criminal offence for a landlord to make a relevant disposal without first serving a Section 5 notice on the tenants, or, having served the notice, without giving the tenants the chance to acquire the property under the Act. There are also provisions for company directors, managers and company secretaries to be held liable if they have consented to or connived in the disposal.

Effect of a disposal in breach of the Act

The disposal remains valid despite the imposition of criminal sanctions. However, the tenants will not be in a worse position as a result. They will have the right to acquire the property from the buyer on the same terms as it was acquired. The new landlord must inform the tenants of his identity no later than the next rent day and also inform them of their rights to acquire from him under the 1987 Act. Again, there are criminal sanctions for failing to comply with either of these obligations. There are also detailed provisions to deal with the possibility that the original purchaser might himself have disposed of his interest before the tenants become aware of what is happening, but the tenants will have a right of acquisition against him on the same terms as before.

Leasehold Advisory Service*

This is an independent agency which provides free advice to lease-holders and landlords on the law affecting residential leasehold property, and in particular with regard to enfranchisement and service charge disputes. Its advice is provided on a self-help basis through the publication of guidance notes and leaflets. It cannot act directly for you, nor can it provide any direct services in surveying, valuation, legal proceedings or conveyancing. It does, however, maintain lists of solicitors and surveyors who specialise in residential landlord and tenant work.

Q *I have a long lease in a block of 25 flats. Should I buy my freehold?*

A Although you cannot acquire the freehold in your own particular flat, you have the right to get together with your neighbours to buy the freehold in the whole block. This would normally mean setting up a limited company to buy the freehold on behalf of all of you.

If all the tenants in the block get on well, this tenants' company may be successful; if you do not get on now, it is unlikely that you will get on when trying to run the company that owns the freehold. Disagreements could lead to problems with the management of the block. Many of the worst-maintained blocks of flats are those controlled by tenants' companies. Tenants often split into factions, arguing about which repairs should be done when and to what standards, and what effect all this will have on the service charge. Often, as a result, very little gets done; a problem landlord has simply been exchanged (at great expense) for a problem tenants' company.

If your lease has less than 50 years left to run, you may well find that you would not be able to sell it as building societies and banks are becoming increasingly reluctant to lend on leases for less than 50 years. Buying the freehold would solve this problem, as you could then grant yourself a new, longer lease.

If you are having problems with the management of the block – getting repairs done and so on – buying the freehold would help solve them. However, once the Commonhold & Leasehold Reform Bill is in force, it will be cheaper for the tenants to exercise the new Right to Manage rather than buy the freehold. It may well be expensive, and the procedure is very complex. However, if the management of the block is acceptable, it may be wiser not to buy the freehold but to buy a new long lease instead. It might be cheaper, and you would not need the co-operation of your neighbours to buy this new lease.

Q *My lease has 30 years left to run. If I buy a new lease for a further 90 years, what happens in 90 years' time when this new lease has only 30 years left to run?*

A It may not be your problem! But even if you or your children are still around then, the answer is simple: you are entitled to another new lease for a further extended period of 90 years.

Chapter 19

Service charge disputes

Rogue landlords, unfortunately, are found in the long-leasehold sector as well as the short-term letting sector and in recent years the problems of some flat-owners, particularly in London, have been well publicised. This chapter looks at the sorts of problems encountered by tenants and suggests some ways of dealing with them.

Note that the statutory protections dealt with below apply no matter who provides the services. The term 'landlord' is therefore used throughout the chapter to identify the person responsible for the provision of the services. Unless otherwise stated, this will include any person or company with this responsibility, such as a management company.

The Commonhold & Leasehold Reform Bill will increase the protections given to tenants and will also introduce a 'Right to Manage' which will entitle tenants to compel the landlord to hand over the management of the block to them.

Major problems faced by tenants

From the tenants' point of view, there are two major, and often interrelated, problems:

- the necessary services are not provided, or are provided to an indifferent standard
- the amount they have to pay for the services is too high.
  Sometimes the services are abysmal *and* the charges extortionate.

Threats of forfeiture

A third problem may ensue from those mentioned above, in that a tenant who dares to object to the standards of the services provided or the level of the service charge levied by withholding the service charge payment may find himself under threat of forfeiture proceedings from the landlord.

Forfeiture is a form of redress available to the landlord when his tenant is in breach of any of the obligations under the lease, such as paying the service charge: it consists of the lease being brought to an end prematurely, without the need for the landlord to pay any compensation for the capital asset that the tenant is losing.

To enforce forfeiture, the landlord would have to go to court, and the tenant might have a defence to the action (the poor services, the excessive charges, or whatever), but what tenant wants to put his home – and the money invested in it – at risk, and what tenant wants to engage in lengthy, expensive and stressful litigation? Most tenants therefore pay up, grumbling to themselves (and anyone else who will listen) about the injustices of the system.

For restrictions on the landlord's right to forfeit see page 257.

Lack of control by tenants

Flat tenants also complain of the lack of control they have over their homes. 'An Englishman's home is his castle', according to the saying – and that goes for the Welshman and Scotsman as well – but a flat-owner is in a far worse position than the owner of a freehold property. If the management of a block of flats is in the hands of the landlord or the landlord's agents, it will be the landlord who decides when the block is to be painted and in what colour; the landlord who decides if and when repairs are to be done, by whom and in what way; the landlord who decides what improvements are to be carried out when and by whom. Indeed, flat-owners may be forgiven for thinking that they are only there to foot the bill for all this.

The solution to the problem of poor provision of services or over-charging is often thought to be giving more control to the tenants. It has to be said, however, that some of the worst-maintained blocks of flats are those which are run by the tenants themselves.

Tenants' management company

Where the management of the flat is in the hands of the tenants it is usually through the medium of a tenants' management company: a company owned and controlled by the tenants. While such a company gives tenants some control over the cost and quality of the services, the control is not absolute: much depends on what the majority of the tenants want, not what each individual wants.

Often, the running of the management company is left in the hands of a few tenants only, perhaps due to the apathy of the majority, and these few volunteers are not always the most capable of running the company efficiently. Sometimes, acrimonious disputes can arise between various factions amongst the tenants. One group wants to replace the lifts, or put in double-glazing, while the other does not. Any compromise reached will be on the basis of the lowest common denominator, which pleases no one. Sometimes no compromise can be reached: if one group wants to replace the window frames with single-glazing, the other with double-glazing, and neither side will yield, the window frames will probably not be replaced at all.

Where a tenant's management company works well, it is often due to the efforts of one or two people. If they leave (or die), things can go badly wrong.

What works well for one set of flat-owners may not work for another. Some of the best-run blocks of flats are those with professional managing agents in charge. Good independent professional agents will have had training and experience in managing property, and such expertise is often worth a lot more than the cost of employing the agent. Some agents charge a percentage of the expenditure, but it is perhaps better if a set sum per flat is charged, as this will avoid any perception that the agents have no incentive to minimise the expenditure.

Problems are most likely to arise if the block is managed by the landlord, or a company owned by the landlord. If you, as a tenant, are happy with the agents, but enfranchise (collectively buy the freehold, with the other tenants) for other reasons, you can, of course, continue to employ the same agents to manage the block if you so wish.

If you are thinking of buying a flat, it makes sense to find out how the block is managed. First impressions are very important: a block with clean hallways and stairways and well-maintained flowerbeds is a good sign. Your solicitor should obtain information about the level of the service charge, but it is as well to make your own enquiries as to the standard of service provided. If possible, ask someone else who lives in the block as well as the seller of the flat; the seller might just be selling because of management problems and may not be inclined to give full details of his reasons for moving. (If a seller actually tells lies about the level of service, or anything else, you may have remedies against him when you discover the truth. However, it is always better to make further enquiries and get at the truth before you buy, when you still have the opportunity of backing out of the purchase.)

Solutions to flat-owners' problems

A mountain of legislation now exists to give flat-owners rights with regard to services and service charges. However, most are dependent on some kind of court action being brought.

Ideally, and at almost all costs, litigation should be avoided. Negotiation is infinitely preferable. Gaining the support of the tenants' association (if there is one) or bringing pressure to bear on a management company at company meetings are important, but as in any kind of negotiation it helps a great deal to know your legal position and the other party's obligations.

Some potential solutions, discussed below, refer to:

- the terms of the lease
- variation of the terms of the lease (Part IV of the Landlord and Tenant Act 1987)
- obtaining information (Landlord and Tenant Act 1985)
- restrictions on the landlord's right to recover costs incurred (Landlord and Tenant Act 1985)
- appointing a manager (Part II of the Landlord and Tenant Act 1987)
- acquisition of the reversion (Parts I and III of the Landlord and Tenant Act 1987; Leasehold Reform, Housing and Urban Development Act 1993)
- exercising the 'Right to Manage' under the Commonhold & Leasehold Reform Bill 2001.

The terms of the lease

First of all, in the case of a dispute, the service charge provisions should be studied carefully to see if there has been any breach of any obligation under them. If so, normal remedies for breach of contract will be available.

Court actions for disrepair
Specific performance
Section 17 of the Landlord and Tenant Act 1985 states:

In proceedings in which the tenant of a dwelling alleges a breach on the part of his landlord of a repairing covenant relating to any part of the premises in which the dwelling is comprised, the court may order specific performance ... whether or not the breach relates to a part of the premises let to the tenant ...

Specific performance is an order of the court which requires the landlord (including, in this context, a management company) to carry out a stated task – repair the roof, or whatever. This is the obvious remedy where the landlord is refusing to carry out necessary work. Note the wording of the section, which allows the order to relate to any part of the building in which the flat is situated.

However, that specific performance is a discretionary remedy. This means that, even if you prove the breach of contract, the court does not have to order it. The court will take into account all the circumstances of the case, including the tenant's conduct, and may decide just to award damages.

Damages
As a general rule, a landlord is not liable to pay damages to his tenant unless he specifically knows of the lack of repair or is in some way put on enquiry.

However, this rule applies only where the repairs are to the premises actually let to the tenant. In the case of repairs to parts of the premises *not* let to the tenant, the landlord's obligation to repair arises as soon as the defect occurs; there is no need for notice to have been given.

In deciding the amount, the court will look at the facts of each case carefully to see what loss the tenant has actually suffered. The following are possible losses which may have been suffered:

- the cost of alternative accommodation
- diminution in value of the premises
- inconvenience and discomfort.

Tenant's right of set-off

Some remedies available for breach of contract do not involve court action. The tenant's initial reaction to a failure to provide the services may well be to refuse to pay the service charge and/or rent. This reaction must be avoided, as you run the risk of the landlord bringing proceedings against you for non-payment, but the law does provide for something similar known as 'set-off'.

Set-off is the right to deduct the amount of any claim you have against someone from money that you owe them. So in this instance a tenant could deduct any loss he has suffered through a breach of the repairing obligations from the service charge or rent due to the landlord. This right can be, and frequently is, taken away by the terms of the lease. However, if the lease merely states that you must pay the rent and service charge 'without deductions' that will not remove the right.

Further, in the case of leases granted on or after 1 July 1995, an effective exclusion of the right to set-off could be void under the Unfair Terms in Consumer Contracts Regulations. These state that a term *may* be void – because it is unfair – if it has the effect of 'obliging the consumer to fulfil all his obligations where the seller or supplier does not fulfil his'.

Deduction from rent of expenditure on repairs by the tenant

Another possible remedy not requiring court action is to do the repairs yourself, and then deduct the cost of those repairs from future payments. However, this right is available only if you have expressly told the landlord that unless he carries out the repairs within a (stated) reasonable time you will do them yourself and deduct the cost from future payments.

Variation of the terms of the lease

If the service charge provisions are defective in some way, it may be possible to vary the terms of the lease. Ideally, this should be done by agreement between the landlord and *all* the tenants. If agreement is not forthcoming it may be possible to apply to the court to vary the terms of the lease under Part IV of the Landlord and Tenant Act 1987.

This is a very little-used procedure, but is available where the lease fails to make satisfactory provision with regard to:

(a) the repair or maintenance of the flat or the building containing it or any other property let to the tenant or over which rights are conferred on him: this could be the case, for example, where some parts of the block or the surrounding grounds are not included within the maintenance obligation; or

(b) the insurance of the flat, building or other property as in (a); or

(c) the repair or maintenance of the installations (whether or not in the same building as the flat) which are reasonably necessary to ensure occupiers have a reasonable standard of accommodation: this would include, for example, a communal central heating boiler; or

(d) the provision or maintenance of services etc. which are reasonably necessary to ensure a reasonable standard of accommodation: this might include the cleaning of hallways, stairways, and so on; or

(e) the computation of the service charge: this might be relevant where the percentage contributions payable by the various tenants do not add up to 100 per cent of the total spent (yes, this does happen!). Surprisingly, it is more usual to find that the contributions come to more than 100 per cent than to less.

Often complaints concern the landlord's right to nominate which insurance company has to be used, but the court cannot under this procedure terminate the landlord's right to do this. However, under Section 43 of the Act (which introduces a new schedule to the Landlord and Tenant Act 1985), tenants are given other rights concerning insurance – for example, where a tenant must use a nominated insurer, he can apply to change the nomination where the insurance available from the nominated insurer is unsatisfactory or the premiums are excessive.

Obtaining information

One particular problem that the law seeks to deal with is the question of information. Tenants often feel that they are being overcharged for this service or that, but have no real proof. 'Does it really cost £X to cut the grass every year?' they may wonder, for example. Information is not a remedy or a solution to a problem in itself, but it may provide ammunition to use against a rogue landlord.

The Landlord and Tenant Act 1985

Tenants paying service charges have various statutory protections, principally under this Act (as amended), over and above any rights given under the lease. The protections apply to leasehold houses as well as flats, but not to freehold premises.

'Service charge' is defined in Section 18 as an amount

payable by a tenant of the dwelling as part of or in addition to the rent (a) which is payable, directly or indirectly, for services, repairs, maintenance or insurance or the landlord's costs of management, and (b) the whole or part of which varies or may vary according to the relevant costs.

The 'relevant costs' are 'the costs or estimated costs incurred or to be incurred by or on behalf of the landlord, or a superior landlord, in connection with the matters for which the service charge is payable'.

Note, however, that this definition of 'service charge' does not at present, include improvements. So if under the terms of your lease you are obliged to pay for any improvements, as opposed to repairs, carried out by the landlord, you will not have the statutory rights relating to those improvements. However, you should check the terms of the lease to see what rights it gives you.

However, the Commonhold & Leasehold Reform Bill will extend the protection of the Act to 'improvements' and also to one-off 'administration charges' e.g. charges for giving consent to carrying out alterations to a flat or for providing information.

Summary of costs

Often the lease will contain provisions with regard to the provision of copy accounts, and so on. But whatever the lease might say, the statute gives the right for a tenant to require, in writing, the landlord to supply him with a written summary of the costs incurred for the previous 12 months or, if the accounts are made up annually, for the last accounting period.

The landlord must comply with the request within one month or within six months of the end of the last 12 months' accounting period, whichever is later.

If there are more than four flats in the dispute, the summary must be certified by a qualified accountant as a fair summary and sufficiently supported by accounts, receipts and other documents which have been produced to him.

To ensure a degree of objectivity, the definition of 'qualified accountant' disqualifies an officer, employee or partner of the landlord or of an associated company or the managing agents.

Within six months of obtaining the summary, the tenant, or the secretary of a recognised tenants' association, is entitled to inspect accounts, receipts and other documents supporting the summary and take copies.

Failure to comply with these provisions is a summary offence.

These provisions are all well and good, provided that the tenants have the expertise to analyse the information when it is provided. And that is the other problem: when it is provided. The information may well come many months after the event – for example, up to six months after the end of the relevant financial year. No 'quick fix' is available.

Commonhold & Leasehold Reform Bill

This will introduce an obligation on a landlord to provide specified details of the service charge accounts, certified by a qualified accountant, without being requested by the tenants. Indeed, the service charge is not payable by the tenants until the information is provided. This is perhaps a strange sanction, as without the service charge payments, the landlord will not have the money to provide the services – and so the tenants will suffer.

Management audit

Under the Leasehold Reform, Housing and Urban Act 1993, Chapter 5, Sections 76–84, the tenants can require a management audit of the service charge functions. This right can be exercised without the need for court action, (unless the landlord refuses to comply with the request), thus enabling the tenant to check whether:

(a) the landlord is discharging his management obligations effectively and efficiently, and

(b) whether the service charge is being applied in an efficient and effective manner.

Tenants qualified to apply for an audit

The right to apply for a management audit of the service charge functions is given to 'qualifying tenants' as defined in the legislation – that is, tenants of dwellings under a long lease under which a service charge is payable, but excluding business leases.

'Long lease' has the same definition as for enfranchisement purposes (see Chapter 18): basically, a term certain exceeding 21 years.

Number of qualifying tenants

The number of qualifying tenants who must join in an application depends upon the number of dwellings in the premises:

- where the premises consist of or include one or two dwellings let to qualifying tenants, *either* (or both) can apply
- where the premises consist of or include three or more dwellings occupied by qualifying tenants, at least two-thirds of the qualifying tenants must apply.

The auditor

The auditor can be either a qualified surveyor or a qualified accountant, so long as he is not a tenant of any part of the premises. He has the right to require the landlord to provide him with information about the service charge and to give him facilities for inspecting and taking copies of the accounts. He also has the right to carry out an inspection of the common parts of the building.

Requesting an audit

The right to have an audit is exercised by an auditor serving a notice on the landlord under Section 80. The notice is validly served if it is served on the person who receives the rent.

If the landlord employs a managing agent, the notice must be served on him.

Landlord's reply

The landlord must supply the information etc. within one month, or state his reasons for refusing to supply it.

The landlord cannot charge directly for supplying the auditor with the requested information which he requests, but he can treat any costs incurred as part of the costs of management, and thus add them into the service charge account. Obviously, the tenants themselves will also have to pay the auditor's fees for carrying out the work.

Application for court order

If the landlord has failed to comply with any aspect of a Section 80 notice within two months, the auditor may apply for a court order requiring compliance by the landlord.

Effect of the audit

The audit will merely identify what the management problems are. It will not provide a remedy for those problems.

Right of tenants to appoint surveyor to advise on service charge

Similar information to that obtainable under a management audit can also be obtained by appointing a surveyor to advise on the service charge. This right was introduced by the 1996 Housing Act following criticisms of the expense of a management audit.

A recognised tenants' association may appoint a surveyor to advise it on any matters relating to the payment of a service charge. The surveyor has extensive rights to inspect the property and of access to documents in the landlord's control to enable him to advise on service charge matters.

Restrictions on the landlord's right to recover costs

Once you have discovered the full facts about the costs being incurred, you can decide whether the landlord is in fact allowed to charge those costs to the service charge account. The Landlord and Tenant Act 1985 places restrictions on the landlord's rights to recover the costs he has incurred, and stresses that they must be 'reasonable'.

Costs can be recovered only to the extent that they are reasonably incurred, and where they are incurred in the provision of services or the carrying out of works, only if those services or works are of a reasonable standard.

Advance payments must be no greater than is reasonable.

Any agreement is void which purports to provide for the question of reasonableness to be determined in a particular way (for example, by the landlord's surveyor) or on particular evidence. However, it is permissible to refer disputes to arbitration.

Any grant – say, from a local authority – paid to the landlord towards the cost of the works must be deducted from the service charge, not kept by him (as has been known).

Costs incurred more than 18 months before the service charge demand is served cannot be recovered unless the tenant has been given written notice of those costs during the 18-month period. This is to stop landlords suddenly producing unexpected demands for cash in relation to old works, which might cause problems for tenants who had not budgeted for such expense.

Determination of reasonableness of service charges

Assuming that, for example, you have discovered that the landlord says that it cost £2,000 last year to cut the grass and you consider that this amount is unreasonable, your first step will be to challenge the landlord. He will probably claim that the sum charged is reasonable. In such circumstances, where landlord and tenant cannot agree or reach a compromise, some third party will have to make the decision. Not so long ago, that would have to have been the court, but as from 1996 the Leasehold Valuation Tribunal (LVT) has had the power to make such decisions.

The LVT is a quasi-judicial public body which sits on a regional basis. Its members are appointed by the Lord Chancellor and consist of surveyors, lawyers and some lay persons. There were various reasons for giving the jurisdiction to the LVT. First, most county court judges will have no real knowledge of flat leases, whereas the LVT should be able to approach cases with a degree of expertise in leasehold matters. Also, the procedure before the LVT is more informal than in court, and this should encourage more people to apply and appear before the tribunal on their own without the need for the expense of legal representation. And as the LVT cannot award costs, there is no risk, should you lose, of having to pay the landlord's costs. (It is likely, however, that in such a case, these will be added to the service charge – but at least that shares them out between all the tenants.)

The jury, figuratively speaking, is still out on the success (or otherwise) of the LVT's involvement in this area. The LVT was not really ready for the extra work involved, although the Lord

Chancellor is now appointing extra members. But there is still a long delay in getting a hearing in many parts of England and Wales, upwards of six months in some cases. And even then, the decision is often reserved – that is, you are not told the result at the end of the hearing, but have to wait for a written decision to be sent to you. This again is often months after the hearing. Also, there appears to be a lack of consistency between the decisions of the various regional tribunals, cases of what seem to be the same facts being decided differently. (It has to be said, however, that if a survey was done of any sorts of decisions by different county courts, this would probably show similar inconsistencies.)

The LVT can be asked to make a declaration that costs were/were not reasonably incurred; that services or works are/are not of a reasonable standard; or that any advance payment is/is not reasonable.

Tenants may also apply for an order that any court costs incurred by the landlord in connection with court proceedings are not to be regarded as relevant costs when the tenants' service charge is calculated. Such an order is intended to stop tenants being penalised in cases where a landlord has sued a tenant (for example, for non-payment of service charges) and has lost. In such proceedings the landlord would normally be ordered to pay the tenant's legal costs. The danger arises that the landlord might then add all the costs – that is, his own costs and those of the tenant which he has been ordered to pay – into the service charge account. This order prevents that from happening.

As well as making a declaration, the LVT has been given a general power to determine whether costs incurred were incurred reasonably, whether services were to a reasonable standard and as to whether the insurance provided or premiums payable are reasonable.

Estimates for work and consultation with tenants

In addition to the reasonableness rule, there are other restrictions on the landlord's right to recover costs incurred.

Where costs are incurred on qualifying works above the limit specified by legislation, the excess is payable only if the 'relevant requirements' have been complied with. This basically involves prior consultation with the tenants before the work is carried out and the expenditure incurred.

The specified limit is currently £50 × the number of flats in the building, or £1,000, whichever is the greater.

'Qualifying works' are works to the cost of which the tenant may be required to contribute under the terms of his lease.

The 'relevant requirements' differ according to whether the tenants are represented by a recognised tenants' association or not. The association can be 'recognised' by a notice in writing by the landlord. This recognition of the association shows that the landlord accepts the association's right to involve itself in matters on behalf of the tenants. If the landlord refuses to do so, application can be made to the local Rent Assessment Committee for it to issue a certificate of recognition. (The RAC and the LVT mentioned above are, as it happens, usually one and the same body.)

'Relevant requirements' for tenants *not* represented by a recognised tenants' association are as follows:

- the landlord must obtain at least two estimates for the works, one from a person wholly unconnected with the landlord
- a notice, together with a copy of the estimates, must be given to each of the tenants or displayed in a place or places where it is likely to come to the notice of all those tenants. This must describe the works to be carried out and invite observations, stating the name and address in the UK of the person to whom they should be sent and the date by which they must be received (this date must not be earlier than one month after the date on which the notice is given or displayed).

'Relevant requirements' for tenants who *are* represented by a recognised tenants' association are these:

- the landlord must give to the secretary of the association a written notice including a detailed specification of the works and specifying a reasonable period in which the association may propose to the landlord the names of one or more persons from whom estimates for the works should be obtained
- at least two estimates must be obtained, one of them from a person wholly unconnected with the landlord
- a copy of the estimates must be given to the secretary of the association
- a notice summarising the proposed work and the estimates must be given to each tenant represented by the association.

This notice must also:

- inform tenants that they have a right to inspect and take copies of a detailed specification and the estimates
- invite observations on those works and estimates
- specify the name and address in the UK of a person to whom the observations may be sent and the date by which they are to be received (this date must be no earlier than one month after the date on which the notice is given).

The landlord must, if requested to do so by a tenant, provide facilities for examining a detailed specification of the works and the estimates free of charge (although the costs of the landlord may be included as management costs in the service charge), and/or taking copies of them on payment of a reasonable charge.

Landlord's obligations concerning comments

Whether or not a tenants' association has been recognised, the landlord must have regard to any observations received in pursuance of the notice and, unless the works are urgent, they must not be begun earlier than the date specified in the notice.

This does *not* mean, however, that the landlord must comply with the observations of the tenants. All that the legislation requires is that he 'has regard' to them. He can quite properly 'have regard' to them and then decide that he is right and that the work should still go ahead. There is still no real control for the tenants. But many critical observations might make the landlord think very carefully about his plans as it could mean that if he goes ahead the tenants might start claiming that the costs were not reasonably incurred. This procedure should at least make landlords think carefully before spending large amounts of their tenants' money, and that cannot be a bad thing.

The requirements outlined above may be dispensed with by the court if satisfied that the landlord has acted reasonably.

Service charge demands

Section 47 of the Landlord and Tenant Act 1987 provides that where a written demand is made for rent or other sums due to the landlord under the tenancy (such as service charges), the following information must be included:

- the name and address of the landlord, and

- if that address is not in England or Wales, an address in England or Wales at which notices, including notices in proceedings, may be served on the landlord.

If the demand does not contain this information, any sum demanded which consists of service charges shall be treated as not due from the tenant until that information is supplied. Hence, the tenant need not pay the service charge if this information is not included. But the tenant is not completely let off the hook; once the information is provided, the money will become due and he will have to pay up.

One problem tenants sometimes have is finding out who their landlord is – and if they do not know who he is, no proceedings can be brought against him. This provision should help solve this.

Restriction on forfeiture for non-payment of service charge

One weapon which landlords have long wielded is the right to forfeit a lease if the tenant is in breach of its terms in some way. This means that the lease is terminated prematurely, without any compensation to the tenant, who thus loses all his investment in the property. Frequently, any tenant making too much of a fuss over the amount of the service charge and threatening non-payment owing to its lack of reasonableness will have been met by a landlord 'reminding' him that the landlord has this right and will use it unless the tenant pays up. And many tenants do, of course, not wanting to run the risk that they may not win if the matter goes to court. No court action is a certainty, and no one wants to gamble with their home.

Some landlords are a little more subtle: they will simply tell the tenant's mortgage lender that the tenant is not paying and that forfeiture is threatened. If this were to happen, the lender would lose its rights over the property and risk not being able to get its loan repaid. So the lender will pay up – and then add the amount to the mortgage account, so the tenant will pay anyway.

The Housing Act 1996 has attempted to put a stop to such intimidation. A landlord cannot exercise forfeiture for failure to pay a service charge unless the amount of the charge has been agreed to by the tenant or determined by the LVT, a court or by arbitration.

Once the amount has been fixed in this way, the landlord may not then forfeit the lease until 14 days have elapsed, commencing with the day after the day of the decision. Any possibility of an appeal is to be ignored in this calculation.

The landlord may serve a notice warning of forfeiture but, if he does, the notice will not be effective unless it contains details of the tenant's rights, as mentioned above. These must be stated in a type-face of similar size and weight to that used to indicate that the tenancy might be forfeited.

This is an important provision. If the tenant disputes the service charge, the landlord cannot forfeit the lease unless the tenant agrees the amount due, or it is settled by the LVT, the court or arbitration. As stated above, the LVT has jurisdiction to determine whether the charge is reasonable or not.

Alternatively, the landlord might sue for the payment of the money and the tenant could then raise the lack of reasonableness as a defence to the claim. But at least this allows the questions as to reasonableness to be ventilated without the tenant fearing that he might lose his home.

Appointment of manager under Part II of the Landlord and Tenant Act 1987

The law recognises that some landlords' attempts at managing blocks of flats are so bad, owing either to negligence or to deliberate policy, that they must be replaced. One way is to apply to the LVT for a manager to be appointed to run the block in place of the land-lord. The landlord remains the owner but someone else takes charge of looking after the block.

Alternatively, the tenants might contemplate buying the freehold from the landlord as a way of getting rid of him permanently (see Chapter 18), but appointing a manager would save the tenants the expense of having to buy him out. However, doing this will require an application to the LVT, which will involve some delay and expense. Appointing a manager can, none the less, be a preliminary step to forcing the landlord to sell his interest to the tenants (see below).

A manager can be appointed if the tribunal is satisfied that:

- the landlord is in breach of an obligation of the tenancy which relates to the management of the premises

- and that those circumstances are likely to continue
- and that it is just and convenient to make an order, *or*
- other circumstances exist which make it just and convenient for an order to be made, *or*
- the court is satisfied that unreasonable service charges have been made or are proposed or likely to be made, and
- that it is just and convenient to make the order.

The manager will then carry out such functions as the court thinks fit.

Hence, a wide variety of circumstances could give rise to the appointment of a manager. The longer-standing and the more serious the landlord's deficiencies (over-charging, bad management, or whatever), the more likely it is to be that the circumstances will continue and the more likely it is that it will be just and convenient to make the order.

Applying for the appointment of a manager

An application for the appointment of a manager can be made by:

- a tenant of a flat
- tenants of premises comprising the whole or part of a building containing two or more flats unless:
  - (a) the current landlord is an 'exempt landlord' (i.e. a local authority or other public-sector landlord), or
  - (b) the current landlord is a 'resident landlord' (i.e. he occupies a flat in the premises as his only or principal residence and has done so for the preceding 12 months and it is not a purpose-built block of flats) or
  - (c) the premises are included within the functional land of a charity.

An application may be made by an individual tenant, although the Act provides that tenants of two or more flats may apply jointly. Obviously, the more tenants in the block who can be shown to support the application, the more likely it is to be granted.

Application is made to the LVT following service of a Preliminary Notice of Intended Application on the Landlord. This must state:

- tenant's name, address of flat and an address for service
- the tenant's intention to apply

- the grounds on which the application is made (see above)
- the matters relied on by the tenant

and require the landlord to take specified steps to remedy breach(es) (if remediable) within a specified reasonable time, further stating that the tenant will refrain from making application to the court if the notice is complied with.

The LVT may dispense with the requirement to serve a Preliminary Notice.

If the notice has been served, the tenant must allow time for compliance (if the breaches are remediable), although the LVT may make an order notwithstanding that the specified period is too short or that the content of the Preliminary Notice is otherwise defective.

The powers of the manager

The manager may be appointed to carry out such functions of management or receivership or both, as the LVT thinks fit. The tribunal order may, *inter alia*:

- transfer existing contractual rights and liabilities to the manager
- authorise the manager to sue on existing or future claims (for example, where a tenant has rent arrears or has defaulted on service charges)
- regulate remuneration: the order may provide for remuneration to be paid to the manager by the landlord, or by the tenants of the premises or by all or any of those persons.

Acquisition of the reversion of the lease

In an extreme case, this step should be seriously considered. Tenants have the right, under Part I of the Landlord and Tenant Act 1987, of first refusal: that is, if the landlord wishes to dispose of his interest to someone else, he must first offer it to the tenants (see Chapter 18).

In cases where there is a history of bad management, compulsory acquisitions may be possible by court order under Part III of the same Act (see below).

In any event, tenants also have a general right to buy the freehold under the Leasehold Reform, Housing and Urban Development Act 1993, albeit at a higher price than under the 1987 Act (this too is covered in Chapter 18).

Note that all this legislation developed piecemeal as particular problems were identified. This means that the qualifying conditions for the 1987 Act and the 1993 Act are not identical, therefore one Act may sometimes apply while the other does not. Hence, the 1987 Act will probably apply to flats situated over a row of shops; the 1993 Act will probably not. The various qualifying conditions must be considered carefully to see whether your situation falls within them.

Compulsory acquisition order under Part III of the Landlord and Tenant Act 1987

This allows tenants to go to court to compel the landlord to sell them his interest in the block where there has been a history of bad management. It is largely redundant owing to the general right to buy the freehold, whether or not bad management is an issue, conferred by the Leasehold Reform Housing and Urban Development Act 1993 (see Chapter 18). However, one advantage of applying under this provision is that the price payable may well be lower than the price payable under the 1993 Act. Also, as the qualifying conditions are different, there may well be circumstances when tenants would qualify under this Act but not under the 1993 Act. This is particularly likely to be the case where the flat is situated in a building of which part is used for non-residential purposes: the classic example would be flats located over a shop or row of shops.

The right to buy is given to qualifying tenants, i.e. those with leases for over 21 years, other than tenants of business premises.

Acquisition will not be possible, however, if the landlord is a resident landlord or the premises are part of the functional land of a charity.

The premises – the block in which the flats are situated – must themselves satisfy various conditions, as follows:

- they must consist of whole or part of a building containing at least two or more flats held by tenants who are qualifying tenants
- the total number of flats held by qualifying tenants must not be less than two-thirds of the total number of flats contained in the premises
- not more than 50 per cent of the internal floor area (excluding common parts) must be occupied or be intended to be occupied

for non-residential purposes. So if your flat is above a row of shops, this will qualify as long as the floor area of the shop part of the building does not exceed 50 per cent of the total floor area.

A Preliminary Notice must be served by at least two-thirds of the qualifying tenants. The contents of this notice are similar to that served when the tenants wish a manager to be appointed (see above).

Grounds for making the order

The court must be satisfied that *either* the landlord is in breach of any obligation owed by him to the applicants under their leases relating to repair, maintenance, insurance or management *and* that the circumstances by virtue of which he is in breach are likely to continue; *or* at the date of the application and throughout the preceding two years there was in force an appointment of a manager under Part II of the 1987 Act (see above).

The landlord's interest will be acquired by a person nominated by the tenants – often a company set up by the tenants for the purpose of acquiring the interest.

If agreement cannot otherwise be reached, the price is to be the 'open-market value' of the landlord's interest, on the assumption that the tenants are not buying or seeking to buy. This method of ascertaining the price is different from that laid down in the 1993 Act (see Chapter 18). The 1993 Act allows the landlord to claim a share of the 'marriage value', which could mean that the price payable under a 1993 Act purchase is considerably more than that under the 1987 Act.

The Right to Manage

The Commonhold & Leasehold Reform Bill will give flat tenants a 'Right to Manage' (RTM), which can be exercised without the need to prove any fault on the part of the landlord. It will thus become for many disgruntled tenants the first choice in seeking to remedy problems with maintenance, etc. Tenants will not need to consider buying the freehold as a method of resolving such problems nor to show fault on the part of the landlord when seeking to appoint a manager under the 1987 Act.

The RTM will be exercised by the tenants setting up a private limited company (an RTM company) to take over the management. It is available in exactly the same circumstances as the right to collectively buy the freehold (see page 221). Thus only 50 per cent of the tenants in the block need be members of the RTM company. The only ground for objection by the landlord (assuming that the qualifying conditions are complied with) is if he is a resident landlord (see page 227) – then the right does not apply. Apart from this, the RTM company can take over the management of the block without the need for any court application. A notice is served on the landlord specifying a date (at least one month away) by which he must admit or contest the claim, and a further date (at least one month after the first date) on which the RTM will commence. There are then complex provisions dealing with the handing over of the management responsibilities and existing service charge contributions to the RTM, and if the landlord does not co-operate, court orders can be obtained to enforce the tenants' rights. The RTM company then has the exclusive right to manage the block and to receive the service charge payments. The landlord will still receive the ground rent.

Although the RTM company will take over the management of the block, there is no reason why it should not then appoint professional managing agents to carry out the day-to-day running of the block. This may well be a sensible option. As has previously been stated, although letting the tenants themselves take charge of the block seems to be seen as a universal panacea for management problems, it often is not. The company has to be run and the block managed on a day-to-day basis. Both of these functions need people, i.e. tenants, willing to find the time and also competent to carry out the various functions. In the absence of such people, things can go badly wrong and the RTM should not be contemplated by flat tenants without a good deal of careful thought as to the implications.

Ground rents for leases

The Commonhold & Leasehold Reform Bill will introduce a provision that the ground rent under a long lease of a dwelling will not be payable unless actually demanded by the landlord. The notice must:

- specify the amount due
- specify the date the tenant must make payment
- specify the date it was due under the lease, if different
- contain any further information which may be prescribed.

The tenant has at least 30 days in which to make payment, but not more than 60 days after the day on which the notice is given. It cannot be before the due date under the lease.

The notice must be in the prescribed form and may be sent by post to the tenant at the dwelling, or such other address in England and Wales notified by the tenant to the landlord.

Note that this provision will apply to leases of houses as well as flats.

Chapter 20

Commonhold

The Commonhold & Leasehold Reform Bill will introduce a new system of freehold ownership called 'commonhold' to England and Wales. This is designed for use in the case of interdependent properties such as flats and will for the first time allow freehold flats to become commonplace.

At the moment, when you buy a flat you usually buy a long lease – say, 99 years. The reason that flats are normally sold leasehold is because of a gap in the law. In the case of a block of flats it is necessary for the repair and maintenance of the structure of the block and the common parts such as hallways, stairways, lifts and car parks to be the responsibility of one person or a management company. It just would not work if each of the tenants was responsible for the repair of their own part of the block – and that would still leave the common parts. But the person or company responsible for the block needs to be reimbursed for all the expenditure, which is why flat-owners have to pay a service charge. Unfortunately, the gap in the present law is that the obligation to pay this service charge is not binding on future flat-owners if they own the freehold in their respective flats. Freeholders cannot be made liable on obligations to pay entered into by previous owners. If there was no liability to pay the service charge, the repairs and maintenance could not be carried out, as the management company just would not have the funds to do the work – with possible disastrous consequences. Leaseholders, however, are obliged to carry on making payments that previous owners made, so flats are sold leasehold and not freehold to ensure the stability and repair and maintenance of the block in the future.

The idea behind commonhold is to change the law so that flats can be sold freehold and the owners made liable to pay the service charge. Future owners of a freehold flat will be liable to pay the service charge, so the present obstacle to freehold flats will be removed. Similar schemes have been in use in other countries (including Scotland) for some time. In the USA they are called 'condominiums' (or 'condos'). (For the main advantage of owning a flat freehold see 'How commonhold will work', below.)

The Bill has all-party support and when it comes into force – possibly sometime in 2002 – it is likely that most new blocks of flats will be sold as commonhold. However, existing leasehold blocks will remain as they are now. It will be possible to convert them into commonhold, but only if the present owner of the freehold and all the flat tenants agree. It is thus likely that most existing blocks of flats will remain leasehold.

How commonhold will work

Where a block of flats is sold as commonhold, each individual flat-owner (called a unit-holder by the Bill) will own the freehold in his individual flat or 'unit'. This will avoid the problem inherent in leases that they decrease in value and become increasingly difficult to sell as they near their termination date. The flat will be the owner's forever, just as a freehold house is.

But there is still the rest of the block to consider – the common parts. The freehold in the common parts of the block will belong to what will be known as a Commonhold Association. This will be a private limited company owned by the flat-owners. Each flat-owner will be a 'member' of the company. So the flat-owners collectively will own the freehold in the block and will thus be responsible for repair and maintenance of it. The position with regard to the common parts will thus be much the same as where the tenants exercise their right to buy the freehold in a block of leasehold flats; the difference will be that the flats – and the common parts – will be owned freehold.

There will also be a Commonhold Community Statement, which will set out the rules of the block. These will include the obligation of the Commonhold Association to repair and maintain the common parts, and the responsibility of the flat-owners, both present and future, to pay the service charge. It is also likely to include provisions familiar to flat-owners (e.g. the flat should be used for residential purposes only and the owners should not cause a nuisance or annoyance to neighbouring owners) and various other rules and regulations ensuring the well-being of all the flat-owners.

Setting up a commonhold

It will be for the developer building a new block of flats to decide whether to sell the flats off freehold (i.e. commonhold) or lease-hold. Most developers of new blocks are likely to go in for commonhold because selling the flats as freehold is probably commercially advantageous: it is thought that freehold flats will sell for more than leasehold ones. Many people have a psychological objection to leases and a corresponding attraction towards freehold land so they may be prepared to pay more for the freehold than they would for a lease.

As far as existing blocks are concerned, again it will be the owner of the freehold (i.e. the present landlord) who will decide whether to convert. As there is no provision for monetary compensation to the landlord on a conversion, it would seem unlikely that many landlords would wish to convert and thus give away a valuable asset, the ownership of the freehold in the block.

The only way that tenants can attempt to force a conversion is first to exercise their right to compel the landlord to sell the free-hold to them (see Chapter 18). As the new owners of the freehold in the block it would then be possible for them to initiate a conver-sion. However, even if they did, the conversion would need the consent of all the tenants and their mortgage lenders. While the mortgage lenders are very much in favour of commonhold and could be expected to agree, it would need only one tenant to refuse to consent for the conversion to be blocked.

Implications of commonhold

It seems likely, therefore, that most existing blocks of flats will remain leasehold.

Over the years, with the increase in the number of commonhold blocks, a two-tier market may develop, with leasehold flats being less attractive to potential buyers than the commonhold ones. As already stated, the public prefers the idea of freehold ownership, so buying a flat which is freehold must be a more attractive purchase than buying a 99-year lease. Although a 99-year lease can be extended, it will cost money and inconvenience, so it would be much better to buy the freehold. It is likely to be the case, therefore, that if there were a choice between a freehold flat and a leasehold one, a buyer would choose the freehold one – and this would be reflected in the price. In the short term, of course, commonhold flats will be few and far between, so any effect on the value of lease-hold flats will be gradual and will become more obvious only as and when more commonhold flats become available.

Service charges

It cannot be assumed that all the problems with service charges and maintenance of blocks of flats will disappear with the introduction of commonhold. The structure and common parts of the block will still need maintaining. This will be the responsibility of the Commonhold Association. But this, in reality, will be just the same as a tenants' management company in a leasehold block. Some work well, others do not. It will all depend upon the availability and competence of people willing to give up their time to manage the block. Appointing professional managing agents to run the block is undoubtedly a good option. Although they will charge a fee, their expertise will often save a lot of time, money and hassle for the flat-owners – and if they do not prove to be satisfactory, they can always be dismissed.

So the introduction of commonhold will be of great significance – but only with regard to new blocks of flats; existing blocks will still suffer from the problems associated with expiring leases (i.e. they will still depreciate in value as the lease gets nearer to its termi-nation date). Whatever the legal arrangements, the flat-owners still need to live together in peaceful co-existence and whether this is possible often depends upon personalities rather than legal struc-tures. Nothing can legislate for the vagaries of human nature.

Chapter 21

Practical tips for landlords and tenants

This chapter covers many of the practical issues affecting landlords and tenants. Some are mentioned, or dealt with in greater detail, elsewhere in the book.

Gas safety

The regulations state that all gas appliances, flues and installation pipework in rental property let to tenants must be properly maintained. It is the landlord's responsibility to do this, and to ensure that appliances are serviced at least once a year by a registered qualified person. The maintenance records must be produced for the tenant on the grant of the tenancy and within 28 days of each inspection. Prospective tenants should ask to see the records before they move in.

Fire safety

If the rental property is furnished the landlord must ensure that all upholstered furniture, including bed bases, mattresses, cushion fillings and covers, has a label on it confirming that it complies with the required fire safety standards. A guide to the Furnishings (Fire) (Safety) Regulations is available from local authorities, CABx or from the DTI's Consumer Safety Publications department.★ Prospective tenants should check for fire safety labels on upholstery before moving in.

Electrical appliances

Electrical appliances in rental property must be safe to use. If there is any doubt, an electrician should be asked to check them out.

Letting mortgaged property

The mortgage lender's consent to granting a tenancy is usually required. If a property is let without such consent the landlord will be in breach of his mortgage terms and the tenant (who will probably be unaware of this requirement) can be evicted by the mortgage lender. Although in practice this rarely happens, tenants should ask the landlord if there is a mortgage and, if there is, whether consent for letting has been obtained. If the property is registered at the Land Registry anyone can find this out. This is done by checking the 'index map' to discover whether the property is registered. If so, a title number will appear and for a small fee a copy of the title details can be obtained.

Letting leasehold property

Permission to sublet should be sought in advance. The lessor will probably require copies of prospective subtenants' references and of the proposed letting agreement.

Houses in multiple occupation

If the rental property is let as more than a single household – for example, to a group of students or nurses – the landlord should check with the local authority to see if it is to be treated as a house in multiple occupation (which is likely if the property is to house more than four unrelated occupants). If so, it may have to be inspected and be registered as an HMO (see Chapter 8).

Tenants' references

Landlords will normally require two referees for each tenant, one of them a character reference, the other from a bank or employer as evidence that the tenant is able to afford the rent. In the case of a company let, a company search may be advisable.

Condition of property

Any landlord who wishes to let property should realise that it is in his own interests to put it into good decorative order, cleared of all personal effects that are not part of the inventory (see below) and thoroughly cleaned throughout. Paintwork should be in good condition, and plumbing and wiring fault-free.

Tenants are normally required to return the property to the landlord in a similar condition to that obtaining when they took possession (see 'Repairs', below), cleaned and with all personal effects and rubbish removed.

Inventories

It is in the interests of both parties to ensure that if property is being let furnished two copies of the inventory (updated by the landlord or his agent as necessary) are made available when the tenant moves in, one copy to be retained, the other to be signed and dated by the tenant, assuming he agrees that everything listed is indeed on the premises, and any defects noted, and returned to the landlord.

Contents of furnished property

The tenant may expect the property to contain all necessary furniture, major appliances (but not, usually, televisions and stereos), kitchen equipment and bedding (i.e. blankets, eiderdowns, pillows and duvets, but not, usually, linen).

Meter readings

Gas and electricity meters need to be read by landlord and tenant at the beginning and end of each tenancy and the relevant service provider notified. The accounts should be put in the name of the tenant. Tenants would be well advised to note the readings on the meters when moving into and out of a property.

Telephone bills

These, and reconnection charges, are the tenant's responsibility and the account is normally in the tenant's name. When vacating, the tenant should notify the telephone company in advance of the date when the telephone may be disconnected (unless otherwise arranged with the landlord) and the tenant's account closed.

Water rates

These are usually paid by the landlord. However, the tenancy agreement can make the tenant liable, so this point needs to be checked in advance by the tenant.

Council tax

The tenant, under the Local Government Finance Act 1992, is obliged to pay this tax and to indemnify the landlord against any liability for this charge following the tenant's departure from the property at the end of the tenancy. Certain exceptions exist, however: for example, where property is let to students.

Insurance

It is the landlord's responsibility to insure the building and the contents he has himself provided, and to comply with the insurance companies' security requirements. The tenant may of course take out insurance to cover his own possessions, particularly any valuable items. Policies are available that are tailored to the needs of private landlords and should ideally cover loss of rental income.

Keys

The landlord should provide a set of keys to the property for each occupant. These and any duplicates should be returned to the landlord at the end of the tenancy.

Viewing of property

It is usual for tenants to allow the landlord or his agents access to the property, by arrangement, during the last 28 days of a tenancy in order to show it to prospective new tenants. The tenancy agreement may include a clause expressly permitting such access.

Access to property

Unless an emergency arises, the landlord should not enter self-contained property lawfully let to a tenant without first obtaining the tenant's permission. For access in respect of non-emergency repairs, the landlord should give the tenant at least 24 hours' notice.

Repairs

In residential tenancies of less than seven years the landlord must maintain the structure and exterior and the facilities for the supply of water, electricity, sanitation and heating. However, many tenancy agreements make the tenant responsible for interior decorations, damage to furniture, and so on. It makes sense for tenants, before entering into a tenancy agreement, to check the condition of these items and to have any existing wear and tear recorded so that the tenant is not made liable for pre-existing defects at the end of the tenancy. A schedule of condition, agreed by both parties and attached to the tenancy agreement, is a good idea.

During the tenancy, if the landlord fails to carry out repairs that he is legally obliged to do (such as repairs to the structure and exterior of the property in tenancies for less than seven years) the tenant can invoke his right of 'self-help' by getting estimates from contractors and sending these to the landlord, at the same time informing the landlord that if he does not have the repairs carried out within a reasonable period (to be specified), the tenant will get them done and deduct the cost from his future rent payments (see Chapter 12).

Deposits

Among the references prospective landlords should seek for prospective tenants is a bank reference, to confirm that he/she will be able to afford the rent agreed. Also, it is usual for the tenant to pay a month's rent in advance and a month's rental as a security deposit. The deposit, to which reference should be made in the tenancy agreement, may be held by a stakeholder (for example, a letting agent, but if the letting agency fails the money could be lost) or put into a joint account held by landlord and tenant. The purpose of the deposit is to cover any outstanding bills, rectify any damage, and pay for breakages and cleaning of carpets, curtains, blankets etc. if soiling is considerable, at the end of the tenancy: the deposit should not be regarded by the tenant as an excuse not to pay the final month's rent. The agreement should allow the landlord to retain the deposit for a short period, perhaps a month, to sort out the property and return the deposit, or the balance of it once any end-of-tenancy expenses have been deducted, to the tenant.

Forwarding address

The landlord is advised to obtain forwarding addresses for outgoing tenants, especially if he has retained part of the deposit against expenditure/outstanding bills (see below). The tenant, even if he has made arrangements to have his mail forwarded by the Post Office, is advised to leave a forwarding address for any item that escapes this arrangement.

Gardens

If the property has a garden, this should be tidy, with a mown lawn and pruned shrubs, at the start of the tenancy. It is in the landlord's own interest to provide basic garden tools, including a mower in good working order, so that the tenant can look after the garden during the tenancy.

Chapter 22

In Scotland: private-sector tenancies

Housing law in Scotland is different from that in England and Wales in many ways. In particular, the Acts of Parliament that apply to Scottish housing are different from those in England and Wales. Nevertheless, there are many similarities. The purpose of this chapter is to explain the law in Scotland as it applies to tenancies in the private sector highlighting the differences between the law in Scotland and that in England and Wales. This is only a summary of the most important aspects of the law and is not comprehensive.

What is a tenancy?

It is important to understand what a tenancy is because most the protection given by Acts of Parliament extends only to tenants. In order to create a tenancy at common law in Scotland, the following factors must be present. If any one of them is missing, there is no tenancy. There must be:

- a landlord (who is either the owner of the property or someone who rents the property from another person)
- a tenant (or two or more joint tenants)
- an agreement between the landlord and tenant that the latter is entitled to exclusively occupy a particular property (which may be part or whole of a house or flat)
- rental for a particular period of time (although if no specific period is agreed and all the other elements noted here are present, the common law will imply a period of one year). At the end of that period, in terms of the common law, the tenancy agreement will automatically renew for the same period unless

either the landlord or tenant decide otherwise. This is called 'tacit relocation'
- rent (which can be in money or in kind).

At common law, the tenancy agreement must be in writing if the tenancy is for a year or more; leases of less than a year can be verbal, although it is in the best interests of both parties to commit the lease to writing. However, as noted below, certain tenants, such as secure tenants and assured tenants, are entitled to a written tenancy agreement.

Unlike England and Wales, where the use of licences is common, licences are not used much in Scotland. This is because the courts have decided that the definition of 'tenancy' is a wide one in Scotland. Thus, many licence agreements offered by landlords in England would be classified as tenancy agreements in Scotland. The difference is important because licensees do not enjoy as many rights as tenants.

What is meant by the private sector?

The private-sector rental market includes all tenancies except where the landlord is a local authority or some other public body. So, the private sector includes housing associations and housing companies as well as individuals. However, when the Housing (Scotland) Act 2001 comes into force (probably in September 2002), all registered social landlords (such as most housing associations and organisations who have had council houses transferred to them) will no longer be treated as being in the private sector. The importance of this is that tenants in the private sector have different rights to those in the public sector (see Chapter 23).

What type of tenancies are there?

Tenants in the private sector may have different types of tenancies according to when they were first entered into and, in the case of assured tenancies, what the landlord and tenant agreed between themselves. The different types of tenancies in the private sector are:

- protected tenancies
- statutory tenancies

- assured tenancies
- short assured tenancies.

Protected tenancies

A tenancy is a protected tenancy under the Rent (Scotland) Act 1984 if all following requirements are satisfied:

- there is a tenancy
- the house or part of it is rented as a dwellinghouse (this can apply to a house or part of a house)
- the house is let to one or more individuals (companies cannot be protected tenants)
- the house is a separate dwelling (see page 19)
- the rateable value must be more than a specified sum (either £600 or £1,500 depending on circumstances)
- the tenancy agreement began before 2 January 1989.

Various categories of tenancies, such as student and holiday lettings, are excluded from the definition of protected tenancies.

A protected tenancy continues in existence until the death of the tenant or his spouse, or any eligible successor, and therefore some protected tenancies are still in existence today. However, because no protected tenancies have been created since 1989, their number is steadily declining, and only a relatively small number of protected tenancies still exist.

Grounds for possession

As is the case in England and Wales (see page 93), where there is a protected tenancy the landlord may repossess a property only by obtaining a court order. The landlord must first serve a notice to quit, giving a minimum of 28 days' notice. Before the court will grant decree for possession, the landlord must prove that one or more of a number of grounds are satisfied. The grounds for possession are either discretionary (where the sheriff *may* grant decree for possession if he is satisfied both that the ground is proved and that it is reasonable to do so) or mandatory (where the sheriff *must* grant decree if the ground is proved).

Discretionary grounds

The discretionary grounds for possession are similar to the grounds in England and Wales (see pages 93–7), and are as follows:

1. rent arrears or breach of the tenancy obligations
2. nuisance, annoyance or using the house for immoral or illegal purposes
3. deterioration of the condition of the dwellinghouse
4. deterioration of the condition of furniture
5. withdrawal of notice to quit by the tenant
6. unlawful assignation or subletting of the whole house
7. house reasonably required by the landlord for occupation by a full-time employee
8. house reasonably required by the landlord for occupation as a residence for himself or a close family member
9. excessive rent charged for a sublet
10. the house is overcrowded.

The last ground applies to situations where the house is so overcrowded as to be dangerous or injurious to the health of the inhabitants and the tenant has failed to take reasonable steps to alleviate the situation by the removal of any lodger or subtenant. In England and Wales, this is a mandatory ground for possession.

Mandatory grounds

The mandatory grounds for possession are:

1. the owner/occupier requires the house as his residence
2. the house is required as the owner's retirement home
3. the letting is an off-season holiday letting
4. the letting is to an educational body (but not students)
5. the letting is on a short tenancy
6. the house is held for occupation by a minister or lay missionary
7–9. the house is required for various agricultural purposes
10. the house is designed and adapted for occupation by a person with special needs and is required for such a person (there is no equivalent ground in the legislation for England and Wales)
11. the landlord is a member of the armed forces and requires the house as his residence.

For most of the mandatory grounds, the landlord must also have served the tenant with a notice before the beginning of the tenancy stating that possession might be recovered on that ground.

Fair rent system

A fair rent system, similar to that in England and Wales, also exists for protected tenancies in Scotland. An application for a fair rent can be made by either the landlord or the tenant or by joint application to a rent officer (who is appointed by the Scottish Ministers). After examining the property, the rent officer will determine a fair rent, taking into account factors such as the area in which the property is situated, the condition of the house and the level of fair rents for similar properties. The rent officer must assume there is no scarcity of accommodation (see pages 99–101).

If either the landlord or the tenant is unhappy with the rent officer's decision, it can be referred to a Rent Assessment Committee, which may confirm, reduce or increase the rent. Both rent officers and Rent Assessment Committees have a duty to consider all the circumstances (other than personal) of each case. In particular, they must apply their 'knowledge and experience of current rents of comparable property in the area'. Once fixed, fair rents are valid for the next three years and the landlord is entitled only to the registered rent. However, a fresh application may be made within three years if there have been substantial changes in circumstances which result in the registered rent no longer being a fair rent.

Succession to protected tenancies

The Rent (Scotland) Act 1984 provides that certain members of the tenant's family may succeed to (i.e., inherit) the tenancy. The right to succeed is restricted and certain criteria must be satisfied. The order of succession which applies where a tenant dies on or after 2 July 1990 is as follows. The tenant's surviving spouse or cohabitee succeeds where the house was that person's only or principal home at the time of the tenant's death. If there is no surviving spouse then a member of the tenant's family who was residing with the tenant at the time of death and for two years beforehand also has a right to succeed. The tenancy that that person will have will be a statutory assured tenancy (see below).

If there are rival claims in either of the above cases, the question of succession will be decided by a sheriff.

Statutory tenancies

A statutory tenancy is one which arises when a tenant remains in possession of a house after the contractual tenancy has been terminated (e.g. by a notice to quit) or a tenant has previously succeeded to the tenancy before 1990. A statutory tenant has similar rights to a protected tenant.

Assured tenancies

Under the Housing (Scotland) Act 1988 a type of tenancy known as an assured tenancy was introduced to Scotland and became operational on 2 January 1989. This is essentially a tenancy at a market rent, with a reduced degree of security of tenure. Significantly, the 1988 Act abolished any method of regulating the rent which a landlord may charge other than by the operation of market forces, i.e. the supply of property and the demand for it. This was part of the government's plan to revitalise the private rented sector in Scotland. Most housing association tenancies are assured tenancies (until the Housing (Scotland) Act 2001 comes into force; probably in September 2002).

A tenancy is an assured tenancy under the Housing (Scotland) Act 1988 if all of the following requirements are satisfied:

- there is a tenancy at common law (see above)
- the house or part of it is rented as a dwellinghouse (this can apply to a house or part of a house)
- the house is let to one or more individuals
- the house is a separate dwelling (see page 19)
- the house is used as the sole or principal residence of the tenant
- the tenancy agreement began on or after 2 January 1989.

Excluded tenancies

The following cannot be assured tenancies:

- tenancies where no rent is paid or where the rent is under £6 per week

- tenancies of shops or licensed premises
- tenancies of agricultural land or agricultural holdings
- lettings to students
- holiday lettings
- tenancies where the landlord is resident
- Crown tenancies
- public-sector tenancies
- shared-ownership agreements
- protected tenancies, housing association tenancies and secure tenancies
- temporary accommodation for the homeless.

Market rent

Assured tenancies allow market forces to operate and rents to be fixed in the market by what landlords are able to charge willing tenants. Therefore, assured tenants, unlike protected tenants (see page 276), do not have the right to apply for a fair rent assessment. Usually, the amount of rent is specified in the tenancy agreement. That is what the tenant must pay.

If the landlord wants to increase the rent, he can do so if there is *any* provision in the tenancy agreement which allows the rent to be increased (e.g. the tenancy agreement says that the rent may be reviewed and increased every 12 months).

If for any reason the assured tenancy has been terminated by a notice to quit, or if the tenancy was inherited, the law about whether the landlord can increase the rent is more complicated. In that situation, if the rent increase provision in the tenancy agreement provides either some sort of formula for determining the new rent or which specifies what the increased rent will be, the landlord can apply that provision without any problem. So if the tenancy agreement says that the rent will rise each year in line with the Retail Price Index, the landlord is entitled to do that. Similarly, if the tenancy agreement says that the rent will increase by £x every 12 months or by x per cent every three years, the landlord is entitled to do so.

However, if there is no such provision, unless the tenant agrees to an increase in rent, the landlord must follow a special, and rather complicated, procedure contained in the Housing (Scotland) Act 1988. The landlord has to serve a formal notice on the tenant (an AT2), giving the tenant notice of the proposed new rent. For a tenancy of six months or more, the minimum notice is six months; for a tenancy of *less* than six months, the required notice period is the length of the tenancy or one month, whichever is the longer. The tenant can refer the notice to a Rent Assessment Committee, before the date on which the new rent is to take effect (see below).

The new rent cannot take effect any earlier than one year from the date of the previous rent increase. If the tenant does nothing, the new rent takes effect from the date specified in the notice. If the landlord wants to increase the rent again in the future, and the tenant does not voluntarily accept an increase, the landlord needs to serve a new AT2 notice. The tenant then has the same rights as before to apply to the Rent Assessment Committee.

The Rent Assessment Committee

When a tenant refers a notice of increase to a Rent Assessment Committee, the committee must consider what rent might reasonably be expected in the open market in a contractual tenancy granted by a willing landlord to a willing tenant. Relevant considerations include the capital value of the house and capital appreciation. In addition, the state of repair of the house and its age, character and locality are considered when deciding on a reasonable rent. Certain factors, such as any improvements by the tenant, will be disregarded.

Once the committee reaches a decision, the new rent is normally due from the date specified in the landlord's notice. However, if the committee feels that this would cause undue hardship to the tenant, it may postpone that date to a date of its choosing.

Assured tenancy agreements

A landlord must draw up a written tenancy agreement (or lease) for an assured tenant, stating the terms on which the tenant occupies the house, and provide the tenant with a copy, free of charge. If the landlord fails to do so, the sheriff may draw up such a lease or alter the document if it is inaccurate. Where the rent is payable weekly, the tenant must also be given a rent book in a specified form.

Succession (or inheritance) on death

When an assured tenant who was the sole tenant dies, the surviving spouse, or someone with whom the deceased lived as husband or wife, can succeed to the tenancy (i.e., inherit it), provided the house was his or her only or principal home at the date of death. The tenancy that the tenant inherits is a statutory assured tenancy. There can be only one succession so if the person who died had himself succeeded to the tenancy, the spouse/cohabitee cannot succeed to the tenancy. If the tenancy had devolved to the spouse in terms of succession law, the landlord is entitled to recover possession of the house, as of right, as long as the action is commenced within a year of the death and the spouse does not have the statutory right of succession.

Security of tenure

The general principle of security of tenure applies in assured tenancies. This means that even if the contractual tenancy has been terminated (e.g. by a notice to quit) the tenant is still entitled to remain in the house. The type of tenancy that the tenant then has is a statutory assured tenancy. The landlord will be entitled to recovery of possession only if he obtains a court order, which he can do only on the grounds noted below.

Recovery of possession

In order for the landlord to obtain an order for recovery of possession of a house let under an assured tenancy, he must do the following things.

1. Serve on the tenant a notice of proceedings stating that he intends to start possession proceedings, specifying the grounds relied on and giving minimum notice before legal proceedings can be started. The minimum period is two weeks where the ground relied on relates to the conduct of the tenant (such as rent arrears) and two months in any other case. In Scotland, a notice is valid for six months. The landlord must start legal proceedings within that time.

2. In addition, unless the contractual tenancy has already been terminated or was a statutory assured tenancy, the landlord must terminate the contractual assured tenancy by serving a notice to quit giving at least 28 days' notice. There are some technical exceptions to this general rule.

3. The landlord must raise an 'action for recovery of possession of heritable property' in the sheriff court for the area in which the

house is located. The procedure used is the 'summary cause procedure'. The action is raised by summons. The summons must state, among other things, the ground(s) on which the landlord wants to recover possession (see below). If the landlord has correctly followed the procedure and the sheriff is satisfied that the ground(s) are made out, he must grant decree. That decree will take effect usually four weeks after the date of decree. If the tenant does not leave voluntarily, sheriff officers are employed to enforce the decree.

Grounds for recovery of possession

As in the case of protected tenants, there are *mandatory* grounds, where the sheriff has no discretion and an order must be granted if the ground is established, and *discretionary* grounds, where the sheriff has discretion and must be satisfied that it is reasonable to grant the order as well as being satisfied that the ground is proved.

Mandatory grounds

These are similar to the grounds under English legislation (see pages 45–51), and are available in the following circumstances:

1. the landlord wants the property for his own home or it was formerly his own home
2. the property is being repossessed by the lender following mortgage default
3. the property is being let as out-of-season holiday accommodation (but not for more than eight months)
4. the property is student accommodation let out-of-term (where tenancy does not exceed 12 months)
5. the property is required for occupation by a minister or full-time lay missionary
6. the landlord intends to demolish or reconstruct the property
7. the tenant dies
8. there are rent arrears of more than three months both at the date of the raising of the action and at the date of the court hearing.

In the case of grounds 1–5, the landlord must also have served a notice on the tenant before the beginning of the tenancy advising him that recovery of possession might be sought on that ground.

Discretionary grounds

If these grounds are used, the landlord must also establish that it is reasonable for the sheriff to grant an order. This will include taking into account all the relevant circumstances affecting both the landlord and the tenant, including their conduct, any possible hardship which might result if the order is granted, and the possibility of the tenant finding other accommodation. The grounds are similar to those under English law, and are as follows:

1. suitable alternative accommodation is available to the tenant (a detailed definition of what this means is given in the 1988 Act).
2. tenant withdraws his notice to quit and continues in possession
3. tenant persistently delays in payment of rent
4. there are rent arrears at date of notice seeking possession and at date of starting proceedings
5. obligations of tenancy broken or not performed
6. deterioration of the condition of the property owing to waste, neglect or default
7. anti-social behaviour, or use of the property for immoral or illegal purposes
8. deterioration of furniture
9. tied accommodation, where employment of the tenant ends.

Short assured tenancies

The Housing (Scotland) Act 1988 also introduced the 'short assured tenancy', which is a distinct form of assured tenancy. The short assured tenant has little security of tenure. In principle, the landlord is entitled, as of right, to recover possession of the house at the end of the tenancy period. The following are the conditions for the creation of a short assured tenancy:

- the tenancy fulfils the requirements of a valid assured tenancy (see above)
- the landlord, before the creation of the tenancy, has served on the tenant a formal notice (the AT5) stating that the proposed tenancy is to be a short assured tenancy and giving various information set out in regulations
- the tenancy is for a fixed period of not less than six months (there is no maximum period).

If at the end of the fixed period neither the landlord nor the tenant takes any action, the tenancy agreement will automatically renew itself for the same period (or one year if the initial period was more than one year). This is known as 'tacit relocation'. The tenant is entitled to a written tenancy agreement.

Determination of rent

The rent is the amount agreed by the landlord and tenant. There is a limited right of challenge open to the tenant if he believes that the rent is too high – he can apply to the Rent Assessment Committee for a determination of the amount. The committee will not lower the rent unless what the tenant pays, judged against rents charged locally, is *significantly higher* than the market rent which the landlord might reasonably expect to be able to obtain. Any rent fixed by a Rent Assessment Committee takes effect from a date set by the committee and the determination lasts for one year.

Recovery of possession

A short assured tenant has no defence to a properly based possession action. The sheriff must grant an order for possession if he is satisfied that all of the following apply:

- the tenancy has reached its termination date
- no tacit relocation is in operation (i.e., a valid notice to quit of at least 40 days has been served by the landlord)
- no further contractual tenancy is in existence
- the landlord has given at least two months' notice to the tenant that he requires possession of the house. The notice can be served during the tenancy, or after the termination date.

The landlord does not need to give any reason why he wants to recover possession and does not have to show that it is reasonable to recover possession. The action for recovery of possession is raised and dealt with in the same way as for assured tenancies (see above).

In addition, because the short assured tenancy is a type of assured tenancy, the landlord is also entitled to seek recovery of possession in the same way as for assured tenancies (see above).

Other aspects of assured and short assured tenancies

The following issues are dealt with in the same way in Scotland as in England and Wales (see Chapter 5):

* permission to grant a tenancy
* payment of rent
* interest on arrears
* council tax
* water charges
* alterations
* insurance
* children and pets
* Unfair Terms in Consumer Contract Regulations 1999
* safety regulations
* deposits
* collecting the rent
* inventories.

However, the sample tenancy agreements are **not** suitable for use in Scotland.

Use of house

The tenant is only entitled, at common law, to use the house as a dwellinghouse. Any other use is a breach of an implied term of the tenancy agreement. It is best, however, to make this explicit in the tenancy agreement.

Irritancy clauses

It is important in the tenancy agreement to specify the circumstances in which the agreement can be terminated by the landlord. This is known as an irritancy clause. The agreement should refer to the circumstances in which the court may grant possession of a house let under an assured tenancy as well as any other circumstances in which the landlord would wish to terminate the tenancy agreement (such as rent arrears, misuse of the house, etc.).

Stamp duty

In Scotland, the tenant cannot be charged for this. Otherwise the position is the same as for England and Wales (see page 82).

Repairs

The landlord's responsibilities are as follows:

- he must provide the house reasonably fit in all respects for human habitation
- he must keep it that way throughout the tenancy
- whenever he becomes aware that repairs are needed, he must carry them out within a reasonable period
- he must keep the house wind- and watertight
- he must keep in good repair the installations in the house for water, gas, electricity, heating, hot water and sanitation
- he must keep in repair the structure and the exterior of the house

The tenant is entitled to withhold rent (but not to spend it) where the landlord has failed in his repairing responsibilities. Alternatively, if the landlord has failed to carry out the repairs after a reasonable period, the tenant can pay for the repairs and deduct the cost from the rent. The landlord cannot avoid his repairing obligations by anything which is contained in the written tenancy agreement.

Assignation and subletting

An assured tenant is not permitted to assign, sublet or part with possession of any part of the property let to him without the landlord's consent. The landlord can refuse permission without reasons or can grant permission with or without conditions.

If a landlord does permit a tenant to sublet part or all of the house, and the tenancy between the tenant and the landlord is subsequently ended, for whatever reason, the subtenant then becomes the tenant of the landlord. That tenancy will be an assured tenancy only if the subtenancy was also an assured tenant.

Harassment and unlawful eviction

Scots law, contained in the Rent (Scotland) Act 1984 and the Housing (Scotland) Act 1988, contains similar provisions to

English law (see Chapter 13) to prevent the harassment and illegal eviction of tenants.

'Unlawful eviction' occurs where any person (not necessarily the landlord) unlawfully deprives the occupier of the house or any part of it, or attempts to do so. Such a person shall be guilty of an offence unless he can prove that he believed, and had reasonable cause to believe, that the tenant had ceased to reside on the premises.

The offence of harassment is committed if actions or omissions are carried out, with the intention of causing the tenant to:

* give up the occupation of the house or any part of it; or
* refrain from exercising any rights or pursuing any remedy to which he is entitled.

Harassment includes acts likely to interfere with the peace or comfort of the tenant or members of his household, and the persistent withholding of services reasonably required for the occupation of the house.

Chapter 23

In Scotland: public-sector tenancies

The Housing (Scotland) Act 2001 was passed in summer 2001. It is expected to come into force in stages and to be in full force by September 2002. The Act makes major changes to the law relating to social housing tenancies (such as council and housing association housing). This chapter describes the law both before the Act comes into force and after. It is only a summary of the main provisions of the law.

Before the Housing (Scotland) Act 2001 comes into force

For the purposes of this chapter, a public-sector tenancy is one in which the landlord is a public authority, such as a local authority (or council), Communities Scotland* (which was known as Scottish Homes until October 2001) or, in a few cases, a housing association, and the tenant is an individual who has rented the house for residential use. Most such tenancies are termed 'secure tenancies'. Secure tenancies are governed by the Housing (Scotland) Act 1987.

What is a secure tenancy?

A tenancy (see page 274) is a secure tenancy if:

- the house is let as a separate dwelling (see page 19)
- the tenant is an individual and the house is his only or principal home
- the landlord is one of a specified list of bodies, e.g. a local authority or Communities Scotland or a housing association (*only* if the tenancy first began before 2 January 1989).

However, certain types of tenancies are excluded from secure tenancy status. They are:

- premises occupied under a contract of employment for the better performance of duties
- a temporary letting to a person moving into an area to take up employment there and for the purpose of enabling him to secure accommodation in the area
- a temporary letting pending development affecting the property
- temporary accommodation during works on the property which the tenant normally occupies as his home
- tenancies granted to the homeless
- agricultural and business premises
- some types of police and fire authority housing
- accommodation forming part of a building held for a non-housing purpose.

Rights and duties of secure tenants

Tenancy agreements

All secure tenants have the right to a written lease or tenancy agreement. It is the landlord's duty to provide such a document and to ensure that it is properly signed. The landlord must also give the tenant a free copy of the lease. There is no particular form that the tenancy agreement must follow. However, landlords can use the Model Secure Tenancy Agreement (published by the Chartered Institute of Housing in Scotland in 1997) if they wish. Neither the landlord nor the tenant is entitled to change the terms of the tenancy agreement without the other's consent. If either party refuses to consent to a change, the other can appeal, in some circumstances, to the sheriff.

Rent

The amount of rent is that stipulated in the tenancy agreement. The rent can be increased at any time by any amount as long as the landlord gives at least four weeks' notice. There is no right of appeal against the amount of the rent increase or the overall level of the rent. If the tenant objects to the rent increase, his only remedy is to give notice to quit.

Repairs

A secure tenant has the same rights to repair as an assured tenant (see page 287). In addition, a secure tenant has the right to have certain small and urgent repairs carried out swiftly in terms of the Secure Tenants (Right to Repair) (Scotland) Regulations 1994. If the repair is not carried out within the timescales laid out in the Regulations, the landlord must pay a small amount of compensation.

Right to buy

A secure tenant has the right to buy his house or flat providing that he has had a minimum of two years' occupation in accommodation let by a secure landlord (not necessarily as a tenant and not necessarily all in the house which is to be bought). A tenant can exercise his right to buy with other members of the family acting as joint purchasers.

The right to buy does not apply to:

- houses specifically designed for the elderly or the disabled
- landlords with fewer than 100 houses
- charities.

The purchase price

The purchase price is the market price less a discount. The market price is determined by a valuer. The discount depends on the length of time that the buyer (or his spouse or cohabitee) has lived in housing subject to a secure tenancy. The occupation need not be as a secure tenant.

The discount

The discount for houses starts at 32 per cent after two years' occupation and rises by 1 per cent for every further year, up to a maximum of 60 per cent. The discount for flats starts at 44 per cent and rises by 2 per cent for every further year, up to a maximum of 70 per cent. In the case of some newer houses, there may be a minimum price below which a house may not be sold.

The procedure

The procedure for buying the house is as follows. The tenant makes an application on a form to buy. The landlord has up to one month to decide whether it has grounds to refuse to sell. If it does, it must serve a refusal notice on the tenant in that time. The tenant can appeal to the Lands Tribunal for Scotland. Otherwise, within two months of the date of application, the landlord must serve on the tenant an offer to sell giving the purchase price and other conditions. There is a right of appeal to the Lands Tribunal for Scotland if the tenant objects to the price or any of the conditions. If the tenant wants to accept the offer, he must do so by a notice of acceptance within two months.

Repayment of discount
If a house is resold within three years of the original purchase, the tenant will normally be required to repay some of the discount, as follows:

- 100 per cent of the discount if the house is sold within one year
- 66 per cent of the discount if the house is sold within two years
- 33 per cent of the discount if the house is sold within three years.

The right to buy on rent-to-mortgage terms
Under the rent-to-mortgage scheme, if a tenant wants to buy his home but has decided that the mortgage payments would be too high, he can obtain help to buy the house. The rent-to-mortgage scheme means that the tenant can become the owner of his home by making mortgage payments which are no higher than the existing rent. The local authority or Communities Scotland gives the tenant a loan for the difference between the level of mortgage which the current rent payments would raise and the discounted purchase price. The loan does not have to be repaid until the house is sold or disposed of. The level of discount is less than under the right-to-buy scheme, ranging from 17 to 45 per cent for a house and from 29 to 55 per cent for a flat. However, various categories of tenant do not qualify for this scheme.

Succession on the death of a tenant
There is a right of succession (a right to inherit) to a secure tenancy on the death of the secure tenant. This is limited to one succession only. Those entitled to succeed are:

- the tenant's spouse or cohabitee (not same-sex cohabitees)
- a surviving joint tenant

- where there is no one in either of the above two categories, a member of the tenant's family who is at least 16 years old and has lived in the house for at least 12 months prior to the tenant's death
- if more than one person is entitled to succeed and the parties cannot agree among themselves who is to succeed, within four weeks of the tenant's death, the landlord can decide who succeeds.

Assignation, subletting and taking in lodgers

If a secure tenant wishes to assign, sublet, give up possession of a house or take in a lodger, he must apply to the landlord in writing. The landlord may not withhold its consent unreasonably and must reply in writing within one month. If it does not reply within that period, permission is deemed to have been given. If the landlord refuses, there is a right of appeal within 21 days to the sheriff. Subtenants do not have a secure tenancy. Nor do they have a protected tenancy or a statutory tenancy under the Rent (Scotland) Act 1984, or an assured tenancy under the Housing (Scotland) Act 1988. They have a common law tenancy (see page 274).

Improvements and alterations

Provided a secure tenant has the landlord's written consent, he may carry out various alterations, improvements or additions to a house. The landlord must not withhold consent unreasonably. However, general repairs and maintenance do not need the landlord's permission, nor does interior decoration. The landlord may not increase the rent on the basis of the tenant's improvements. In some cases, it is possible for a tenant to obtain compensation for the cost of the works from the landlord at the end of the tenancy.

Transfer of tenancies and allocations

Whether a secure tenant is entitled to a transfer of a tenancy depends on the landlord's allocations policy. All housing associations and local authorities must publish their allocations policy. The policy should deal with transfers among tenants of tenancies. If the tenant disagrees with the landlord's decision on an allocation matter, the only remedy is judicial review in the Court of Session.

Terminating a secure tenancy

There are five main ways in which a secure tenancy can be terminated:

- the landlord and tenant agree in writing
- the tenant gives four weeks' notice to the landlord
- the tenant abandons the tenancy (no court order required)
- no one is eligible or willing to succeed to a tenancy
- the landlord obtains a court order for recovery of possession.

If the landlord wishes to obtain recovery of possession by court order, the procedure is as follows:

- service on the tenant of a notice giving him at least four weeks' notice of intention to take proceedings for recovery of possession (the notice must give details of the ground(s) on which the landlord will rely in court), and
- commencement of court proceedings by serving a summons on the tenant within six months of the date specified in the notice.

The form of action is known as a 'summary cause' and is dealt with by the sheriff court for the area.

Grounds for possession

The Housing (Scotland) Act 1987 sets out certain criteria which must be satisfied before a sheriff will grant an order for recovery of possession. The landlord must establish either a mandatory or a discretionary ground for recovery of possession.

Discretionary grounds

In the following cases, the sheriff has discretion to decide whether it is reasonable to grant an order. If he is not satisfied, the sheriff may refuse to make such an order. The discretionary grounds are:

1. non-payment of rent or breach of tenancy conditions
2. conviction for using the property for immoral or illegal purposes
3. waste, neglect and default leading to deterioration in the condition of the property
4. deterioration of the condition of furniture due to ill-treatment by the tenant
5. absence for a continuous period of six months or more/cessation of occupation as principal home

6. grant of tenancy induced by a false statement
7. nuisance or annoyance (serious anti-social conduct).

Mandatory grounds

If the landlord establishes a mandatory ground for recovering possession of a property, the sheriff has no discretion to refuse the order. However, the landlord must show that suitable alternative accommodation will be available to the tenant when the order takes effect. The mandatory grounds are:

8. nuisance or annoyance (less serious anti-social conduct)
9. overcrowding
10. demolition or other substantial works
11. premises designed or adapted for special needs
12. houses designed or provided with, or located near, facilities for people with special social support needs
13. housing association providing housing for special categories of tenants (the old, infirm, disabled, etc.)
14. the landlord's interest in the house is that of a tenant and the lease has been terminated or will terminate within six months
15. the landlord is an Islands council and the house is held for education purposes and is required for those purposes, and the council cannot provide an alternative house, and the tenant is or was employed by the council in its functions as an Education Authority, and such employment is being terminated
16. the landlord wishes to transfer the secure tenancy of a house to a tenant's spouse, former spouse or cohabitee. In this case, the sheriff must be satisfied both that it is reasonable to make an order *and* that suitable accommodation will be available to the tenant.

Tenant's choice

The Housing (Scotland) Act 1988 provides a 'tenant's choice' scheme which gives most public-sector tenants the right to transfer to an approved landlord, such as a housing association or a private landlord. An individual tenant may decide that he wishes to allow his house to be transferred. If so, the approved landlord requires the consent of the tenant and must then apply to acquire the house from the existing owner. The house is valued in accordance with a pre-determined formula, then the tenant is given a copy of the offer to sell (giving details of price and conditions) and has the right to negotiate and agree the terms of a new assured tenancy before the transfer of ownership is finalised. This scheme has not been much used. Where transfers of housing stock have taken place in Scotland, it has usually been done under separate legislation in the 1987 Act allowing councils and Communities Scotland (the former Scottish Homes) to transfer their housing stock to housing associations or housing companies. This process is known as Large Scale Voluntary Transfer (LSVT).

Under this process, when a council or Communities Scotland wishes to sell part or all of its housing to a housing association or housing company, it must first carry out widespread consultation with the tenants. Then it must conduct a ballot. The Scottish Ministers must approve the LSVT. They will do so only if a majority of those voting have voted in favour. In most cases, the tenants and the Scottish Ministers have approved the LSVT. On transfer, the tenants lose their status as secure tenants and become assured tenants. However, the right to buy is preserved.

After the Housing (Scotland) Act 2001 comes into force

The Housing (Scotland) Act 2001 introduces major changes to the governance of social housing and the rights and duties of tenants housed by local authorities, Communities Scotland (the former Scottish Homes) and registered housing associations. The following describes the main aspects of the law as it will apply once the Act is fully in force (which is expected to be by September 2002).

For the purposes of this chapter, a public-sector tenancy is one in which the landlord is a public authority such as a local authority (or local council), Communities Scotland or a registered housing association, and the tenant is an individual who has rented the house for residential use. Most such tenancies are termed 'Scottish secure tenancies'. Scottish secure tenancies are governed by the Housing (Scotland) Act 2001.

What is a Scottish secure tenancy?

A tenancy (see page 274) is a Scottish secure tenancy if:

- the house is let as a separate dwelling (see page 19)
- the tenant is an individual and the house is his only or principal home
- the landlord is a local authority, a registered social landlord (mostly housing associations), a water or sewerage authority or any other landlord prescribed by the Scottish Ministers, and
- the tenancy was created after the coming into force of the 2001 Act or
- the tenancy was created before the coming into force of the 2001 Act and the Scottish Ministers have decided that that tenancy will be a Scottish secure tenancy; and
- it is not a short Scottish secure tenancy (see below).

In practice, the vast majority of secure tenancies will automatically convert into Scottish secure tenancies some time in 2002, as will the majority of assured tenancies held by housing association tenants.

However, certain types of tenancies are excluded from Scottish secure tenancy status. The exclusions are:

- premises occupied under a contract of employment for the better performance of duties
- some types of police and fire authority housing
- student lettings
- temporary accommodation during works on the property which the tenant normally occupies as his home
- tenancies granted to the homeless
- accommodation for offenders under local authority supervision
- shared ownership agreements
- accommodation forming part of a building held for a non-housing purpose
- agricultural and business premises
- accommodation in property not owned by the landlord and where the terms of the lease prohibit the creation of a Scottish secure tenancy.

Rights and duties of Scottish secure tenants

Tenancy agreement

The Scottish secure tenancy landlord must provide the tenant with a free copy of a properly signed tenancy agreement. The Scottish Ministers have published a Model Scottish Secure Tenancy

Agreement and official guidance about the content of all Scottish secure tenancy agreements. The terms of the tenancy agreement cannot be changed without both the landlord and tenant agreeing. In certain restricted cases, where one party to the agreement does not agree to change the agreement, there is a right of appeal to the sheriff.

Rent

The Scottish secure tenancy landlord can increase the rent or any other charge under the tenancy by giving at least four weeks' written notice. An increase may be made at any time. There is no restriction on the amount of the increase. However, before the landlord increases the rent, it must first consult with all its tenants and have regard to what they say.

Repairs

As for secure tenants (see page 291). However, the 1994 Right to Repair Regulations which apply to secure tenants will be modified.

Right to buy

The right to buy for Scottish secure tenants who first became tenants after the Housing (Scotland) Act 2001 came into force is much less generous than for secure tenants. However, those Scottish secure tenants who used to be secure tenants will retain the old right to buy terms and conditions (see above).

The right-to-buy scheme for Scottish secure tenants is different from that for secure tenants in the following ways:

- five years' occupation is required instead of two years before the right to buy is acquired
- the starting point for the discount is 20 per cent for houses and flats
- the maximum discount is £15,000 or 35 per cent, whichever is the lesser
- the right to buy is suspended where legal proceedings have begun for possession of the house on the grounds of anti-social behaviour
- the right to buy is suspended where the tenant has council tax or rent arrears

- the right to buy extends to housing association houses: however, it will not come into effect until 2011 and there are many exceptions from the right to buy.

Succession (or inheritance)

When the tenant dies, the tenancy can be inherited by one of the following people. The order of priority is as follows.

Level one: spouse or cohabitee if the house was the only or principal home at death (and was for the previous six months in case of cohabitees); or joint tenant.

If no one qualifies, then:

Level two: member of family over 16 if the house was the only or principal home of that person.

If no one qualifies, then:

Level three: a person who gave up permanent accommodation in order to care for the tenant or member of the family and live in the house as his only or principal home.

If there is a dispute as to who should succeed, the landlord will decide. The tenancy can be inherited *twice* under these provisions. The term 'cohabitee' includes same-sex couples.

Assignation, subletting, joint tenants, mutual exchange and lodgers

If the tenant wants to assign the tenancy, sublet part of it, take in a lodger, convert the sole tenancy to a joint tenancy, or exchange the house with another Scottish secure tenant, he must obtain the permission of the landlord. The landlord must not unreasonably refuse permission and must reply to such a request within four weeks. If it does not, permission is deemed to have been granted. There is a right of appeal to the sheriff against an unreasonable refusal.

Improvements and alterations

As for secure tenants (see above).

Terminating a Scottish secure tenancy

There are six main ways in which a Scottish secure tenancy can be terminated:

- the landlord and tenant agree in writing
- the tenant gives four weeks' notice to the landlord
- the tenant abandons the tenancy (no court order required)
- no one is eligible or willing to succeed to a tenancy
- the landlord obtains a court order for recovery of possession
- the tenancy is converted to a short Scottish secure tenancy (see below).

Grounds for possession

The Housing (Scotland) Act 2001 sets out the grounds which must be satisfied before a sheriff will grant an order for recovery of possession. The grounds are very similar to those for secure tenants (see above). There is the same distinction between mandatory and discretionary grounds. In considering, in a discretionary case, whether it is reasonable to grant decree, the sheriff must consider all relevant circumstances including:

- nature, frequency and duration of the wrongdoing that is alleged
- whether other people were responsible for the conduct leading to the repossession action
- the effect of the conduct on other people
- what the landlord did before the raising of the action to stop the conduct complained of.

Short Scottish secure tenancies

From the date that the 2001 Act comes into force, public-sector landlords will be able, in certain restricted situations, to offer new tenants a short Scottish secure tenancy (SSST) rather than a Scottish secure tenancy. Short Scottish secure tenants have fewer rights than Scottish secure tenants. The main differences between the two types of tenancies are as follows:

- the SSST is for a fixed period of at least six months
- at the end of the fixed period, the landlord is entitled, as of right, to recover possession in the courts. The landlord will not have to prove one of the grounds for recovery of possession of a Scottish secure tenancy (although, if it wishes, it can also use that route). The landlord will not have to prove that it is reasonable for the court to grant decree

- there is no right to buy
- there is no right of succession
- the landlord must serve a notice on the tenant before the tenancy is granted telling him that the tenancy is a SSST.

SSSTs can be granted only in certain circumstances. However, the landlord is allowed to offer a Scottish secure tenancy instead of an SSST even if one of the following circumstances applies:

- a member of the tenant's family is subject to an anti-social behaviour order (under the Crime and Disorder Act 1998)
- the tenant has, within the last three years, been evicted on the grounds of anti-social behaviour
- it is a temporary letting to person seeking accommodation
- it is a temporary letting pending development of the house
- accommodation for homeless persons
- it is providing accommodation for a person requiring housing support services
- the house is leased by the landlord from some other body who does not permit Scottish secure tenancies to be granted over that house.

In addition, the landlord can convert an SSST into a Scottish secure tenancy by the service of a notice on the tenant. This can be done only when the tenant or a member of his household has become subject to an anti-social behaviour order. In that case, and in the case of the second of the situations noted above, the tenancy will automatically convert to a Scottish secure tenancy after 12 months unless a notice of proceedings is served in that time. There is a right of appeal to the sheriff by a person who is aggrieved at having his tenancy converted to an SSST or who has been offered an SSST.

Assured tenancies: grounds for possession

This is the full, verbatim listing of the grounds for possession available under assured tenancies as laid out in Schedule 2 of the Housing Act 1988.

Mandatory grounds

Ground 1: owner-occupier
Not later than the beginning of the tenancy the landlord gave notice in writing to the tenant that possession might be recovered on this ground or the court is of the opinion that it is just and equitable to dispense with the requirement of notice, and (in either case):

(a) at some time before the beginning of the tenancy, the landlord who is seeking possession or, in the case of joint landlords seeking possession, at least one of them occupied the dwellinghouse as his only or principal home; or

(b) the landlord who is seeking possession or, in the case of joint landlords seeking possession, at least one of them requires the dwellinghouse as his or his spouse's only or principal home and neither the landlord (or, in the case of joint landlords, any one of them) nor any other person who, as landlord, derived title under the landlord who gave the notice mentioned above, acquired the reversion on the tenancy for money or money's worth.

Ground 2: mortgagee exercising power of sale
The dwellinghouse is subject to a mortgage granted before the beginning of the tenancy; and

(a) the mortgagee is entitled to exercise a power of sale conferred on him by the mortgage or by Section 101 of the Law of Property Act 1925; and

(b) the mortgagee requires possession of the dwellinghouse for the purpose of disposing of it with vacant possession in exercise of that power; and

(c) either notice was given as mentioned in ground 1 above or the court is satisfied that it is just and equitable to dispense with the requirement of notice.

Ground 3: out-of-season holiday accommodation

The tenancy is a fixed-term tenancy for a term not exceeding eight months; and

(a) not later than the beginning of the tenancy the landlord gave notice in writing to the tenant that possession might be recovered on this ground; and

(b) at some time within the period of 12 months ending with the beginning of the tenancy, the dwellinghouse was occupied under a right to occupy it for a holiday.

Ground 4: out-of-term student accommodation

The tenancy is a fixed-term tenancy for a term not exceeding 12 months; and

(a) not later than the beginning of the tenancy the landlord gave notice in writing to the tenant that possession might be recovered on this ground; and

(b) at some time within the period of 12 months ending with the beginning of the tenancy, the dwellinghouse was let on a tenancy falling within paragraph 8 of Schedule 1 to this Act.

Ground 5: minister of religion's house

The dwellinghouse is held for the purpose of being available for occupation by a minister of religion as a residence from which to perform the duties of his office; and

(a) not later than the beginning of the tenancy the landlord gave notice in writing to the tenant that possession might be recovered on this ground; and

(b) the court is satisfied that the dwellinghouse is required for occupation by a minister of religion as such a residence.

Ground 6: demolition or reconstruction

The landlord who is seeking possession or, if that landlord is a registered housing association or charitable housing trust, a superior landlord, intends to demolish or reconstruct the whole or a substantial part of the dwellinghouse or to carry out substantial works on the dwellinghouse or any part thereof or any building of which it forms part, and the following conditions are fulfilled:

(a) the intended work cannot reasonably be carried out without the tenant giving up possession of the dwellinghouse because:

    (i) the tenant is not willing to agree to such a variation of the terms of the tenancy as would give such access and other facilities as would permit the intended work to be carried out; or

    (ii) the nature of the intended work is such that no such variation is practicable; or

    (iii) the tenant is not willing to accept an assured tenancy of such part only of the dwellinghouse (in this sub-paragraph referred to as 'reduced part') as would leave in the possession of his landlord so much of the dwellinghouse as would be reasonable to enable the intended work to be carried out and, where appropriate, as would give such access and other facilities over the reduced part as would permit the intended work to be carried out; or

    (iv) the nature of the intended work is such that such a tenancy is not practicable; and

(b) either the landlord seeking possession acquired his interest in the dwellinghouse before the grant of the tenancy or that interest was in existence at the time of that grant and neither that landlord (or, in the case of joint landlords, any of them) nor any other person who, alone or jointly with others, has acquired that interest since that time for money or money's worth

(c) the assured tenancy on which the dwellinghouse is let did not come into being by virtue of any provision of Schedule 1 to the Rent Act 1977, as amended by Part 1 of Schedule 4 to this Act or, as the case may be, Section 4 of the Rent (Agriculture) Act 1976, as amended by Part II of that Schedule.

For the purposes of this ground, if, immediately before the grant of the tenancy, the tenant to whom it was granted or, if it was granted to joint tenants, any of them was the tenant or one of the joint tenants of the dwellinghouse concerned under an earlier assured tenancy or, as the case may be, under a tenancy to which Schedule 10 to the Local Government and Housing Act 1989 applied, any reference in paragraph (b) above to the grant of a tenancy is a reference to the grant of that earlier assured tenancy or, as the case may be, to the grant of the tenancy to which the said Schedule 10 applied.

For the purposes of this ground 'registered housing association' has the same meaning as in the Housing Associations Act 1985 and 'charitable housing trust' means a housing trust, within the meaning of that Act, which is a charity, within the meaning of the Charities Act 1960.

For the purposes of this ground, every acquisition under Part IV of this Act shall be taken to be an acquisition for money or money's worth; and in any case where:

(i) the tenancy (in this paragraph referred to as 'the current tenancy') was granted to a person (alone or jointly with others) who, immediately before it was granted, was a tenant under a tenancy of a different dwellinghouse (in this paragraph referred to as 'the earlier tenancy'), and

(ii) the landlord under the current tenancy is the person who, immediately before that tenancy was granted, was the landlord under the earlier tenancy, and

(iii) the condition in paragraph (b) above could not have been fulfilled with respect to the earlier tenancy by virtue of an acquisition under Part IV of this Act (including one taken to be such an acquisition by virtue of the previous operation of this paragraph), the acquisition of the landlord's interest under the current tenancy shall be taken to have been under the Part and the landlord shall be taken to have acquired that interest after the grant of the current tenancy.

Ground 7: death

The tenancy is a periodic tenancy (including a statutory periodic tenancy) which has devolved under the will or intestacy of the former tenant and the proceedings for the recovery of possession are begun not later than 12 months after the death of the former tenant or, if the court so directs, after the date on which, in the opinion of the court, the landlord or, in the case of joint landlords, any one of them became aware of the former tenant's death.

For the purposes of this ground, the acceptance by the landlord of rent from a new tenant after the death of the former tenant shall not be regarded as creating a new periodic tenancy, unless the landlord agrees in writing to a change (as compared with the tenancy before the death) in the amount of the rent, the period of the tenancy, the premises which are let or any other term of the tenancy.

Ground 8: substantial rent arrears

Both at the date of the service of the notice under Section 8 of this Act relating to the proceedings for possession and at the date of the hearing

(a) if rent is payable weekly or fortnightly, at least eight weeks' rent is unpaid;

(b) if rent is payable monthly, at least two months' rent is unpaid;

(c) if rent is payable quarterly, at least one quarter's rent is more than three months in arrears; and

(d) if rent is payable yearly, at least three months' rent is more than three months in arrears;

and, for the purpose of this ground, 'rent' means rent lawfully due from the tenant.

Discretionary grounds

Ground 9: alternative accommodation

Suitable alternative accommodation is available for the tenant or will be available for him when the order for possession takes effect.

Ground 10: rent arrears

Some rent lawfully due from the tenant:

(a) is unpaid on the date on which the proceedings for possession are begun; and

(b) except where subsection (1)(b) of Section 8 of this Act applies, was in arrears at the date of the service of the notice under that section relating to those proceedings.

Ground 11: persistent delay
Whether or not any rent is in arrears on the date on which proceedings for possession are begun, the tenant has persistently delayed paying rent which has become lawfully due.

Ground 12: breach of covenant
Any obligation of the tenancy (other than one related to the payment of rent) has been broken or not performed.

Ground 13: waste or neglect
The condition of the dwellinghouse or any of the common parts has deteriorated owing to acts of waste by, or the neglect or default of, the tenant or any other person residing in the dwellinghouse and, in the case of an act of waste by, or the neglect or default of, a person lodging with the tenant or a subtenant of his, the tenant has not taken such steps as he ought reasonably to have taken for the removal of the lodger or subtenant.

Ground 14: nuisance
The tenant or a person residing in or visiting the dwellinghouse:

(a) has been guilty of conduct causing or likely to cause a nuisance or annoyance to a person residing, visiting or otherwise engaging in a lawful activity in the locality, or
(b) has been convicted of:
  (i) using the dwellinghouse or allowing it to be used for immoral or illegal purposes, or
  (ii) an arrestable offence committed in, or in the locality of, the dwellinghouse.

Ground 14A
The dwellinghouse was occupied (whether alone or with others) by a married couple or a couple living together as husband and wife and:

(a) one or both of the partners is a tenant of the dwellinghouse;
(b) the landlord who is seeking possession is a registered social landlord or a charitable housing trust;
(c) one partner has left the dwellinghouse because of violence or threats of violence by the other towards (i) that partner or (ii) a

member of the family of that partner who was residing with that partner immediately before the partner left, and

(d) the court is satisfied that the partner who has left is unlikely to return.

For the purposes of this ground 'registered social landlord' and 'member of the family' have the same meaning as in Part I of the Housing Act 1996 and 'charitable housing trust' means a housing trust within the meaning of the Housing Associations Act 1985, which is a charity within the meaning of the Charities Act 1993.

Ground 15: damage to furniture

The condition of any furniture provided for use under the tenancy has, in the opinion of the court, deteriorated owing to ill-treatment by the tenant or any other person residing in the dwellinghouse and, in the case of ill-treatment by a person lodging with the tenant or by a subtenant of his, the tenant has not taken such steps as he ought reasonably to have taken for the removal of the lodger or subtenant.

Ground 16: former employee

The dwellinghouse was let to the tenant in consequence of his employment by the landlord seeking possession, or a previous landlord under the tenancy, and the tenant has ceased to be in that employment.

For the purposes of this ground, at a time when the landlord is or was the Secretary of State, employment by a health service body, as defined in Section 60(7) of the National Health Service and Community Care Act 1990, shall be regarded as employment by the Secretary of State.

Ground 17: false statement

The tenant is the person, or one of the persons, to whom the tenancy was granted and the landlord was induced to grant the tenancy by a false statement made knowingly or recklessly by (a) the tenant, or (b) a person acting at the tenant's instigation.

Schedule 2A
Assured tenancies: non-shortholds

Tenancies excluded by notice

1. (1) An assured tenancy in respect of which a notice is served as mentioned in sub-paragraph (2) below.
   (2) The notice referred to in sub-paragraph (1) above is one which:
   - (a) is served before the assured tenancy is entered into,
   - (b) is served by the person who is to be the landlord under the assured tenancy on the person who is to be the tenant under that tenancy, and
   - (c) states that the assured tenancy to which it relates is not to be an assured shorthold tenancy.
2. (1) An assured tenancy in respect of which a notice is served as mentioned in sub-paragraph (2) below.
   (2) The notice referred to in sub-paragraph (1) above is one which:
   - (a) is served after the assured tenancy has been entered into,
   - (b) is served by the landlord under the assured tenancy on the tenant under that tenancy, and
   - (c) states that the assured tenancy to which it relates is no longer an assured shorthold tenancy.

Tenancies containing exclusionary provision

3. An assured tenancy which contains a provision to the effect that the tenancy is not an assured shorthold tenancy.

Tenancies under Section 39

4. An assured tenancy arising by virtue of Section 39 above, other than one to which subsection (7) of that section applies.

Former secure tenancies

5. An assured tenancy which became an assured tenancy on ceasing to be a secure tenancy.

Tenancies under Schedule 10 to the Local Government and Housing Act 1989

6. An assured tenancy arising by virtue of Schedule 10 to the Local Government and Housing Act 1989 (security of tenure on ending of long residential tenancies).

Tenancies replacing non-shortholds

7. (1) An assured tenancy which:
   - (a) is granted to a person (alone or jointly with others) who, immediately before the tenancy was granted, was the tenant (or, in the case of joint tenants, one of the tenants) under an assured tenancy other than a shorthold tenancy ('the old tenancy')
   - (b) is granted (alone or jointly with others) by a person who was at that time the landlord (or one of the joint landlords) under the old tenancy, and
   - (c) is not one in respect of which a notice is served as mentioned in sub-paragraph (2) below
   (2) The notice referred to in sub-paragraph (1)(c) above is one which:
   - (a) is in such form as may be prescribed
   - (b) is served before the assured tenancy is entered into
   - (c) is served by the person who is to be the tenant under the assured tenancy on the person who is to be the landlord under that tenancy (or, in the case of joint landlords, on at least one of the persons who are to be joint landlords), and
   - (d) states that the assured tenancy to which it relates is to be a shorthold tenancy.

8. An assured tenancy which comes into being by virtue of Section 5 above on the coming to an end of an assured tenancy which is not a shorthold tenancy.

Sample agreement for letting a whole house on a shorthold tenancy

Note: do not use this agreement without first reading Chapters 2, 3 and 5. Alternative or optional clauses are enclosed in square brackets [ ]. Be careful when inserting or deleting these clauses. If you delete any clauses, remember to re-number the subsequent clauses.

Date:

Parties

The Landlord: whose address for service is

The Tenant: whose address is

(1) DEFINITIONS

1.1 'the Agreement': this tenancy agreement, including any variation or amendment of it

1.2 'the Contents': the Landlord's fixtures, fittings, furniture and contents listed in the attached inventory

1.3 'the Deposit': £... (.... ...... pounds)

1.4 'the House': *(insert full postal address of property to be let)*

1.5 'the Interest Rate': .... (...) per cent per year above the base lending rate from time to time of .... Bank plc. *(insert name of your Bank)*

1.6 'the Landlord's Bank Account': account number ...... in the name of .... at the .... Bank plc of ......, sort code... *(insert full name and address and sort code of your bank)*

1.7   'the Rent': ... (... pounds) each month, payable in advance on the .... day of each month, the first payment payable today

1.8   'the Term': [.... months from and including ... *(specify commencement date)*] [*OR* a monthly/weekly periodic tenancy from and including *(specify commencement date)*]

(2)   THE TENANCY

The Landlord lets the House and the Contents to the Tenant for the Term.

(3)   THE TENANT'S OBLIGATIONS

The Tenant agrees with the Landlord (and if there is more than one tenant they agree jointly and individually) to comply with the obligations in Schedule I.

(4)   THE LANDLORD'S OBLIGATION

As long as the Tenant complies with the Tenant's obligations, the Landlord agrees not to interfere with the Tenant's use and enjoyment of the House.

(5)   AGREEMENTS AND DECLARATIONS

5.1   Any money payable to the Landlord by the Tenant is recoverable as rent.

5.2   Schedule II applies to the Deposit.

5.3   Subject to clause 5.4, if:

5.3.1   the Tenant complies with the Tenant's obligations, and

5.3.2   the House is uninhabitable due to fire or any other risk against which the Landlord may have insured

the Tenant may

(a)   stop paying the Rent until the House is reinstated [and
(b)   if the House is not reinstated within two months, serve at least four weeks' notice on the Landlord, expiring on any day, terminating the tenancy from that day.] *(This alternative is required only for a fixed-term tenancy)*

5.4   Clause 5.3 does not apply if the insurance money is irrecoverable because of any act or omission by the Tenant or anyone living in or visiting the House.

5.5   The Landlord may keep keys to the House.

5.6   Sections 11–14 of the Landlord and Tenant Act 1985 (as amended) apply to the Agreement. These require the Landlord to keep in repair the structure and exterior of the House and certain installations inside the House for the supply of water, gas, electricity and for sanitation.

5.7   Section 196 of the Law of Property Act 1925 (as amended) applies to notices served under the Agreement. This allows notices to be left at, or sent by registered or recorded delivery post, to the recipient's last known address. In the case of notices to be served on the Tenant, they can be left at or sent by registered or recorded delivery post to the House.

5.8   The Tenant consents to Housing Benefit being paid direct to the Landlord.

5.9   Subject to clause 5.9.4

5.9.1 the Landlord may increase the Rent at any time during the Term by giving to the Tenant at least 14 days' notice in writing prior to a rent payment day specifying the new rent.

5.9.2 the Tenant will then pay the increased amount as the Rent on and from that rent payment day.

5.9.3 if the Tenant does not agree to the amount specified, he may give the Landlord not less than two months' notice in writing, expiring on any day, terminating the tenancy from that day.

5.9.4 the Landlord cannot increase the Rent under this provision by more than 5 per cent or within 12 months of the commencement of the Term or within 12 months of a previous increase.

5.10   If at any time the Landlord:

5.10.1 requires the House for occupation by himself or any member of his family; or

5.10.2   wishes to sell the House with vacant possession; or

5.10.3   has died and the Landlord's Personal Representatives require vacant possession either to sell the House or so that it can be occupied by a beneficiary under the Landlord's will or intestacy

then the Landlord may terminate the tenancy by giving to the Tenant not less than two month's notice in writing expiring at any time.

5.11   If at any time the Tenant wishes to terminate the tenancy, he may do so by giving the Landlord not less than two months' notice in writing expiring at any time.

(6)   NOTICES

The Landlord notifies the Tenant that the Agreement is intended to create an assured shorthold tenancy within the meaning of Section 19A of the Housing Act 1988.

(7)   LANDLORD'S RIGHT OF RE-ENTRY

[not be used for a periodic tenancy]

7.1   Subject to clauses 7.2 and 7.3

7.1.1   If the Tenant does not:

7.1.1.1   pay the Rent (or any part) within 14 days of the due date; or

7.1.1.2   comply with the Tenant's obligations; or

7.1.2   if any of the circumstances mentioned in Grounds 2 and 8 of Part I of Schedule 2 or Grounds 10–15 of Part II of Schedule 2 of the Housing Act 1988 arise the Landlord may re-enter the House and end the tenancy.

7.2   Subject to clause 7.3

7.2.1   if anyone lives at the House; or

7.2.2   if the tenancy is an assured tenancy, the Landlord must obtain a court order for possession of the House before re-entering it.

7.3   the Landlord retains all his other rights in respect of the Tenant's obligations under the Agreement.

(8)   STAMP DUTY CERTIFICATE

The parties certify that there is no prior agreement to which this tenancy agreement gives effect.

THE PARTIES HAVE TODAY SIGNED THIS TENANCY AGREEMENT AS A DEED.

Schedule I

TENANT'S OBLIGATIONS

1.   To pay to the Landlord the Rent by banker's standing order to the Landlord's Bank Account according to the terms of the Agreement.

2.   To pay to the Landlord on demand:

2.1   interest at the Interest Rate on the Rent (and other money payable under this clause) if the Rent and other money is not paid on time; and

2.2   any increase in the Landlord's insurance premium due to a breach of clause 11.4 below; and

2.3   sufficient money to make up the Deposit to its original amount; and

2.4   the costs incurred by the Landlord in:

2.4.1   replacing locks and keys if the Tenant loses keys or breaches clause 8.3 below; and

2.4.2   rectifying any breaches of the Tenant's obligations.

2.5   the Landlord's legal and other costs and expenses (including VAT) incurred in:

2.5.1   recovering Rent or other money from the Tenant; and

2.5.2   enforcing the Agreement; and

2.5.3   serving any notice on the Tenant; and

2.5.4   recovering possession from the Tenant.

2.6   the Deposit.

3. To pay to the Landlord the Landlord's reasonable legal costs and expenses properly incurred in negotiating, preparing, executing and stamping the Agreement and counterpart.

4. To pay:

4.1 the council tax for the House; and

4.2 the water, sewerage, and environmental charges for the House; and

4.3 all charges for gas and electricity used at the House and for any telephone installed at the House; and

4.4 the television licence fee for the House.

5. To use the House as a home for one family only.

6. To keep the House and Contents clean, tidy and in good decorative repair, and in particular to:

6.1 remove rubbish from the House each day; and

6.2 protect the House and Contents from frost; and

6.3 ensure all rooms at the House are properly ventilated at all times; and

6.4 clean all the windows (both inside and out) at least once a month; and

6.5 vacuum-clean all carpets at least once a week; and

6.6 unblock drains, pipes, sinks, basins and baths; and

6.7 remove all vermin; and

6.8 keep the garden tidy; and

6.9 mow any grass once a week in the growing season.

7. To comply with notices from the Landlord to remedy breaches of clause 6 within a reasonable time.

8. Not to or allow anyone else to:

8.1 damage the House or Contents; or

8.2 remove the Contents from the House; or

8.3   change the locks at the House; or

8.4   alter, add or attach anything to the House; or

8.5   tamper with water, telephone, electrical or gas systems and installations serving the House; or

8.6   overload, block up or damage any drains, pipes, wires or cables serving the House;

8.7   assault or abuse the Landlord, the landlord's agents or any members of the Landlord's family.

9.   To notify the Landlord immediately in writing of:

9.1   any vermin, defects or disrepair in the House or the Contents; and

9.2   any notices about the House delivered to the House.

10.   To permit the Landlord and his agents to enter the House at all reasonable times and on reasonable notice having been given to:

10.1   inspect the House and Contents; or

10.2   repair the House; or

10.3   repair or replace the Contents; or

10.4   replace locks; or

10.5   comply with any legal obligations; or

10.6   show prospective buyers or tenants the House.

11.   Not to do or allow at the House anything which:

11.1   might annoy others; or

11.2   is dangerous; or

11.3   is illegal or immoral; or

11.4   might prejudice the Landlord's insurance cover or increase the premiums.

12.   Not to or allow others to:

12.1   keep any birds or animals at the House other than in secure cages or containers; or

12.2   play or use any musical or electrical instrument or any other means of reproducing sound so that it can be heard outside the House.

13.   Not to leave the House vacant for more than 72 hours without:

13.1   draining all water supplies to the House; and

13.2   turning off the gas and electricity supplies at the mains.

14.   To ensure that at all times the windows and doors are properly secured.

15.   Not to:

15.1   assign; or

15.2   sublet; or

15.3   part with; or

15.4   share possession of the House or any part of it without the Landlord's prior consent in writing, such consent not to be unreasonably withheld.

16.   At the determination of the tenancy to return to the Landlord:

16.1   the House and the Contents in a clean and tidy condition in accordance with the Tenant's obligations; and

16.2   all keys to the House.

Schedule II

THE DEPOSIT

1.   The Landlord holds the Deposit as security for:

1.1   unpaid Rent or other money due to the Landlord; and

1.2   unpaid accounts for gas, electricity, telephone, water and Council Tax; and

1.3   any other breach of the Tenant's obligations; and

1.4   any Housing Benefit repayable to the Local Authority, and

1.5   any other claims made against the Landlord because of any acts or omissions of the Tenant.

2. The Landlord may at any time take money from the Deposit:

2.1 to cover the items listed in clause 1 above; and

2.2 to pay on the Tenant's behalf the charges in clause 4 of Schedule I; and

2.3 to pay for gas, electricity, telephone and water services to be re-connected, if disconnected due to the Tenant.

3. Subject to clause 2 above, if the Landlord:

3.1 sells his interest in the House; and

3.2 pays the Deposit (or balance of it, if any) to his buyer,

the Tenant shall release the Landlord from all claims and liabilities in respect of the Deposit.

4. The Landlord may retain the Deposit until the local authority confirms that no Housing Benefit paid to the Landlord is repayable.

5. Subject to clauses 2, 3 and 4 above, if the Tenant:

5.1 complies with the Tenant's obligations; and

5.2 vacates the House,

the Landlord must repay the Deposit (or the balance of it, if any) without interest to the Tenant (or where the Tenant is more than one person) to any of them within 28 days of the Tenant vacating the House.

(Lease)

SIGNED AS A DEED

BY THE LANDLORD: *(Signature of landlord)*

IN THE PRESENCE OF: *(Signature of witness)*
(Name and address of witness)

(Counterpart)

SIGNED AS A DEED

BY THE TENANT: *(Signature of tenant)*

IN THE PRESENCE OF: *(Signature of witness)*
(Name and address of witness)

Sample agreement for letting a whole house on an ordinary assured tenancy with a ground 1 notice

Note: do not use this agreement without first reading Chapter 3. Alternative or optional clauses are enclosed in square brackets [ ]. Be careful when inserting or deleting these clauses. If you delete any clauses, remember to re-number the subsequent clauses.

Date:

Parties

The Landlord: whose address for service is

The Tenant: whose address is

(1)   **DEFINITIONS**

1.1   'the Agreement': this tenancy agreement, including any variation or amendment of it

1.2   'the Contents': the Landlord's fixtures, fittings, furniture and contents listed in the attached inventory

1.3   'the Deposit': £... (.... ...... pounds)

1.4   'the House': *(insert full postal address of property to be let)*

1.5   'the Interest Rate': .... (...) per cent per year above the base lending rate from time to time of .... Bank plc. *(insert name of your Bank)*

1.6   'the Landlord's Bank Account': account number ...... in the name of .... at the .... Bank plc of ......, sort code... *(insert full name and address and sort code of your bank)*

1.7   'the Rent': … (… pounds) each month, payable in advance on the …. day of each month, the first payment payable today

1.8   'the Term': [… . months from and including … *(specify commencement date)*] [*OR* a monthly/weekly periodic tenancy from and including *(specify commencement date)*]

(2)   THE TENANCY

The Landlord lets the House and the Contents to the Tenant for the Term.

(3)   THE TENANT'S OBLIGATIONS

The Tenant agrees with the Landlord (and if there is more than one tenant they agree jointly and individually) to comply with the obligations in Schedule I.

(4)   THE LANDLORD'S OBLIGATION

If the Tenant complies with the Tenant's obligations, the Landlord agrees not to interfere with the Tenant's use and enjoyment of the House.

(5)   AGREEMENTS AND DECLARATIONS

5.1   Any money payable to the Landlord by the Tenant is recoverable as rent.

5.2   Schedule II applies to the Deposit.

5.3   Subject to clause 5.4, if:

5.3.1   the Tenant complies with the Tenant's obligations, and

5.3.2   the House is uninhabitable due to fire or any other risk against which the Landlord may have insured

the Tenant may

(a) stop paying the Rent until the House is reinstated [and
(b) if the House is not reinstated within two months, serve at least four weeks' notice on the Landlord, expiring on any day, terminating the tenancy from that day.] *(This alternative is required only for a fixed-term tenancy)*

5.4   Clause 5.3 does not apply if the insurance money is irrecoverable because of any act or omission by the Tenant or anyone living in or visiting the House.

5.5   The Landlord may keep keys to the House.

5.6   Sections 11–14 of the Landlord and Tenant Act 1985 (as amended) apply to the Agreement. These require the Landlord to keep in repair the structure and exterior of the House and certain installations inside the House for the supply of water, gas, electricity and for sanitation.

5.7   Section 196 of the Law of Property Act 1925 (as amended) applies to notices served under the Agreement. This allows notices to be left at, or sent by registered or recorded delivery post to, the recipient's last known address. In the case of notices to be served on the Tenant, they can be left at or sent by registered or recorded delivery post to the House.

5.8   The Tenant consents to Housing Benefit being paid direct to the Landlord.

5.9   Subject to clause 5.9.4

5.9.1   the Landlord may increase the Rent at any time during the Term by giving to the tenant at least 14 days' notice in writing prior to a rent payment day specifying the new rent.

5.9.2   the Tenant will then pay the increased amount as the Rent on and from that rent payment day.

5.9.3   if the Tenant does not agree to the amount specified, he may give the Landlord not less than two months' notice in writing, expiring on any day, terminating the tenancy from that day.

5.9.4   the Landlord cannot increase the Rent under this provision by more than 5 per cent or within 12 months of the commencement of the Term or within 12 months of a previous increase.

5.10   If at any time the Landlord:

5.10.1 requires the House for occupation by himself or any member of his family; or

5.10.2   wishes to sell the House with vacant possession; or

5.10.3   has died and the Landlord's Personal Representatives require vacant possession either to sell the House or so that it can be occupied by a beneficiary under the Landlord's will or intestacy

then the Landlord may terminate the tenancy by giving to the Tenant not less than two months' notice in writing expiring at any time.

5.11   If at any time the Tenant wishes to terminate the tenancy, he may do so by giving the Landlord not less than two months' notice in writing expiring at any time.

(6)   NOTICES

6.1   The Landlord notifies the Tenant that the Agreement is intended to create an assured tenancy within the meaning of Section 1 of the Housing Act 1988.

6.2   The Landlord notifies the Tenant that possession of the House may be recovered under:

[Insert whichever paragraphs are appropriate, and re-number accordingly]

6.2.1   Ground 1 of Part I of Schedule 2 of the Housing Act 1988.

This ground requires the court to order possession of the House where the Landlord has previously occupied the House as his only or principal home or where the Landlord requires the House as his or his spouse's only or principal home; and

6.2.2   Ground 2 of Part I of Schedule 2 of the Housing Act 1988.

This ground requires the court to order possession of the House where:

(a) the House is subject to a mortgage or charge granted before the beginning of the tenancy; and
(b) the lender is entitled to exercise a power of sale; and
(c) the lender requires possession of the House in order to dispose of it with vacant possession when exercising the power of sale.

6.2.3   Ground 3 of Part I of Schedule 2 of the Housing Act 1988.

This ground requires the court to order possession of the House where:

(a) the tenancy is for a fixed term not exceeding eight months; and
(b) at some time within the 12 months prior to the letting the House was occupied for holiday purposes.

6.2.4   Ground 4 of Part I of Schedule 2 of the Housing Act 1988.

This ground requires the court to order possession of the House where:

(a) the House is held for the purpose of being available as a residence for a Minister of Religion from which to perform his duties; and
(b) the court is satisfied that the House is so required.

[(7)   LANDLORD'S RIGHT OF RE-ENTRY

[not required in a periodic tenancy]

7.1   Subject to clauses 7.2 and 7.3

7.1.1   If the Tenant does not:

7.1.1.1 pay the Rent (or any part) within 14 days of the due date; or

7.1.1.2 comply with the Tenant's obligations; or

7.1.2   if any of the circumstances mentioned in Grounds 2 and 8 of Part I of Schedule 2 or Grounds 10–15 of Part II of Schedule 2 of the Housing Act 1988 arise the Landlord may re-enter the House and end the tenancy.

7.2   Subject to clause 7.3

7.2.1   if anyone lives at the House; or

7.2.2   if the tenancy is an assured tenancy, the Landlord must obtain a court order for possession of the House before re-entering it.

7.3   The Landlord retains all his other rights in respect of the Tenant's obligations under the Agreement.

(8) STAMP DUTY CERTIFICATE

The parties certify that there is no prior agreement to which this tenancy agreement gives effect.

THE PARTIES HAVE TODAY SIGNED THIS TENANCY AGREEMENT AS A DEED.

Schedule I

TENANT'S OBLIGATIONS

1.　　To pay to the Landlord the Rent by banker's standing order to the Landlord's Bank Account according to the terms of the Agreement.

2.　　To pay to the Landlord on demand:

2.1　　interest at the Interest Rate on the Rent (and other money payable under this clause) if the Rent and other money is not paid on time; and

2.2　　any increase in the Landlord's insurance premium due to a breach of clause 11.4 below; and

2.3　　sufficient money to make up the Deposit to its original amount; and

2.4　　the costs incurred by the Landlord in:

2.4.1　　replacing locks and keys if the Tenant loses keys or breaches clause 8.3 below; and

2.4.2　　rectifying any breaches of the Tenant's obligations.

2.5　　the Landlord's legal and other costs and expenses (including VAT) incurred in:

2.5.1　　recovering Rent or other money from the Tenant; and

2.5.2　　enforcing the Agreement; and

2.5.3　　serving any notice on the Tenant; and

2.5.4　　recovering possession from the Tenant.

2.6　　the Deposit.

3. To pay to the Landlord the Landlord's reasonable legal costs and expenses properly incurred in negotiating, preparing, executing and stamping the Agreement and counterpart.

4. To pay:

4.1 the council tax for the House; and

4.2 the water, sewerage, and environmental charges for the House; and

4.3 all charges for gas and electricity used at the House and for any telephone installed at the House; and

4.4 the television licence fee for the House.

5. To use the House as a home for one family only.

6. To keep the House and Contents clean, tidy and in good decorative repair, and in particular to:

6.1 remove rubbish from the House each day; and

6.2 protect the House and Contents from frost; and

6.3 ensure all rooms at the House are properly ventilated at all times; and

6.4 clean all the windows (both inside and out) at least once a month; and

6.5 vacuum-clean all carpets at least once a week; and

6.6 unblock drains, pipes, sinks, basins and baths; and

6.7 remove all vermin; and

6.8 keep the garden tidy; and

6.9 mow any grass once a week in the growing season.

7. To comply with notices from the Landlord to remedy breaches of clause 6 within a reasonable time.

8. Not to or allow anyone else to:

8.1 damage the House or Contents; or

8.2 remove the Contents from the House; or

8.3   change the locks at the House; or

8.4   alter, add or attach anything to the House; or

8.5   tamper with water, telephone, electrical or gas systems and installations serving the House; or

8.6   overload, block up or damage any drains, pipes, wires or cables serving the House;

8.7   assault or abuse the Landlord, the landlord's agents or any members of the Landlord's family.

9.   To notify the Landlord immediately in writing of:

9.1   any vermin, defects or disrepair in the House or the Contents; and

9.2   any notices about the House delivered to the House.

10.   To permit the Landlord and his agents to enter the House at all reasonable times and on reasonable notice having been given to:

10.1   inspect the House and Contents; or

10.2   repair the House; or

10.3   repair or replace the Contents; or

10.4   replace locks; or

10.5   comply with any legal obligations; or

10.6   show prospective buyers or tenants the House.

11.   Not to do or allow at the House anything which:

11.1   might annoy others; or

11.2   is dangerous; or

11.3   is illegal or immoral; or

11.4   might prejudice the Landlord's insurance cover or increase the premiums.

12.   Not to allow others to:

12.1   keep any birds or animals at the House other than in secure cages or containers; or

12.2   play or use any musical or electrical instrument or any other means of reproducing sound so that it can be heard outside the House.

13.   Not to leave the House vacant for more than 72 hours without:

13.1   draining all water supplies to the House; and

13.2   turning off the gas and electricity supplies at the mains.

14.   To ensure that at all times the windows and doors are properly secured.

15.   Not to:

15.1   assign; or

15.2   sublet; or

15.3   part with; or

15.4   share occupation of the House or any part of it without the Landlord's prior consent in writing, such consent not to be unreasonably withheld.

16.   At the determination of the tenancy to return to the Landlord:

16.1   the House and the Contents in a clean and tidy condition in accordance with the Tenant's obligations; and

16.2   all keys to the House.

Schedule II

THE DEPOSIT

1.   The Landlord holds the Deposit as security for:

1.1   unpaid Rent or other money due to the Landlord; and

1.2   unpaid accounts for gas, electricity, telephone, water and council tax; and

1.3   any other breach of the Tenant's obligations; and

1.4   any Housing Benefit repayable to the Local Authority, and

1.5   any other claims made against the Landlord because of any acts or omissions of the Tenant.

2. The Landlord may at any time take money from the Deposit:

2.1 to cover the items listed in clause 1 above; and

2.2 to pay on the Tenant's behalf the charges in clause 4 of Schedule I; and

2.3 to pay for gas, electricity, telephone and water services to be re-connected, if disconnected due to the Tenant.

3. Subject to clause 2 above, if the Landlord:

3.1 sells his interest in the House; and

3.2 pays the Deposit (or balance of it, if any) to his buyer,

the Tenant shall release the Landlord from all claims and liabilities in respect of the Deposit.

4. The Landlord may retain the Deposit until the local authority confirms that no Housing Benefit paid to the Landlord is repayable.

5. Subject to clauses 2, 3 and 4 above, if the Tenant:

5.1 complies with the Tenant's obligations; and

5.2 vacates the House,

the Landlord must repay the Deposit (or the balance of it, if any) without interest to the Tenant (or where the Tenant is more than one person) to any of them within 28 days of the Tenant vacating the House.

(Lease)

SIGNED AS A DEED

BY THE LANDLORD: *(Signature of landlord)*

IN THE PRESENCE OF: *(Signature of witness)*
(Name and address of witness)

(Counterpart)

SIGNED AS A DEED

BY THE TENANT: *(Signature of tenant)*

IN THE PRESENCE OF: *(Signature of witness)*
(Name and address of witness)

Sample agreement for letting part of a house, not on an assured or a shorthold tenancy

Note: do not use this agreement without first reading Chapter 3. Alternative or optional clauses are enclosed in square brackets [ ]. Be careful when inserting or deleting these clauses. If you delete any clauses, remember to re-number the subsequent clauses.

If you are letting the *whole* of a house on a non-shorthold tenancy (see Chapters 5 and 6), you will need to delete the provisions relating to 'the House' and the 'shared facilities' and amend the description at 1.1. All other references to 'the Flat' in the agreement will also need changing.

Date:

Parties

The Landlord: whose address for service is

The Tenant: whose address is

(1) DEFINITIONS

1.1   'the Flat': (*insert full postal address and location of flat: e.g. 'First-floor flat at 6 Coronation Street, Weatherfield WF7 8UH, comprising kitchen, bathroom, living room and bedroom'; OR 'Flat 5, 6 Coronation Street, Weatherfield WF7 8UH'; OR 'Front bed-sitting room at …'*)

1.2   'the Term': [… months from and including (*specify commencement date)*] [OR a monthly/weekly periodic tenancy from and including (*specify commencement date*)]

1.3 'the Rent': £ .... (. . . . . pounds) for each month, payable in advance on the . . . of each month, the first payment payable today

1.4 'the Contents': the Landlord's fixtures, fittings, furniture and contents in the Flat listed in the attached inventory

1.5 'the Deposit': £ .... (. . . . . pounds);

1.6 'the Interest Rate': . . . . (. . . .) per cent a year above the lending rate for the . . . . Bank plc

1.7 'the Landlord's Bank Account': account number . . . ., in the name of . . . . at the . . . . Bank plc of . . . ., sort code 00 00 00

1.8 the Agreement': this tenancy agreement, including any variation or amendment of it

1.9 'the House': the Landlord's house at *(insert address)* of which the Flat forms part

1.10 'the Landlord's Possessions': any goods or property (whether or not belonging to the Landlord) located in the House

[1.11 'the Shared Facilities': the kitchen, lavatory, bathroom, living room, hall and stairs used in common with the Landlord or other tenants] *(Delete as appropriate)*

(2)   THE TENANCY

The Landlord lets the Flat [together with the use of the Shared Facilities] and the Contents to the Tenant for the Term.

(3)   THE TENANT'S OBLIGATIONS

The Tenant agrees with the Landlord (and if there is more than one tenant they agree jointly and individually) to comply with the obligations in Schedule I.

(4)   THE LANDLORD'S OBLIGATION

If the Tenant complies with the Tenant's obligations, the Landlord agrees not to interfere with the Tenant's use and enjoyment of the Flat [or the Shared Facilities]

(5)   AGREEMENTS AND DECLARATIONS

5.1   Any money payable to the Landlord by the Tenant is recoverable as rent.

5.2   Schedule II applies to the Deposit.

5.3   Subject to clause 5.4, if:

5.3.1   the Tenant complies with the Tenant's obligations; and

5.3.2   the Flat is uninhabitable due to fire or any other risk against which the Landlord may have insured

the Tenant may

(a)   stop paying the Rent until the Flat is reinstated; [and
(b)   if the Flat is not reinstated within two months, serve at least four weeks' notice on the Landlord, expiring on any day, terminating the tenancy from that day.] *(This alternative is required only for a fixed-term tenancy)*

5.4   Clause 5.3 does not apply if the insurance money is irrecoverable because of any act or omission by the Tenant or anyone living in or visiting the Flat.

5.5   The Landlord may keep keys to the Flat.

5.6   Sections 11–14 of the Landlord and Tenant Act 1985 (as amended) apply to the Agreement. These require the Landlord to keep in repair the structure and exterior of the Flat and certain installations inside the Flat for the supply of water, gas, electricity and for sanitation.

5.7   Section 196 of the Law of Property Act 1925 (as amended) applies to notices served under the Agreement. This allows notices to be left at, or sent by registered or recorded delivery post to, the recipient's last known address. In the case of notices to be served on the Tenant, they can be left at or sent by registered or recorded delivery post to the Flat.

5.8   The Tenant consents to Housing Benefit being paid direct to the Landlord.

5.9   Subject to clause 5.9.4

5.9.1   the Landlord may increase the Rent at any time during the Term by giving to the Tenant at least 14 days' notice in writing prior to a rent payment day specifying the new rent.

5.9.2   the Tenant will then pay the increased amount as the Rent on and from that rent payment day.

5.9.3   if the Tenant does not agree to the amount specified, he may give the Landlord not less than two months' notice in writing, expiring on any day, terminating the tenancy from that day.

5.9.4   the Landlord cannot increase the Rent under this provision by more than 5 per cent or within 12 months of the commencement of the Term or within 12 months of a previous increase.

5.10   If at any time the Landlord:

5.10.1   requires the Flat for occupation by himself or any member of his family; or

5.10.2   wishes to sell the Flat with vacant possession; or

5.10.3   has died and the Landlord's Personal Representatives require vacant possession either to sell the Flat or so that it can be occupied by a beneficiary under the Landlord's will or intestacy

then the Landlord may terminate the tenancy by giving to the Tenant not less than two months' notice in writing expiring at any time.

5.11   If at any time the Tenant wishes to terminate the tenancy, he may do so by giving the Landlord not less than two months' notice in writing expiring at any time.

(6)   LANDLORD'S RIGHT OF RE-ENTRY

(do not use in a periodic tenancy)

6.1   Subject to clauses 6.2 and 6.3

6.1.1   If the Tenant does not:

6.1.1.1   pay the Rent (or any part) within 14 days of the due date; or

6.1.1.2 comply with the Tenant's obligations; or

6.1.2 if at any time the tenancy created by this Agreement is an assured or assured shorthold tenancy within the Housing Act 1988 and any of the circumstances mentioned in Grounds 2 and 8 of Part I of Schedule 2 or Grounds 10–5 of Part II of Schedule 2 of the Housing Act 1988 arise

the Landlord may re-enter the Flat and end the tenancy.

6.2 Subject to clause 6.3

6.2.1 if anyone lives at the Flat; or

6.2.2 if the tenancy is at any time an assured or an assured shorthold tenancy,

the Landlord must obtain a court order for possession of the Flat before re-entering it.

6.3 the Landlord retains all his other rights in respect of the Tenant's obligations under the Agreement.]

(7) STAMP DUTY CERTIFICATE

The parties certify that there is no prior agreement to which this tenancy agreement gives effect.

THE PARTIES HAVE TODAY SIGNED THIS TENANCY AGREEMENT AS A DEED.

Schedule I

TENANT'S OBLIGATIONS

1. To pay to the Landlord the Rent by banker's standing order to the Landlord's Bank Account according to the terms of the Agreement.

2. To pay to the Landlord on demand:

2.1 interest at the Interest Rate on the Rent (and other money payable under this clause) if the Rent and other money is not paid on time; and

2.2 any increase in the Landlord's insurance premium due to a breach of paragraph 11.4 below; and

2.3   sufficient money to make up the Deposit to its original amount; and

2.4   the costs incurred by the Landlord in:

2.4.1   replacing locks and keys if the Tenant loses keys or breaches clause 8.3 below; and

2.4.2   rectifying any breaches of the Tenant's obligations.

2.5   the Landlord's legal and other costs and expenses (including VAT) incurred in:

2.5.1   recovering Rent or other money from the Tenant; and

2.5.2   enforcing the Agreement;

2.5.3   serving any notice on the Tenant; and

2.5.4   recovering possession from the Tenant.

2.6   the Deposit.

3.   To pay the Landlord the Landlord's reasonable legal costs and expenses properly incurred in negotiating, preparing, executing and stamping the Agreement and counterpart.

4.   To pay:

4.1   the council tax for the Flat; and

4.2   the water, sewerage, and environmental charges for the Flat; and

4.3   all charges for gas and electricity used at the Flat and for any telephone installed at the Flat; and

4.4   the television licence fee for the Flat.

5.   To use the Flat as a home for one [person] [family] only.

6.   To keep the Flat and Contents in good decorative repair [and the Flat and Contents and Shared Facilities clean and tidy], and in particular to:

6.1   remove rubbish from the Flat [and the Shared Facilities] each day; and

6.2   protect the Flat and Contents from frost; and

6.3   ensure all rooms at the Flat are properly ventilated at all times; and

6.4   clean all the windows of the Flat (both inside and out) at least once a month; and

6.5   vacuum-clean all carpets in the Flat at least once a week; and

6.6   unblock drains, pipes, sinks, basins and baths in the Flat [and the Shared Facilities]; and

6.7   remove all vermin.

7.   To comply with notices from the Landlord to remedy breaches of clause 6 within a reasonable time.

8.   Not to or allow anyone else to:

8.1   damage the House or the Flat or the Contents or the Landlord's Possessions; or

8.2   remove the Contents from the Flat or the Landlord's Possessions from the House; or

8.3   change the locks at the Flat or the House; or

8.4   alter, add or attach anything to the Flat; or

8.5   tamper with water, telephone, electrical or gas systems and installations serving the House or the Flat; or

8.6   overload, block up or damage any drains, pipes, wires or cables serving the House or the Flat;

8.7   assault or abuse the Landlord, the landlord's agents or any members of the Landlord's family.

[8.8   prevent or hinder the Landlord or anyone authorised by him from using the Shared Facilities]

9.   To notify the Landlord immediately in writing of:

9.1   any vermin, defects or disrepair in the Flat or the Contents [or the Shared Facilities]; and

9.2   any notices about the Flat delivered to the Flat.

10.   To permit the Landlord and his agents to enter the House at all reasonable times and on reasonable notice having been given to:

10.1   inspect the Flat and Contents; or

10.2   repair the Flat; or

10.3   repair or replace the Contents; or

10.4   replace locks; or

10.5   comply with any legal obligations; or

10.6   show prospective buyers or tenants the Flat.

11.   Not to do or allow at the Flat [or in the Shared Facilities] anything which:

11.1   might annoy the Landlord or others; or

11.2   is dangerous; or

11.3   is illegal or immoral; or

11.4   might prejudice the Landlord's insurance cover or increase the premiums.

12.   Not to or allow others to:

12.1   keep any birds or animals at the Flat other than in secure cages or containers; or

12.2   play or use any musical or electrical instrument or any other means of reproducing sound [in the Shared Facilities or] so that it can be heard outside the Flat.

[12.3   use any bathroom, kitchen or lavatory forming part of the Shared Facilities for any purpose other than as a bathroom, kitchen or lavatory respectively.]

[12.4   use any hallway or stairway forming part of the Shared Facilities other than as a means of access on foot to and from the Flat]

13.   Not to leave the Flat vacant for more than 72 hours without:

13.1   draining all water supplies to the Flat; and

13.2   turning off the gas and electricity supplies at the mains.

14.   To ensure that at all times the windows and doors of the Flat are properly secured.

15.   Not to:

15.1   assign; or

15.2   sublet; or

15.3   part with; or

15.4   share possession of

the Flat or any part of it without the landlord's prior consent in writing, such consent not to be unreasonably withheld.

16.   At the determination of the tenancy to return to the Landlord:

16.1   the Flat and the Contents in a clean and tidy condition in accordance with the Tenant's obligations; and

16.2   all keys to the Flat and to the House.

Schedule II

THE DEPOSIT

1.   The Landlord holds the Deposit as security for:

1.1   unpaid Rent or other money due to the Landlord; and

1.2   unpaid accounts for gas, electricity, telephone, water and council tax; and

1.3   any other breach of the Tenant's obligations; and

1.4   any Housing Benefit repayable to the Local Authority, and

1.5   any other claims made against the Landlord because of any acts or omissions of the Tenant.

2.   The Landlord may at any time take money from the Deposit:

2.1   to cover the items listed in clause 1 above; and

2.2   to pay on the Tenant's behalf the charges in clause 4 of Schedule I; and

2.3   to pay for gas, electricity, telephone and water services to be re-connected, if disconnected due to the Tenant.

3.   Subject to clause 2 above, if the Landlord:

3.1   sells his interest in the Flat; and

3.2   pays the Deposit (or balance of it, if any) to his buyer,

the Tenant shall release the Landlord from all claims and liabilities in respect of the Deposit.

4.   The Landlord may retain the Deposit until the local authority confirms that no Housing Benefit paid to the Landlord is repayable.

5.   Subject to clauses 2, 3 and 4 above, if the Tenant:

5.1   complies with the Tenant's obligations; and

5.2   vacates the Flat,

the Landlord must repay the Deposit (or the balance of it, if any) without interest to the Tenant (or where the Tenant is more than one person) to any of them within 28 days of the Tenant vacating the Flat.

(Lease)

SIGNED AS A DEED

BY THE LANDLORD: *(Signature of landlord)*

IN THE PRESENCE OF: *(Signature of witness)*
(Name and address of witness)

(Counterpart)

SIGNED AS A DEED

BY THE TENANT: *(Signature of tenant)*

IN THE PRESENCE OF: *(Signature of witness)*
(Name and address of witness)

Sample guarantee agreement for residential tenancies

Note: do not use this agreement without first reading Chapter 5. Alternative or optional clauses are enclosed in square brackets [ ].

Date:

Parties

The Landlord:

   of *(address/es)*

The Tenant:

   of *(address/es)*

The Guarantor:

   of *(address/es)*

The House: *(address)*

The Agreement: the tenancy agreement entered into between the Landlord and the Tenant dated . . . . and any amendment or variation of it and any new or further agreement granting a tenancy which is entered into between the Landlord and the Tenant

IT IS AGREED AS FOLLOWS:

1.   In consideration of the Landlord granting the Tenant a tenancy of the House upon the terms of the Agreement the Guarantor guarantees:

1.1   the payment by the Tenant of the rent and any other monies payable by the Tenant under the Agreement; and

1.2   the performance and observance by the Tenant of all the other terms contained or implied in the Agreement.

2.   The Guarantor covenants with the Landlord as follows:

2.1   If the Tenant defaults in the payment of the rent or any other monies payable under the Agreement I/we will immediately upon written demand by the Landlord pay to the Landlord the full amount owing from the Tenant.

2.2   If the Tenant defaults in the performance or observance of any of the terms contained or implied in the Agreement, I/we will immediately upon written demand by the Landlord pay to the Landlord all losses, damages, expenses and costs which the Landlord has suffered because of the Tenant's breaches.

3.   It is agreed that this Guarantee cannot be revoked by the Guarantor:

3.1   for so long as the tenancy created by the Agreement continues; or

3.2   during the continuance of any further tenancy entered into expressly or impliedly between the Landlord and the Tenant.

4.   This Guarantee is not to be revoked by:

4.1   the death of the Guarantor [or any of the Guarantors]; or

4.2   the death of the Tenant [or any of the Tenants]; or

4.3   the bankruptcy of the Tenant [or any of the Tenants].

5.   This Guarantee continues in operation

5.1   notwithstanding any alteration of the terms of the Agreement including any increase in the amount of the rent payable for the House; and

5.2   in relation to any new or further tenancy entered into between the Tenant and the Landlord; and

5.3   in relation to any statutory periodic tenancy which may arise in the Tenant's favour under the Housing Act 1988; and

5.4   notwithstanding that the Agreement may be terminated by agreement, court order, notice, re-entry, forfeiture or otherwise; and

5.5   notwithstanding any arrangement made between the Landlord and the Tenant (whether or not with the Guarantor's consent) nor by any indulgence or forbearance shown by the Landlord to the Tenant.

6   This Guarantee constitutes the Guarantor as principal debtor.

7.   Any demand by the Landlord under the terms of this Guarantee shall be validly made if sent by registered or recorded delivery post or left at the address(es) specified above as the Guarantor's address or such other address(es) as the Guarantor may notify to the Landlord.

8.   Where there is more than one Guarantor, the Guarantor's obligations will be joint and individual.

9.   Where there is more than one Tenant, references in this Guarantee to 'the Tenant' shall be construed as referring to all or both or either or any of the persons so named.

SIGNED AS A DEED

BY THE LANDLORD: *(Signature of landlord)*

IN THE PRESENCE OF: *(Signature of witness)*

SIGNED AS A DEED

BY THE GUARANTOR: *(Signature of guarantor)*

IN THE PRESENCE OF: *(Signature of witness)*

Addresses and websites

**Association of Residential Letting
Agents (ARLA)**
ARLA Administration
Maple House
53–55 Woodside Road
Amersham
Buckinghamshire HP6 6AA
Hotline: (01923) 896555
Website: www.arla.co.uk
Email: info@arla.co.uk

**Campaign for the Abolition of
Residential Leasehold (CARL)**
PO Box 26369
London N8 7ZL
Website: www.carl.org.uk
Email: charlotte@carl.org.uk

Child Poverty Action Group
94 White Lion Street
London N1 9PF
Tel: 020-7837 7979
Fax: 020-7837 6414
Website: www.cpag.org
Email: staff@cpag.demon.co.uk

Communities Scotland
Thistle House
91 Haymarket Terrace
Edinburgh EH12 5HE
Tel: 0131-313 0044
Fax: 0131-313 2680
Website:
www.communitiesscotland.gov.uk

Court Service
Southside
105 Victoria Street
London SW1E 6QF
Tel: 020-7210 2266
Website: www.courtservice.gov.uk
Email: customerservice@courtservice.
gsi.gov.uk

DTI Consumer Safety Publications
Admail 528
London SW1W 8YT
Tel: (0870) 150 2500
Fax: (0870) 150 2333
Website: www.dti.gov.uk/publications
Email: publications@dti.gsi.gov.uk

Independent Housing Ombudsman
Website:
www.ihos.org.uk/tds/about.htm

Inland Revenue
Website: www.inlandrevenue.gov.uk

Leasehold Advisory Service (LEASE)
70–74 City Road
London EC1Y 2BJ
Tel: 020-7490 9580
Fax: 020-7253 2043
Website: www.lease-advice.org
Email: info@lease-advice.org

National Association of Estate Agents (NAEA)
Arbon House
21 Jury Street
Warwick
Warwickshire CV34 4EH
Tel: (01926) 496800
Fax: (01926) 400953
Website: www.naea.co.uk
Email: info@naea.co.uk

Royal Institution of Chartered Surveyors (RICS)
Parliament Square
12 Great George Street
London SW1P 3AD
Tel: 020-7222 7000
Fax: 020-7222 9430
Website: www.rics.org.uk
Email: info@rics.org.uk

Royal Institution of Chartered Surveyors in Scotland (RICS Scotland)
9 Manor Place
Edinburgh EH3 7DN
Tel: 0131-225 7078
Fax: 0131-240 0831
Website: www.rics.org.uk

Index

agricultural tenancies 22, 99, 121

almshouses 121

alternative accommodation, provision of 52, 97, 306

anti-social behaviour 54, 55, 93, 124, 131, 307

armed forces, landlord in 99

assignment
  prohibitions against 28–9, 79, 95
  in Scotland 287, 293, 299
  secure tenancies 128

assured shorthold tenancies 16–39, 70–88
  death of a tenant 29–31
  deemed shortholds 106–7
  excluded tenancies 21–3
  expiry of fixed term 34
  granting a new tenancy 70–88
  key features 16
  leaving before expiry of term 35, 37
  legislative regime 13–14
  long shortholds 26
  minimum fixed term 104–5
  'new' shortholds (granted on or after 28 February 1997) 14, 15, 17–23, 38
  'old' shortholds (granted before 28 February 1997) 13–14, 14, 17, 38, 40, 104–6, 107
  possession rights and proceedings 16, 17, 33, 34, 35–6, 42, 74, 172–9, 185, 198–9
  prescribed shorthold notice 105–6
  registered social landlords 136
  rent 24–8, 37, 106
  requirements 17–21
  sample tenancy agreement 311–19
  security of tenure 14, 16, 70

subtenancies 19, 28–9, 32
  termination 14, 35, 105
  transferring and subletting 28–9
  see also fixed-term tenancies; periodic tenancies

assured tenancies 14, 15, 16, 35, 36, 38, 40–61
  death of the tenant 50–1, 57, 305–6
  definition 41
  'fully assured tenancies' 14, 15
  granted 15 January 1989 to 28 February 1997 13, 14, 41, 107
  granted on or after 28 February 1997 41
  key features 16
  legislative regime 13
  new lettings 107
  non-shortholds 309–10, 331–40
  possession grounds and proceedings 40–1, 42–3, 44–57, 59–60, 70, 179–83, 185, 199, 235–6, 302–10
  reasons for granting 41–3
  registered social landlords 136
  rent 42, 57, 58
  resident landlord 58
  sample agreement 320–30
  in Scotland 279–84, 284–8
  security of tenure 13, 14, 16, 40, 42, 44, 70, 136, 198, 235
  serving notice of 41, 44
  subtenancies 57–8
  succession rights 60–1
  surrender 44
  transferring and subletting 57

bedsits and flatlets 11
  see also flats

break clauses 76, 81
Building Regulations 113
business tenancies 19, 22, 121
buy-to-let mortgage schemes 11

Campaign Against Residential Leasehold
        (CARL) 168
children 59, 81
clearance areas 153
cohabitees 29, 30
commonhold 7, 265–8
    implications 267–8
    and service charges 266, 268
    setting up 267
Commonhold Associations 266
Commonhold and Leasehold Reform Bill
        2001 7, 213, 217, 218, 219, 222, 223,
        226, 227, 228, 231, 232, 233, 234,
        235, 241, 242, 249, 250, 262, 263,
        265, 266
Communities Scotland 296
company lets 65–6, 92
corner shops with accommodation 22
'corresponding day rule' 35
council tax 11, 77, 113, 118–19, 271–2
council tax benefit 118–19
council tenancies see local authority lettings
Criminal Law Act 1977 159
Crown property 23, 227

death of a tenant 13, 29–31
    assured tenancies 50–1, 57, 305–6
    fixed-term tenancies 29–30
    periodic tenancies 30–1
    see also succession rights
Defective Premises Act 1972 142
demolition or reconstruction of property
        49–50, 126, 153, 304–5
deposits 11, 29, 76, 80, 85–6, 273
    excessive deposits 87
    Tenancy Deposit Scheme 86–7
disabled persons 126
domestic violence, tenant's, as grounds
        for possession 55, 124, 307–8

electrical safety 84, 154, 269
employees, letting to 56, 95–6, 121, 125,
        126, 308
enfranchisement
    cost 230–1, 232
    death of tenant and 218

'desire notice' 219
excluded buildings 227–8
flats 221, 221–41, 223–6, 223–32,
        228–32, 236–41
    high-value houses 216–17
    houses 213–20
    houses held on trust 217–18
    landlord opposition 229–30
    marriage value 230, 231
    price of the freehold 220
    qualifying tenant 217, 223–4, 237–8
    residence qualification 225–6
    tenants' right of first refusal 236, 238
    transfer of rights 219
Environmental Protection Act 1990
        141–2, 150–2
eviction see harassment and unlawful
        eviction; possession proceedings

fair rent system 24, 25, 91, 97, 99–101,
        108, 138, 139
    landlord application 100
    registering 101
    tenant application 100
false statements by tenants 56–7, 125, 308
fire safety 84, 111, 269
fixed-term tenancies 9–10, 74, 81, 91,
        121, 143
    death of a tenant 29–30
    ending the tenancy 191
    rent 25–7
    subletting 32
flats
    acquisition of reversion of lease
        260–1
    appointing a manager 258–60
    bad management history 261–2
    buying the freehold (enfranchisement)
        221, 223–32, 236–41
    commonhold 265–8
    compulsory acquisition of landlord's
        interest 261–2
    definition 223–4
    extending the lease 222, 226, 230, 233–6
    house conversions 33, 215
    long leases 221–41, 265
    professional managing agents 244, 263
    public-sector accommodation 132, 228
    purpose-built 33
    repairs and maintenance 145–6, 221
    Right to Manage (RTM) 235, 242, 262–3
    service charges 221, 242–64

tenant management companies 240, 244
forwarding addresses 273
furnished lettings 143, 206–7, 271, 308
furniture, damage to 55, 94, 125, 308

gardens 78, 273
gas and electricity bills 11
gas safety 83–4, 154, 269
granny flats 224
ground rent 213, 218, 263–4
guarantee agreements 68, 341–3

harassment and unlawful eviction
        157–69, 170, 197
    breach of contract 160
    civil proceedings 159–65
    compensation 159, 162
    court action 165–8
    criminal sanctions 157–9
    damages awarded 162–4
    emergency relief 165
    injunctions 164–5, 169
    landlord bullying 168
    in Scotland 287–8
    trespass 160–1
    violence 157, 160–1
head leases 31, 32
high-value properties, tenancies of 21
holiday lettings 21, 22, 70, 91, 171, 207
    out-of-season 43, 47–8, 303
homeless persons, tenancies granted to 121
hostels 110, 171
Housing Act 1985 122, 126, 152–4, 171, 185
Housing Act 1988 13, 16, 17, 21, 23, 24,
        28, 30, 40, 82, 90, 91, 103, 136,
        161–2, 171
Housing Act 1996 13, 15, 36, 38, 137,
        171, 257
housing associations 23, 126, 135–6, 229,
        307, 308
    co-operative housing associations 135,
        138
    local authority transfers 137
    possession grounds and proceedings
        136, 139, 185, 191
    rents 139
    repairs and maintenance 139
    in Scotland 296, 297
    security of tenure 138
    tenancies granted before 15 January
        1989 137, 138

tenancies granted on or after 15
        January 1989 136, 138, 139
    tenant's guarantee 136, 139
    unregistered 138
    see also registered social landlords
housing benefit 66–7, 114–18
    entitlement 115
    payment 114, 117–18
    payment direct to landlord 66–7, 117
    restrictions on amount of benefit 115–17
Housing Corporation 135
housing ombudsman service 136–7
Housing (Scotland) Act 1988 279, 284, 295
Housing (Scotland) Act 2001 275, 279,
        289, 296
Housing for Wales 135

illegal or immoral purposes, using a
        house for 55, 93, 124, 131, 307
improvements to the property 78, 113,
        129, 142, 293
income support 66
Independent Housing Ombudsman 86
injuries as a result of defective premises
        142, 147, 155
insurance
    insurer's consent to letting 71–2
    multiple occupation properties 113
    property and contents insurance 78, 272
inventories 62, 65, 76, 87–8, 271
irritancy clauses 286

keys 272

Landlord and Tenant Act 1927 28
Landlord and Tenant Act 1985 77, 85,
        143, 144–8, 248, 252
Landlord and Tenant Act 1987 80,
        236–40, 256, 258, 260, 261
landlord/tenant relationship 10–12
landlords
    access to property 148, 272
    charity as landlord 126, 223
    granting a tenancy where landlord is
        resident 89
    requires property for own or family
        occupation 16, 96–7, 98
    resident landlord exception 15, 19, 23,
        32–4, 58, 91, 191
    sharing facilities with 19
Leasehold Advisory Service 240

leasehold property, letting 270
Leasehold Reform Act 1967 214
Leasehold Reform, Housing and Urban
    Development Act 1993 221, 250,
    260, 261
Leasehold Valuation Tribunal (LVT)
    253–4, 255, 258, 259, 260
leases 9, 31, 32, 47, 72
    deeds 73
    enfranchisement 214, 217, 218, 219,
        220, 221, 223–6, 228–32, 236–41
    expiry 214, 235–6
    extending the lease 214, 222, 226, 230,
        233–6, 241
    head leases 31, 32
    lease-backs 228–9
    long leases of flats 221–41
    long leases of houses 213–20
    premiums 73, 234
    rent 214, 216
    subleases 72, 79
    see also tenancies
letting a property
    company lets 65–6, 92
    deciding the rent 83
    deposits 11, 29, 80, 85–6, 273
    finding a tenant 62–9
    guarantors 68
    letting agents 62–4, 65–6, 68, 83, 86, 87
    misrepresentation 68–9
    mortgagee's consent 12, 71, 270
    practical tips 269–73
    premiums 29
    references 12, 62, 63, 64, 65, 67–8, 270
    see also tenancy agreements
limited companies, letting to 20
local authority lettings 23, 120–34, 185, 191
    see also secure tenancies
lodgers 10, 29, 95, 128, 134, 293, 299

maisonettes 224
marriage value 230, 231, 234, 262
meter readings 271
ministers of religion, housing for 43, 49,
    99, 303
mortgages
    buy-to-let mortgages 11, 200–1
    mortgagee exercises power of sale
        46–7, 98, 302–3
    mortgagee's consent to letting 12, 47,
        71, 270

rent-to-mortgage scheme 292
multiple occupation (HMOs) 11, 110–13,
    270
    landlord obligations 111
    legal definition 110
    registration schemes 111, 112
    regulations 111, 112–13
    tenant responsibilities 111

National Trust property 227
non-shorthold tenancies 89, 331–40
    see also assured tenancies
notice to quit 10, 122–3
nuisance 11, 54–5, 60, 78, 93, 113, 124,
    131, 151–2, 307
    statutory nuisance 151–2

Occupiers Liability Act 1957 142
overcrowding 112, 126
owner-occupiers 42–3, 45–6

peppercorn rent 233
periodic tenancies 9, 10, 24, 30–1, 34,
    75–6, 81, 91, 121, 122, 128, 143
    ending the tenancy 191–2
    rent 27
pets 59, 81, 134
planning permission 72–3, 113
possession, grounds for
    assured shorthold tenancies 36
    assured tenancies 40, 42–3, 44–57,
        235–6, 302–10
    discretionary grounds 40, 41, 45, 51–7,
        93–7, 123–7, 306–9
    mandatory grounds 40, 41, 42, 45–51,
        97–9, 302–6
    'reasonableness' 51, 172, 182–3, 191, 192
    Rent Act tenancies 13, 50, 91, 93
    in Scotland 276–8, 282–4, 294–5, 300
    secure tenancies 123–7
    statutory tenancies 92–9
possession proceedings 11, 170–99
    accelerated possession procedure 17,
        43, 174–9, 195
    court orders 45, 170, 171, 192–3,
        194–5, 197
    defence or counterclaims 197–9
    enforcement of possession orders 194–5
    excluded licences or tenancies 171–2,
        196
    legal costs 194

in Scotland 276–8, 282–4, 285, 286
termination notices 122–3, 172–4,
    178–9, 179–82, 195, 196, 198–9
see also under types of tenancy
premiums 29, 73, 234
private sector tenancies 8, 13–15
    in Scotland 274–88
see also types of tenancy
problems, common 11–12
property development businesses 68–9
Property Misdescriptions Act 1991 68–9
protected shorthold tenancies 23–4, 103–4
protected tenancies 13, 91–2, 183–5, 198
protected tenancies (Scotland) 276–9
Protection from Eviction Act 1977 157–9,
    161
public sector tenancies 8, 120–34, 190–1
    in Scotland 289–301
    see also housing associations; registered
        social landlords; secure tenancies

qualifying tenant 217, 223–4, 237–8

redevelopment areas 126
references 12, 62, 63, 64, 65, 67–8, 270
registered social landlords 9, 135, 307, 308
    complaints against 136–7
    tenancies granted on or after 15
        January 1989 136
    tenant's guarantee 136
    tenant's right to buy 139
relevant disposals 238–9
rent
    arrears 11, 16, 17, 51, 52–3, 58, 76, 93,
        123–4, 306
    board or service payments included in 91
    cash or cheque payment 64–5
    collecting 87
    contractual increases 24
    in excess of £25,000 per year 21, 89
    fair rent system 24, 25, 91, 97, 99–101,
        108, 138, 139
    ground rent 213, 218, 263–4
    housing associations 139
    housing benefit paid direct to landlord
        66–7, 117
    increases 24, 24–6, 38, 57, 58, 80, 101–2
    'local reference rent' 116
    low rents 21–2, 91, 147, 216, 224
    over-payments 102
    payment intervals 76

peppercorn rent 233
persistent delays in paying 53, 307
'property-specific rent' 117
'reasonable market rent' 115–16
registered rents 101–2
rent books 87
rent control 13, 106, 128–9
rent officers 13, 100, 115, 116, 117
rent referrals 26–8, 43, 74, 80, 106
rent review provision 37, 76, 80
rent-free accommodation 171
Scotland 278, 280–1, 285, 290, 298
setting the rent 83
statutory increases 25
withholding rent for repairs 247
see also under types of tenancy
Rent Act 1977 21, 25, 99, 108, 171
Rent Act tenancies 13, 14, 23–4, 50, 51
    death of a tenant 91
    fair rent system 24, 97, 99–101, 108
    granting a new tenancy 89, 90
    lettings prior to 15 January 1989 90–104
    possession rights and proceedings 51,
        91, 94, 183–5, 199
    security of tenure 14, 91, 92
    succession rights 91, 102–3, 108–9
Rent Assessment Committee 16, 24, 25,
    26–8, 32, 42, 43, 57, 74, 80, 106,
    255, 281, 285
Rent (Scotland) Act 1984 278
rent-a-room scheme 207
rent-to-mortgage scheme 292
repairs and maintenance 11, 77–8,
    140–56, 272–3
    closing order 153
    common parts 144
    demolition order 153
    flats 145–6, 221
    HMO regulations 111
    housing associations 139
    improvements, distinct from 142
    landlord's obligations 12, 77, 85, 129,
        142, 143, 145–6, 148, 156, 272
    landlord's right of access 148
    legislation 141–2
    non-structural internal repairs and
        decoration 78
    property to be fit for habitation 148,
        151, 152–3
    remedies against landlord 148–54,
        154–6, 247, 248

repair notice 153
requirement for notice 147
right-to-repair scheme 149–50
safety regulations 83–4, 154, 269
in Scotland 287, 291, 298
secure tenancies 129, 149–50, 155
self-help scheme 148, 149, 273
standards of repair 147
statutory nuisance 150–2
structure and exterior repairs 77, 85,
129, 145–6, 156
tenant's obligations 78, 142–3, 144,
147, 272
'waste or neglect' 53–4, 94, 125, 307
residential licences 10, 18, 171, 275
right to buy scheme 132–3
discounts 132, 133
preserved right to buy 137
price 132–3
registered social landlord tenants 139
residence qualification 132
in Scotland 291–2, 298–9

safety regulations 83–4, 154, 269
sale of the property 94–5, 98
Scotland 274–301
assignation and subletting 287, 293, 299
assured tenancies 279–84
fair rent system 278
harassment and unlawful eviction 287–8
housing associations 296, 297
possession grounds and proceedings
276–8, 285, 286, 294–5, 300
private sector tenancies 274–88
protected tenancies 276–9
public sector tenancies 289–301
rent 278, 280–1, 285, 290, 298
right to buy 291–2, 298–9
secure tenancies 289–301
short assured tenancies 284–8
short Scottish secure tenancy (SSST)
300–1
statutory tenancies 279
succession rights 278–9, 281, 292–3,
299
tenancy agreements 281, 286, 290, 297–8
'tenant's choice' scheme 295–6
Section 5 notice 239
Section 8 notice 45
Section 21 notice 35
secure tenancies 120–9

assignment 128
definition 120
exceptions to 121
introductory tenancy scheme 129–31
landlord condition 120, 121
licence to occupy 120
lodgers and subletting 128, 134
possession grounds and proceedings
122–7, 130–1, 133
rent 121, 128–9
repairs and maintenance 129, 149–50,
155
right to buy scheme 132–3
right-to-repair scheme 149–50
in Scotland 289–301
security of tenure 122, 198
succession rights 127–8
tenant condition 120, 121
tenants' improvements 129
Secure Tenants of Local Housing
Authorities (Right to Repair)
Regulations 1994 129
security of tenure
assured shorthold tenancies 14, 16, 70
assured tenancies 13, 14, 16, 40, 42, 44,
70, 136, 198, 235
housing associations 138
Rent Act tenancies 13, 14, 91, 92
in Scotland 282
secure tenancies 122, 198
subtenancies 32
service charges 221, 242–64, 265
administration charges 249
and commonhold 266, 268
computation 248
definition 249
estimates and tenant consultation 254–6
forfeiture proceedings 243, 257–8
independent advice on 252
information, provision of 248–50
management audit 250–2
reasonableness 252–4
restrictions on landlord's right to
recover costs 252–3
tenant's right of set-off 247
terms of the lease/variation of terms
246–8
written demands 256–7
service occupants 56
sharing accommodation and facilities
19–20

short assured tenancies (Scotland) 284–8
short Scottish secure tenancy (SSST)
    300–1
shortholds *see* assured shorthold tenancies
soft furnishings safety 84
specific performance order 148–9
squatters and trespassers 171
stamp duty 82–3, 287
statutory tenancies 13, 92–3, 183–5
statutory tenancies (Scotland) 279
student lettings 22, 113, 121
    out-of-term 43, 48–9, 303
subtenancies 31–2
    assured tenancy, creation of 32, 57–8
    duration of 31
    permission for 72, 128
    prohibitions 28–9, 31, 32, 79, 95
    in Scotland 293, 299
    security of tenure 32
succession rights
    assured tenancies 60–1
    cohabitees 30
    fixed-term tenancies 29–30
    intestacy 30, 31, 128
    periodic tenancies 30–1
    Rent Act tenancies 91, 102–3, 108–9
    same-sex couples 30, 127
    in Scotland 278–9, 281, 292–3, 299
    secure tenancies 127–8
surrender 44

tax
    capital allowances 206
    capital gains tax 208–9, 210
    dealing with the Inland Revenue 211–12
    deductible expenses 203–6
    holiday lettings 207
    income tax 201–8, 209–10
    letting landlord's own home 209–11
    losses 208
    profit calculation 202–3
    rent-a-room relief 207
telephone bills 11, 271
television aerials and satellite dishes 129
tenancies
    exclusive possession 10
    fixed or ascertainable period 9–10,
        25–7, 29–30, 32, 74, 81, 91, 121,
        143, 191
    key features 9
    legal definition 7, 9–10

periodic tenancies 9, 10, 25, 27, 30–1,
    34, 75–6, 81, 91, 121, 122, 128,
    143, 191–2
private sector tenancies 8, 13–15
public sector tenancies 8, 120–34, 190–1
    under Scottish law 274–5
    see also types of tenancy
tenancy agreements
    address for service 80
    alterations to the property 78
    assignment of the tenancy 79
    breach of contract 53, 307
    break clauses 76, 81
    children and pets 81
    council tax 77
    description of the property 68, 76
    duration of term 9, 74–5
    express terms 141
    forfeiture clauses 76, 81–2
    implied terms 141, 143–8
    insurance of property 78
    inventory of contents 62, 65, 76, 87–8,
        271
    lodgers 95
    non-shorthold tenancies 89
    oral agreements 36–7, 73
    rent 24, 25, 76–7, 80, 83
    repairs and maintenance 77–8, 141,
        142–3, 144
    sample agreements 311–43
    in Scotland 281, 286, 290, 297–8
    shorthold tenancies 75–82
    subletting 28–9, 31, 32, 79, 95
    'unfair' terms 81
    Unfair Terms in Consumer Contracts
        Regulations 1999 75–6, 81, 87
    use of property 78
    water charges 77
    written agreements 37, 73–4, 75
Tenancy Deposit Scheme 86–7
'tenant's choice' scheme (Scotland) 295–6
trespass 160–1
trust, houses held on 217–18
trusts as landlords 126

Unfair Terms in Consumer Contracts
    Regulations 1999 75–6, 79, 80, 81,
    87, 247
use of property, restrictions on 78, 286

water charges 11, 77, 271
winter lets 43, 48